Watercolor Mixing

the 12-Hue Method

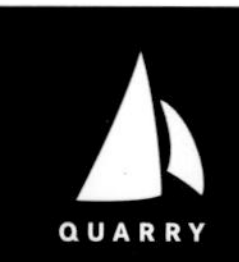

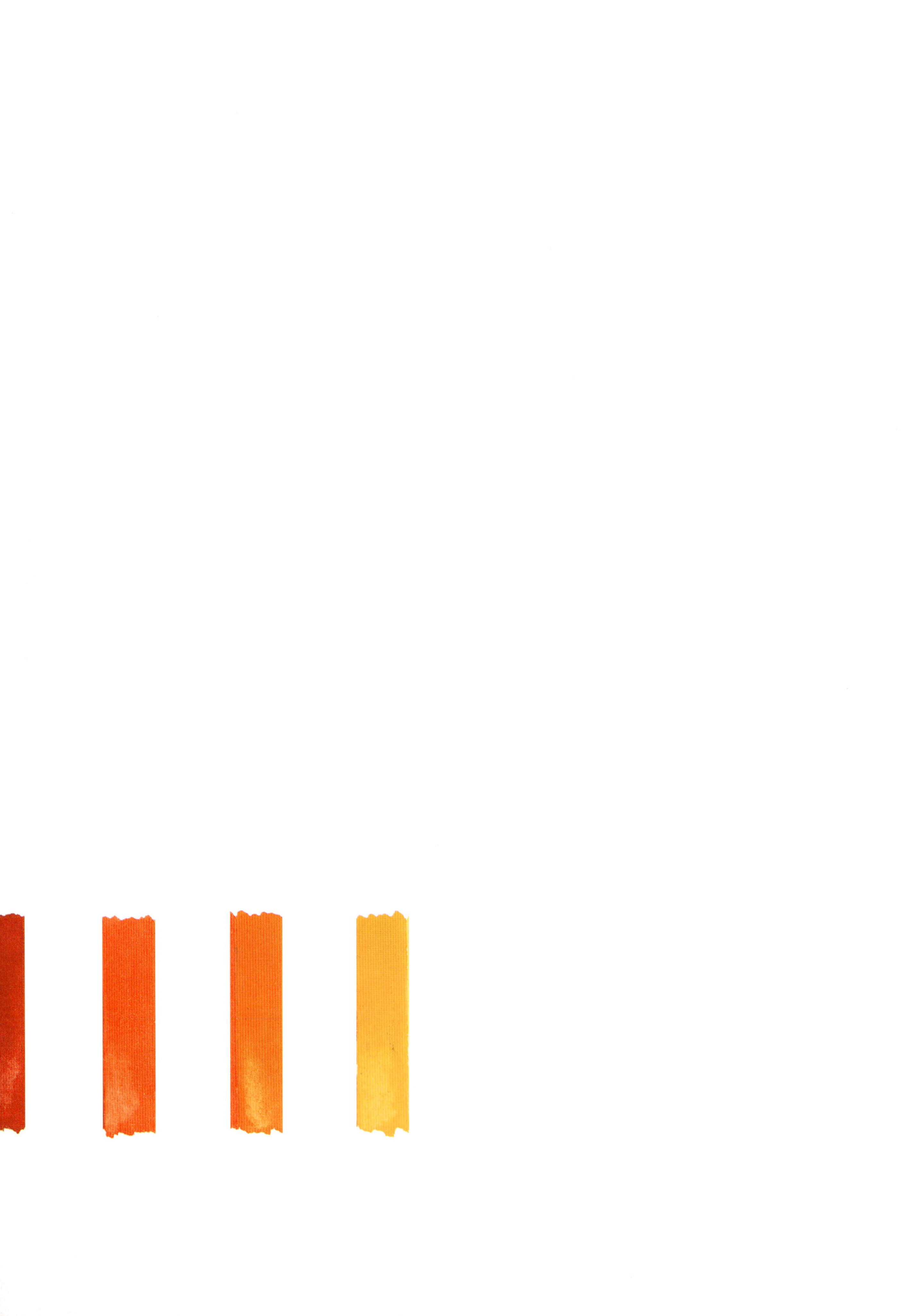

Watercolor Mixing

the 12-Hue Method

Christopher Willard

GLOUCESTER MASSACHUSETTS

QUARRY BOOKS

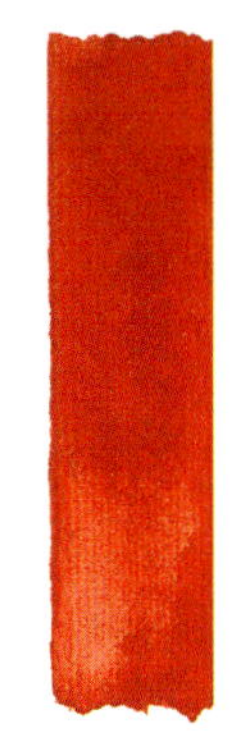
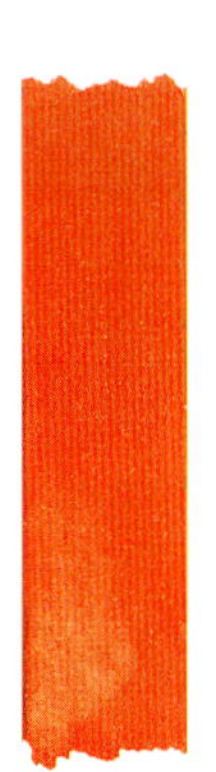
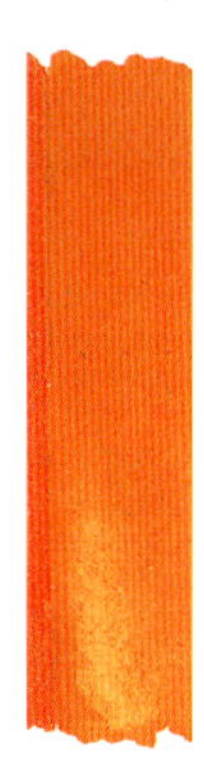
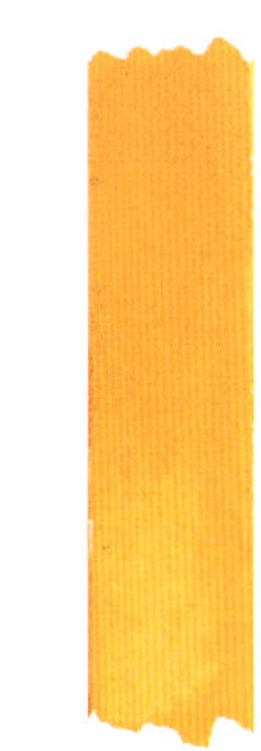

First published in the United States of America by
Rockport Publishers, Inc.
33 Commercial Street
Gloucester, Massachusetts 01930-5089
Telephone: (978) 282-9590
Facsimile: (978) 283-2742
www.rockpub.com

ISBN 1-56496-605-4

10 9 8 7 6 5 4 3 2 1

Cover Design: Lisa Catalone
Book Design: Cathy Kelley
Layout: SYP Design & Production
All Watercolor Diagrams by Christopher Willard.

Printed in China.

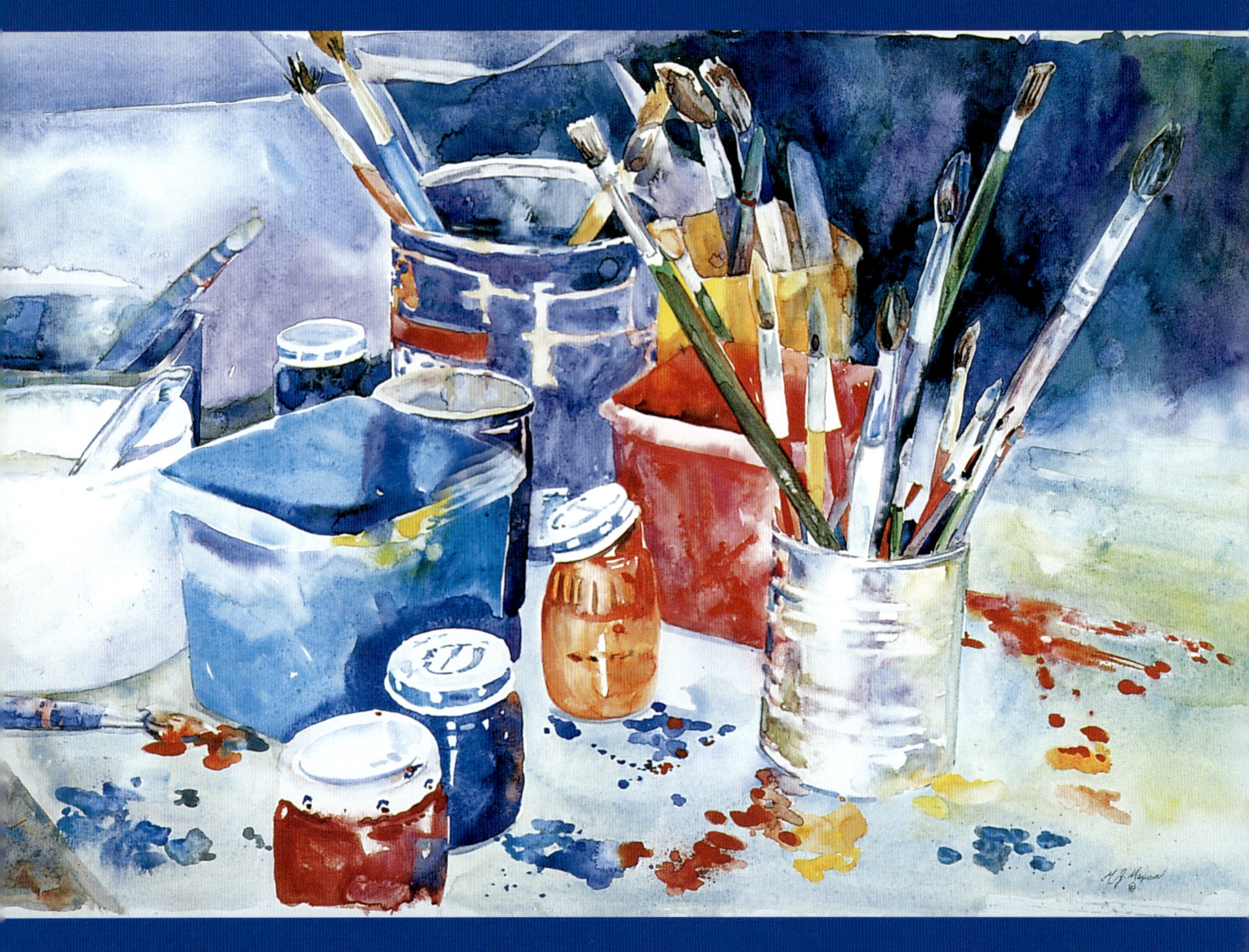

Acknowledgments

This book came about through the support and hard work of many people. I am indebted to my agent Lew Grimes, who believed in my idea from the start and who provided continual encouragement. To the many people at Rockport Publishers who helped guide my rough drafts to a final form I express a sincere thanks. A debt of gratitude is owed to Laurel Smith for looking over the unfinished manuscript and offering a number of pertinent observations. I thank Sherry French for assisting me in my search for artists. There are countless others who deserve appreciation because they fostered my interest in color and tested my ideas: family, friends, artists, teachers, and students.

The most grateful acknowledgment is given to the outstanding artists who generously agreed to provide the images of their paintings that illustrate this book.

I dedicate this book to my son Etienne, whose inquisitive eye and intellectual curiosity are constant inspirations.

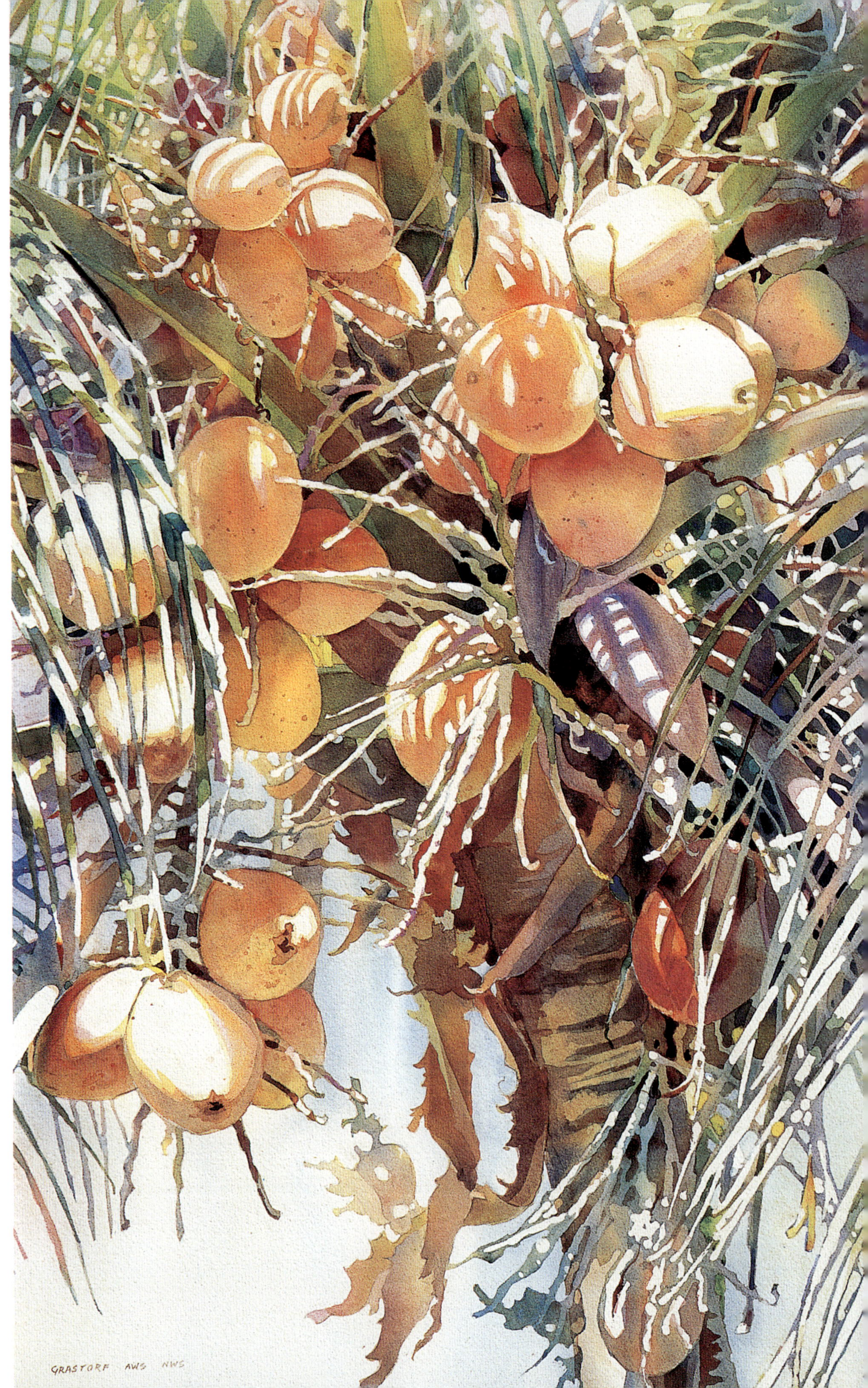
GRASTORF AWS NWS

Contents

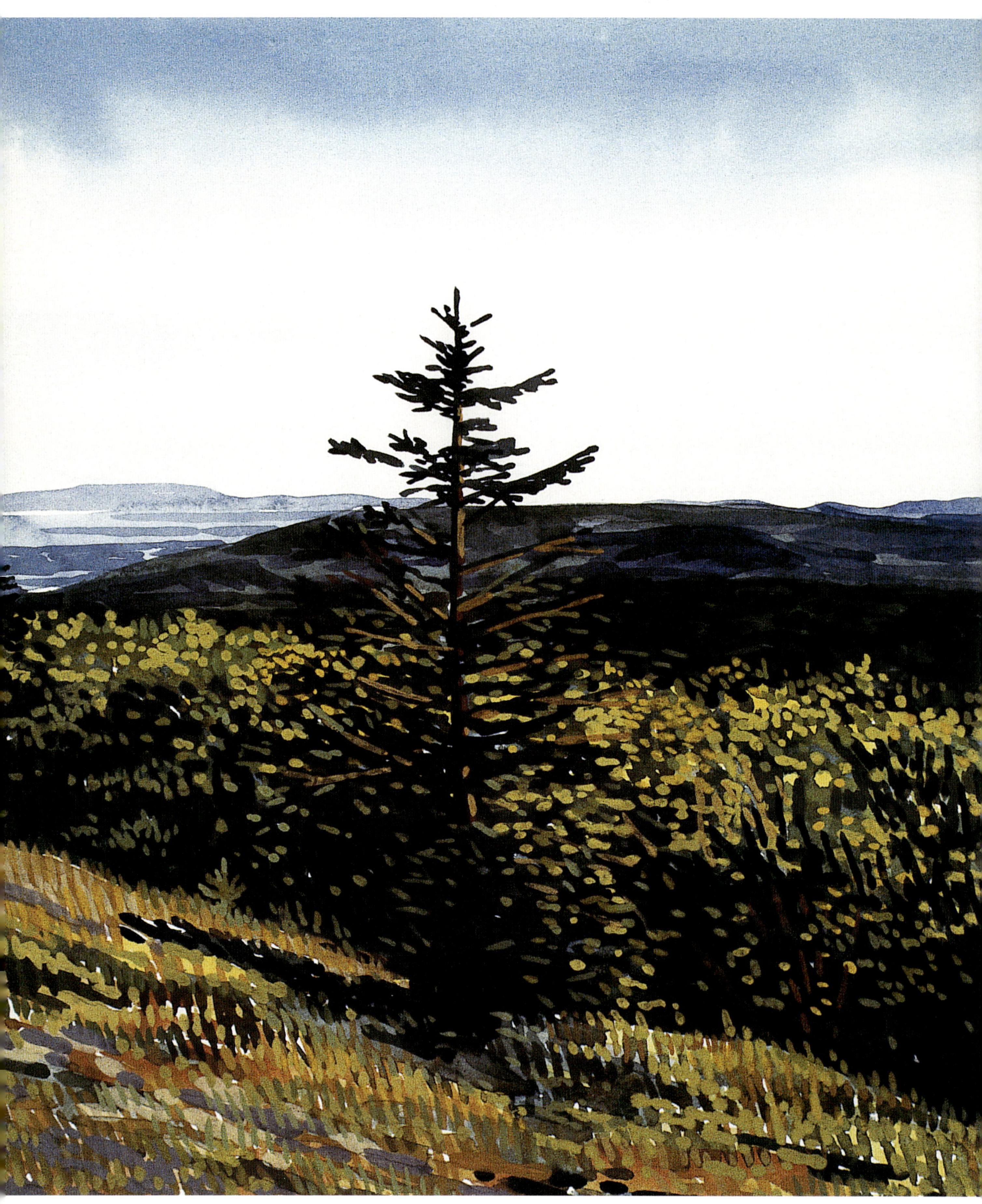

Introduction

"The first process in the art of the painter is the composition of colors."

—Theophilus, from *De Diversis Artibus*, c. 1125

Ask artists how they choose their colors for paintings and many will say they just put down what they see. Others will remark they feel like using certain colors on a particular day. These answers suggest that color is often an aspect of painting that artists find intuitive rather than planned. They carefully choose their brushes and papers, they do detailed drawings of their subjects, and then they jump right in with the paint—never stopping to really question what colors they apply. Their process of using color for maximum effect is mainly one of hit or miss. At the same time, almost every artist I talk with, whether beginning or advanced, expresses the desire to know more about color so they can use it more successfully in their works.

Color is a tricky thing. Almost everyone sees in color, and vision experts have proven that an amazing seventy percent of human sensory information comes in through the eyes. ALL this information is color information, because the eyes see in color. Yet, even though it is easily seen, color is hard to fully understand. As I look outside, I see a color that appears to be greenish, brownish, grayish and orangeish all at the same time. This color is difficult to describe without the correct words, difficult to mix without knowing what colors to use, and difficult to put into a painting.

Watercolorists are required to pay special attention to their color usage because they work in a medium that does not allow much room for mistakes. It is almost impossible to completely switch one color for another after the first has dried. One mistake with a second layer of color or a tricky color, like the one described above, can ruin an otherwise great painting. This is why understanding color is of special significance to the watercolorist.

Like most artists, there was a time when I used color solely in an intuitive manner. In undergraduate school, I took a color course where students moved sheets of colored papers around, but such exercises didn't seem to relate to my own paintings. I applied paint as

LEFT: ***Study for Looking East*** **by James Linehan, *9" x 8" (23cm x 20cm)***

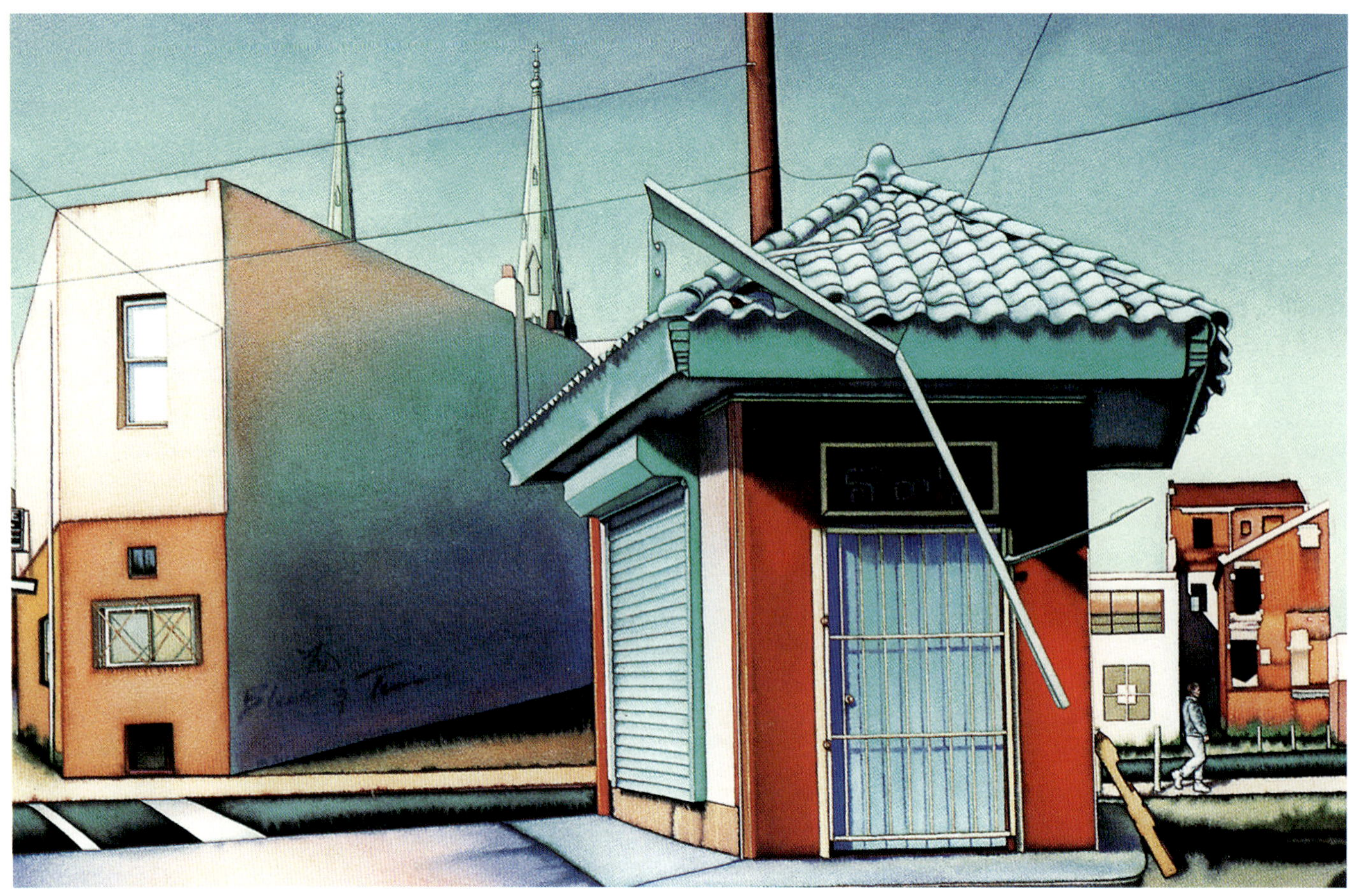

Buttonwood Blues **by Ann DeLaurentis,** ***24" x 36" (61cm x 91cm)***

blends, bleeds, strokes and stipples; I never used colored papers. Furthermore, studying color sounded akin to a theoretical science rather than a practical tool relevant to creating art.

As a result, my own paintings were hit or miss when it came to color. One might be good while others showed masses of muddy mingling where I had tried my hardest to capture an exact light sensation. I knew my works were lacking something because the masterful color compositions found in paintings by the great artists I admired completely outshone my attempts.

I struggled for years using color in a haphazard way, and one day decided to reduce my paintings to two colors in an attempt to control what I was doing. Suddenly, a whole new world opened up to me. In limiting my colors I found, surprisingly, I could say more because I was forced to learn everything about how those two colors worked together. From that point, I became interested in finding out what the other colors could do, and before I knew it color became a wonderful obsession. I read books on color. I found artists who used color well and I picked their brains. I spoke at internation-

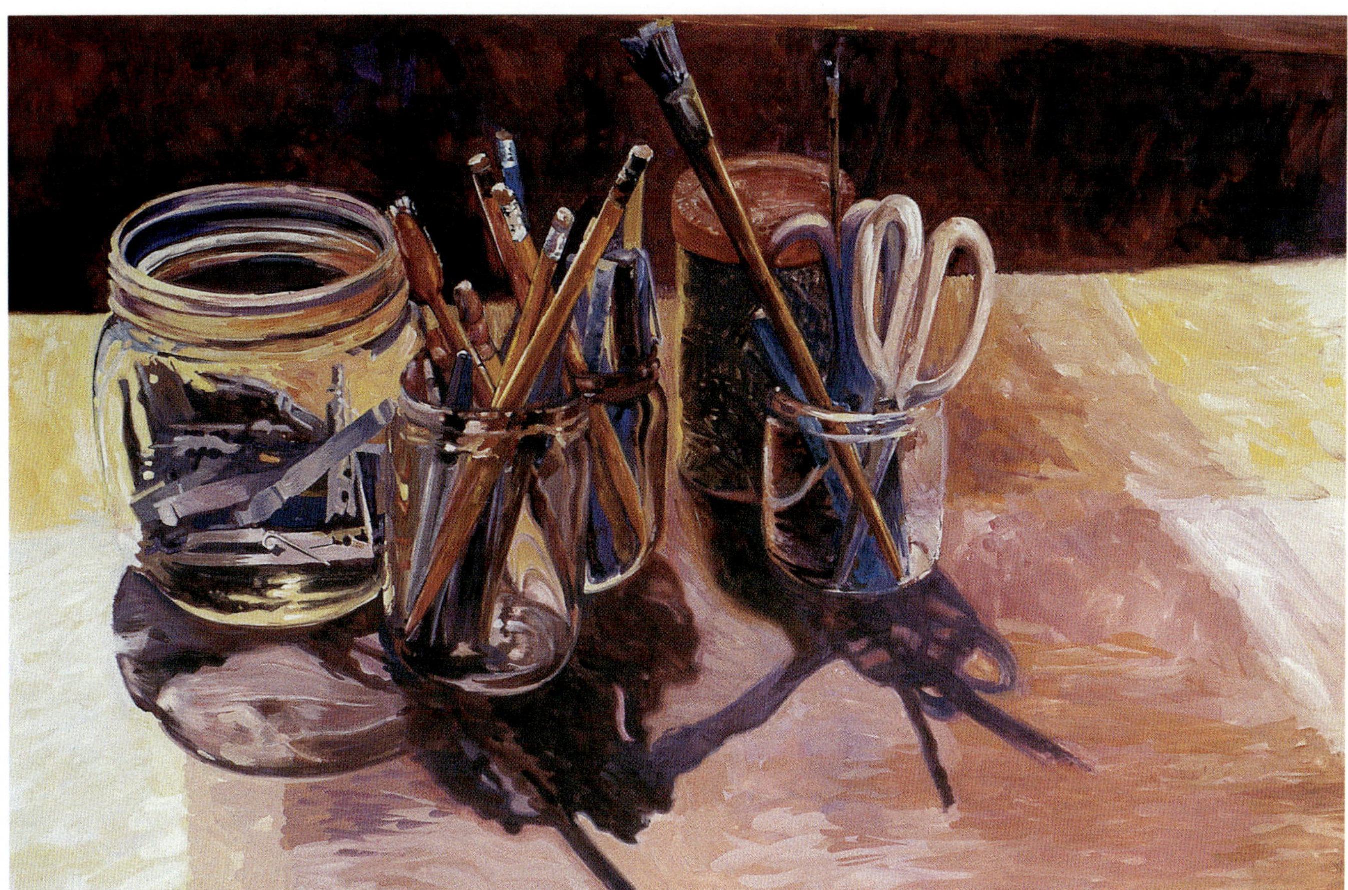

Job Jars **by Mary Maxam,** ***20" x 22" (51cm x 56cm)***

al conferences on color. Color became fascinating and indispensable. Most importantly, color became something I understood as fundamental to my own painting. The more I learned, the easier it became to use colors. Yet, even with all that knowledge, color still retains its uniquely mysterious quality.

This book will show any reader how to use color to create paintings that are amazingly luminous and striking, and that possess what I call the "wow effect." This is a point I will continually emphasize. My goal is to show how artists can use color successfully in their art once they have learned a few simple principles. Colors in paintings are colors in combinations. Once readers know how to describe colors and various ways of combining them, they are well on their way to creating terrific paintings.

Learning color is like learning a language. At first, a few simple nouns and verbs suffice. One can use these to construct a sentence like "She has brown hair." This is where most artists are with color; they rely on simple statements to represent their ideas. But once one decides to become more expressive, to revise the statement to "her flowing auburn tresses," some extra knowledge is needed.

Color knowledge gives artists the ability to make an outstanding statement when once a simple statement was all they knew. And knowing about color does not mean giving up an intuitive approach, just as knowing rules of grammar does not prevent the writing of a great novel charged with emotion. It is a combination of the inspired heart and the educated eye that finally allows artists to employ particular color preferences in striking and harmonious combinations.

Color knowledge is also power and opportunity. It is the power to reach a goal with less frustration, and it is the opportunity to create incredibly strong, color-based paintings. It provides painters with options they might never have thought of without specific direction.

This is not a strict how-to book that says a cadmium yellow light must be placed near a viridian green to create a sunlit leaf. The problem with such exacting prescriptions is that they teach color only for specific situations. When artists are faced with a completely different scene in a new color key, it becomes difficult for them to translate that specific information to the fresh scene. Nor is this a book that spends hours describing why one color, such as yellow, won't mix to a nice green with a certain blue—although I do briefly discuss that problem in Chapter 3. This book starts out immediately with twelve colors that form bright mixtures.

Color Mixing: The 12-Hue Method gives readers the fundamentals without a lot of useless information. Information is geared toward the practicing artist, and to specific problems of painting. The guidelines are easy to learn, easy to use, and are so important that a veritable library of color books might be condensed down to the basics presented here. It is the understanding and use of these basics that help make the paintings of master artists admired today. My goal is to cut through the red tape, stimulate the grey matter, and help readers paint blue-chip watercolors that make viewers green with envy.

I believe that artists who use the basics found in my book will go on to create some of the best paintings of their careers. It doesn't matter if the reader paints every day or once a week, is a beginner or an expert. Each principle is presented simply and in clear language so it may be quickly understood and immediately used in a painting. I am confident that beginning painters reading

OPPOSITE: ***Boundaries*** **by Ashley Peter,** ***30" x 22" (76cm x 56cm)***

this book can learn to be pros at using color with a minimum of time invested in these ideas. I'm also confident that more advanced painters will discover fresh, never-considered color concepts that they will wish to try in new works. Moreover, the elements here are so important that they will guide artists throughout their careers.

I've designed the book to be a studio companion, offering practical outlines for experimentation and success. Each concept is illustrated with paintings by talented artists, and along the way key points are singled out in "recipes for success" for quick reference. The book is also full of interesting discussions that make it something that one will want to read through leisurely over a cup of tea. However, don't blame me if a chapter is so inspiring you run off to the studio to try an idea and forget all about that tea.

I learned what is important about color and painting the hard way, and through diligent study over many years. My goal is to clearly show every reader how to use color as one of the most useful tools of the paint box. I will know I've succeeded if artists who read this book go on to create paintings that are particularly impressive for their use of color. I'm confident they will be.

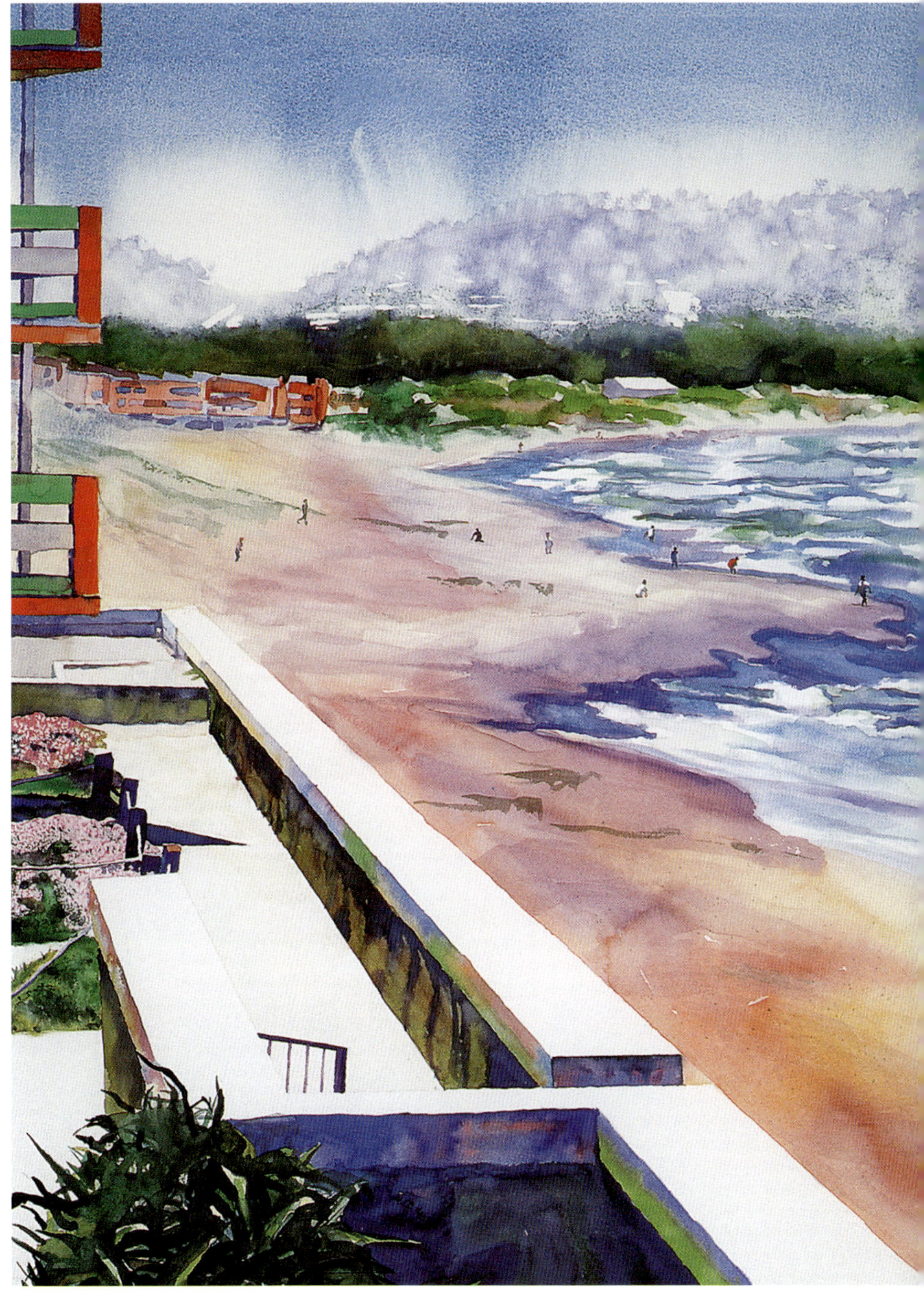

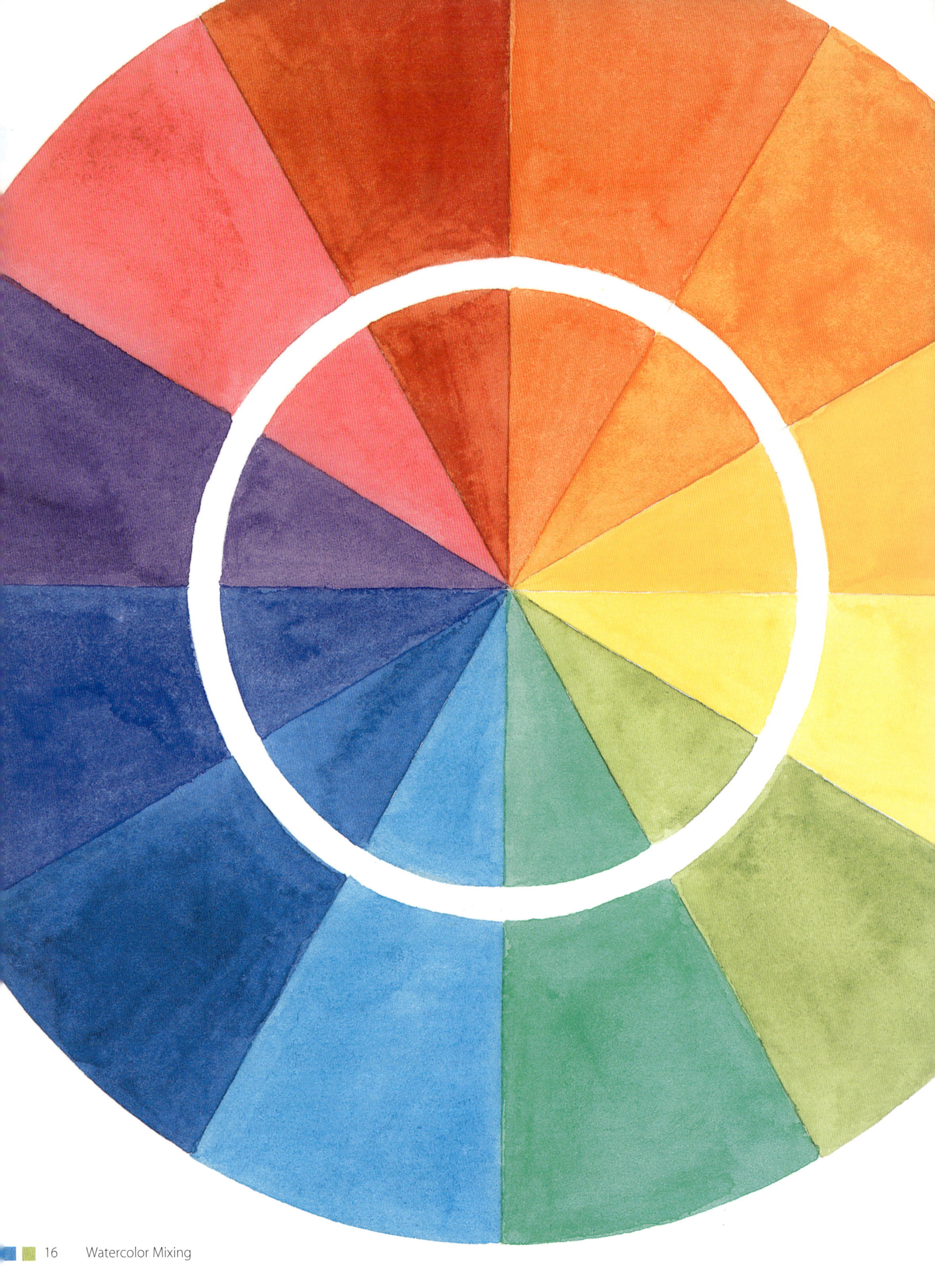

1

Reinventing the Color Wheel

Color is one of the most important elements of watercolor. When color is used well, a painting boasts an amazing vibrancy and energy. Yet, unfortunately, not every painting has such wonderful color. This book presents a method of painting using twelve hues designed for the purpose of achieving energetic and colorful paintings. My objective is to show you how you can make each of your of your watercolors elicit what I call the "wow effect." The wow effect occurs when your color is working so well that someone who looks at the painting literally exclaims, "Wow!"

It is customary for some artists to use every color in every painting. If we consider the analogy of cooking, those same artists would not want to throw every spice into a soup because it would have an unappetizing, jumbled flavor. Similarly, tossing just any color into a painting creates a unappealing confusion of colors. Each color tries to dominate the composition with garish results.

The wow effect arises when we use a few colors knowledgeably instead of thoughtlessly throwing in every color and crossing our fingers.

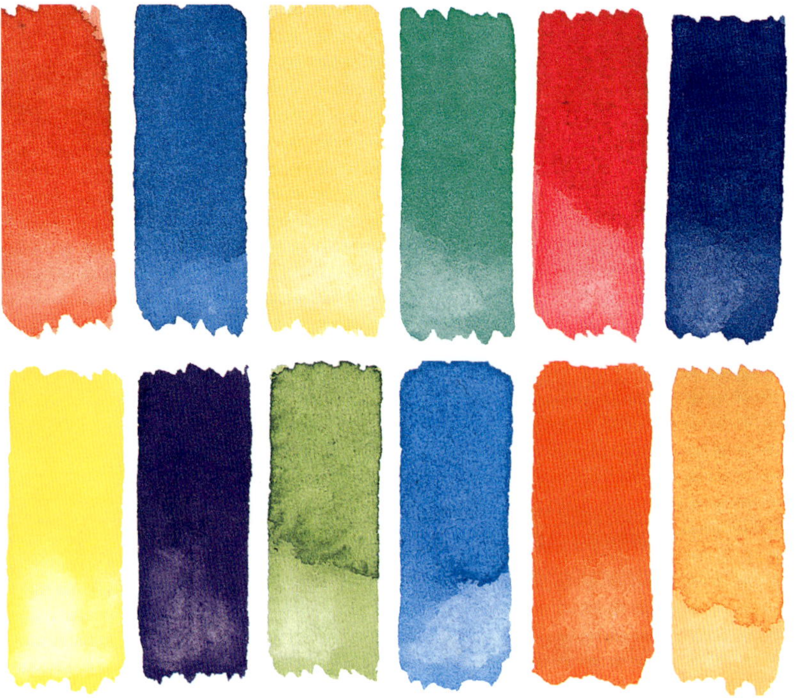

Diagram 1.1 Twelve hues that span the spectrum of colors. These are arranged by their pigment name and their color wheel name below.

Pigment name	**Color-wheel name**
Cadmium Red	Deep Red
Cadmium Red	Light Red-orange
Cadmium Orange	Orange
Cadmium Yellow	Yellow-orange
Cadmium Yellow	Pale Yellow
Sap Green	Yellow-green
Phthalo Green	Green
Cerulean Blue	Blue-green
Phthalo Blue	Blue
French Ultramarine	Blue Blue-violet
Dioxazine Violet	Violet
Quinacridone Red	Red-violet

Table 1.1 These colors may be arranged into a color wheel as shown in the diagram below.

Our first goal will be to reinvent the color wheel as a way to limit our colors. Limiting colors means that right from the start we cannot use every color in a painting because they are no longer on our palette. I have chosen twelve commonly found watercolors that I think represent the entire spectrum of color in a balanced manner (diagram 1.1).

We confine our palette to twelve colors not to save money on paint, but to allow us to learn the secrets of mixing and placement that are guaranteed to produce maximum color impact (diagram 1.2).

At first glance you might wonder why our color wheel does not show all the colors of the real world. For example, brown, a color found everywhere in the real world, is not included on the wheel. This is because some colors are mixture colors rather than pure colors. Chapter 5, Toning Colors for Harmony and Glow, includes a section on how to mix browns that are generally more brilliant than tube browns as well as some other mixing techniques.

The western musical scale consists of only twelve tones. These vary in pitch, lowness and highness, just as we can vary the lightness or darkness of a color. The sounds may also be blended together as chords just as we blend colors to form a new mixture color. Yet with only these few simple tones Beethoven created his symphonies and Mozart his concerti. Likewise, I believe that we can achieve countless beautiful variations of colors by mixing only our original twelve.

At first, it will be helpful to use the same colors I have chosen so you can check your results against the diagrams. At the end of this chapter, we will look at how you can slightly modify this group of colors or even how to begin choosing your own set of twelve colors.

Speaking about Color

First, we need to learn how to talk about color together. If I say I am thinking of a pale red, do I mean a red that has white in it, a light red from the tube, a thin red wash of paint, or merely a pink?

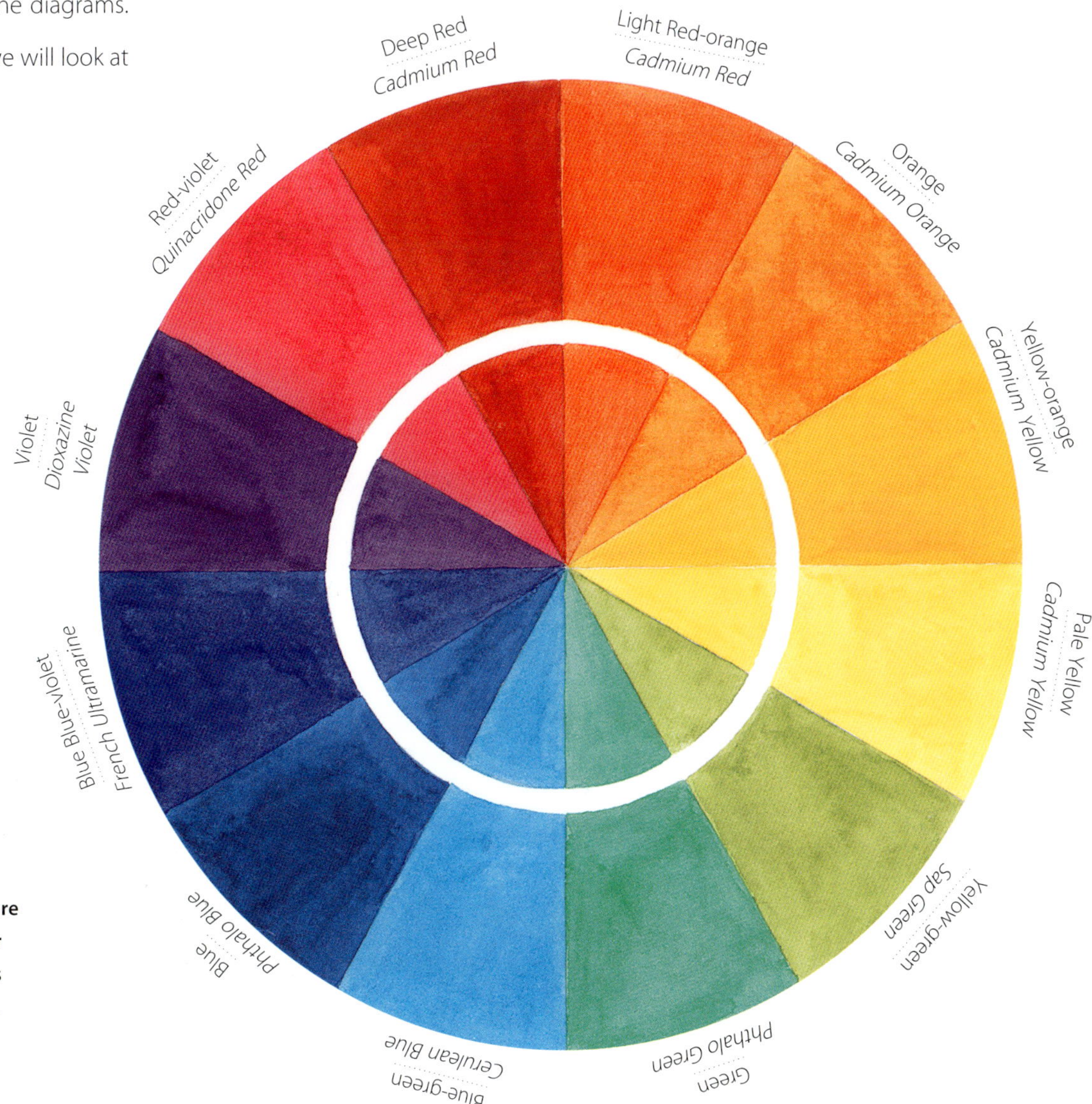

Diagram 1.2 The twelve colors are arranged into a reinvented color wheel with their pigment names next to their color wheel names.

Diagram 1.3 How exactly do we describe this red?

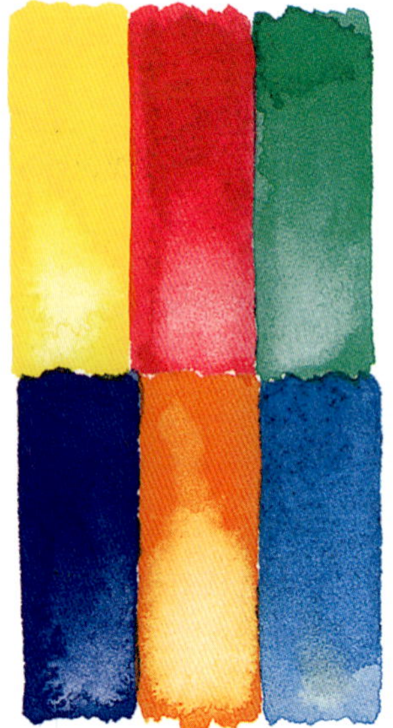

Diagram 1.4 A grouping of different hues. Hue is the chromatic content of color that we indicate by its name.

Common color names are not helpful either. Is the color I am thinking of a vermilion, carnelian, crimson, poppy, scarlet, or a more outdated term such as amaranth? It can get downright confusing.

Rather than learn millions of color names, we can describe any color with only three simple words. If you have ever had someone point out and describe a color that at first you did not see, you know that understanding colors helps us to see more colors.

HUE is the first word. Quite simply, it means the color of the paint. Red is a hue, blue is another hue. So if I mention a red hue, I am really using a fancy word to talk about a red color. Diagram 1.5 shows a grouping of different hues.

VALUE describes the lightness or darkness of a color. A red that has white added to it is a red of lighter value. If it has some black in it, it is a red of darker value. Some colors, such as yellow, are of a lighter value right out of the tube, while others—viridian green or ultramarine blue—are naturally a darker value. Diagram 1.6 shows different values of purple and green. Note the hues purple and green do not change, only the lightness or darkness changes.

SATURATION refers to a color's purity or greyness. A red straight from tube is a saturated color. Think of it as saturated or drenched with full color. A greyish color is a desaturated color. As we begin mixing grey with a tube red, we are gradually

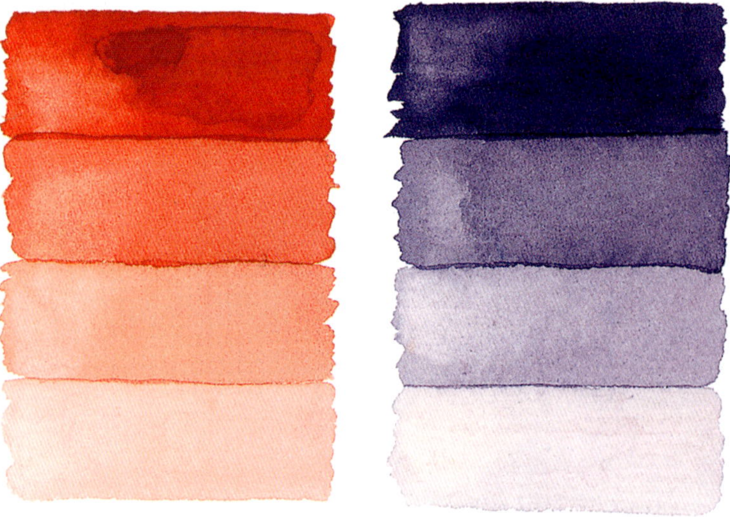

Diagram 1.5 The values of the violet and the red are becoming lighter as more water is added to the color.

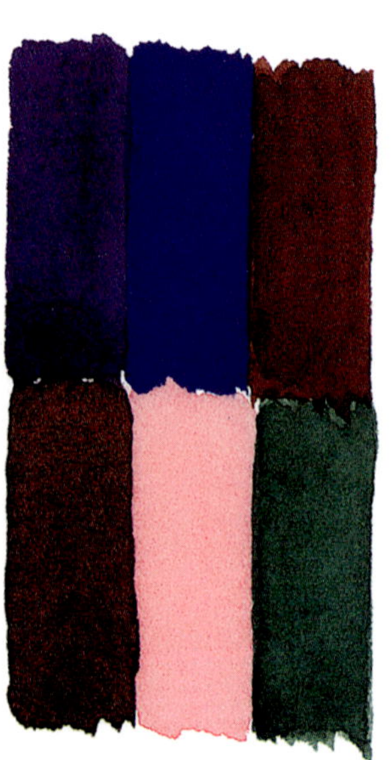

Diagram 1.6 Value can be used for sharp contrast when we make most of the painting dark and a small part of the painting light.

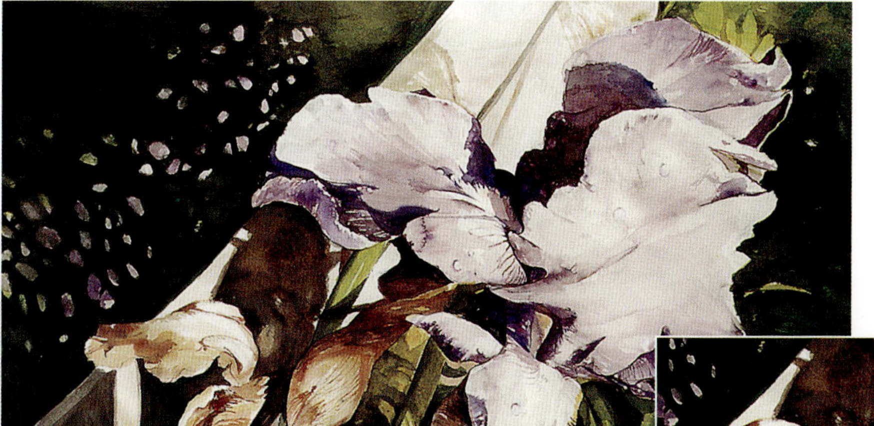

Morning Iris by Nancy Carey, *30" x 22" (76cm x 56cm)*
The dark greens surrounding the light violet irises provides a strong value contrast that give the painting a crisp sparkle. The juxtaposition of the desaturated red-orange and green makes the yellow greens and saturated violets appear super bright. This is called a contrast of saturation.

desaturating the red. If this sounds confusing, remember this: A saturated color is a pure color, a desaturated color is a greyish color. Diagram 1.8 shows blue and an orange that are desaturated with grey. The hues do not change, only the greyness of the blue and orange changes.

Using our three terms, a rose by any other name would be a fully saturated, slightly bluish red hue of a medium dark value.

RECIPE FOR SUCCESS

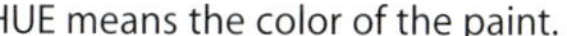

Learn how to describe colors with these three terms:

HUE means the color of the paint.

VALUE means the lightness or darkness of the color.

SATURATION refers to the purity of a color. A saturated color is a pure color, a desaturated color is a greyish color.

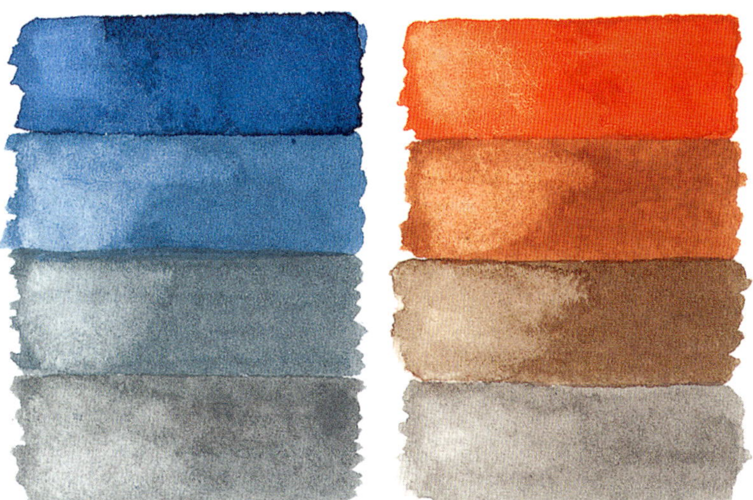

Diagram 1.7 The blue and orange are becoming desaturated with the addition of grey.

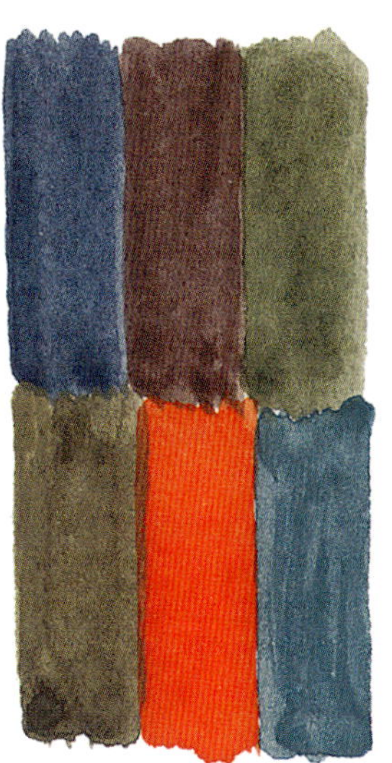

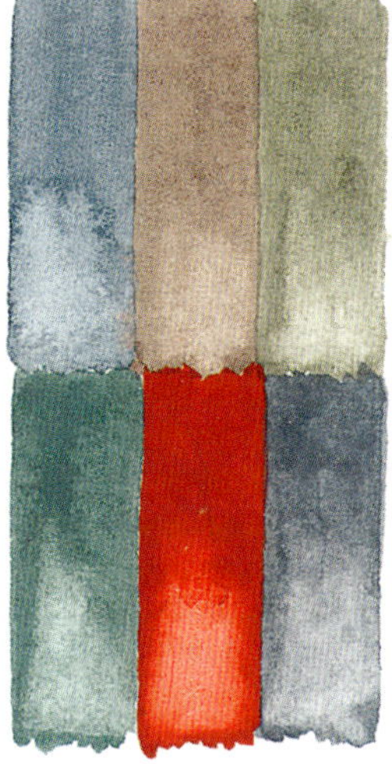

Diagram 1.8 The saturated orange and red work well when surrounded by a variety of desaturated colors.

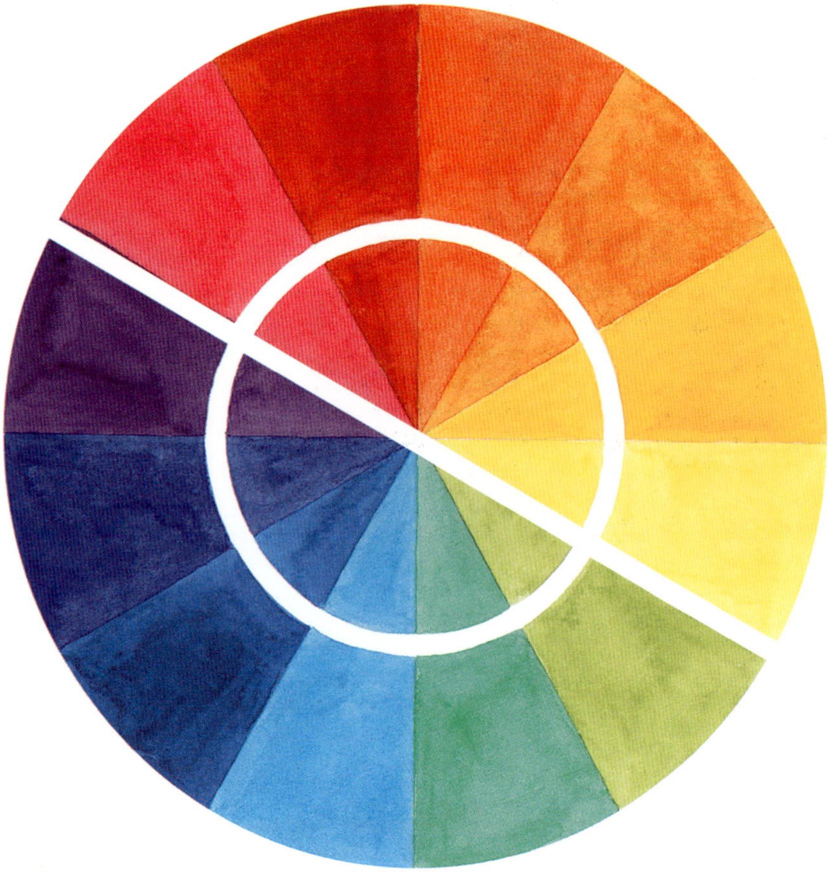

Bisecting the Color Circle

Draw a line straight through the middle of the color wheel to separate the reds, oranges and yellows from the greens, blues and violets; this bisects the colors.

The two groups of colors are often said to be warm and cool. While the idea of bisecting the color wheel is a good one, pinning one side as warm or cool can limit your growth as a painter. In diagram 1.11 we see two oranges, yet one appears warmer than the other. How can it be that variations of one hue from the warm side of the wheel appear both warm and cool?

Diagram 1.12 shows two blues; typically blue is called a cool color, but, once

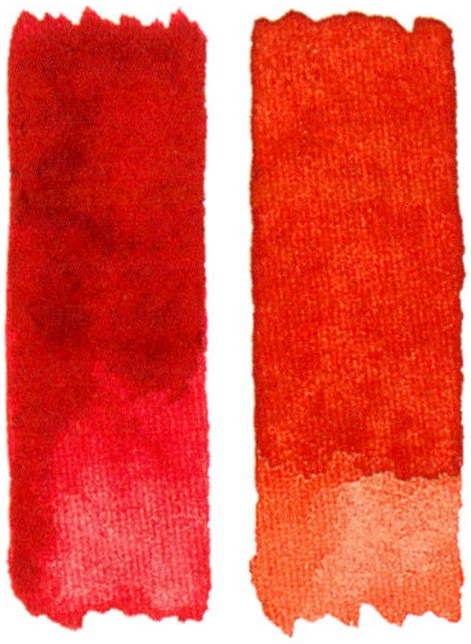

Diagram 1.9 **This color wheel is bisected into what are typically called warm and cool colors.**

Diagram 1.10 **The orange on the left appears cool and the orange on the right appears warm.**

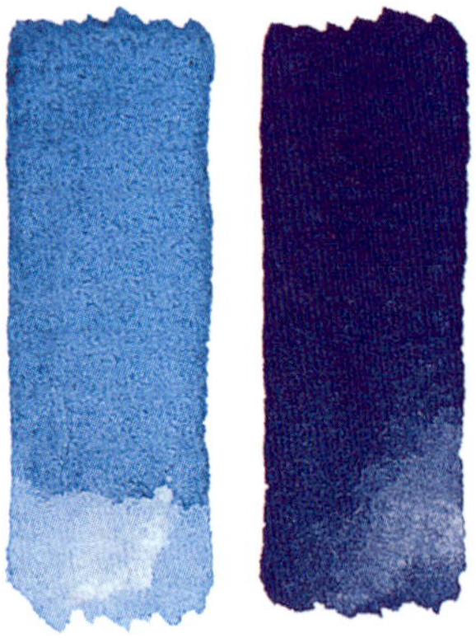

Diagram 1.11 **The blue on the left appears warm and the blue on the right appears cool.**

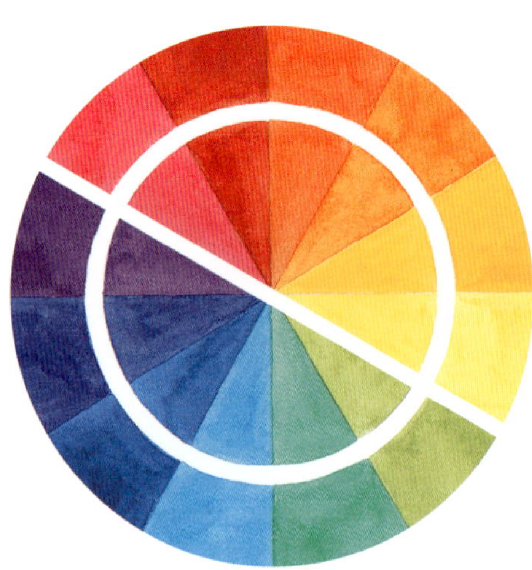

Diagram 1.12 **We can bisect the color wheel at any point. Here we are separating it along the red/green line.**

again, one appears warmer and the other cooler. I think it is better to realize each hue can have variations that can appear either warm or cool. The blues in diagram 1.12 have such individual qualities. For example, we can use the cooler French ultramarine blue on the right in shadow areas and we can use the warmer cerulean blue on the left in the sunlit areas of our painting.

Breaking traditional rules about warm and cool colors gives us freedom. We can now bisect the color wheel anywhere. For example, we can draw a line through diagram 1.13 to find two different groups of colors.

Contrasting each group in a painting will create a very powerful impact. For example, we might consider our painting as having two sides. On the left side we can paint colors from the yellow-orange to violet side of the wheel. On the right side we can paint colors from the yellow to blue-violet side of the wheel.

Kay Smith's *Blue Green Chair with Clay Goat* (above right) is a terrific example of how bisecting a color wheel works in a painting.

The left side of *Blue Green Chair with Clay Goat* by Kay Smith contains mostly greens, blue-greens, and blues, while the right side is made of greater amounts of red and red-orange. In this case, the color wheel is bisected along the blue-green /yellow-orange line. Intermingled on each side are small touches of colors from the opposite side of the wheel. The touch of red on the chair cushion comes from the opposite side of the wheel and, because it is kept small, it provides exciting contrast.

Not every stroke needs to be preplanned when you try this. Just work as you usually do, but keep this book open and the idea in mind. The more you try to use these ideas consciously in your work, the more natural they will eventually become.

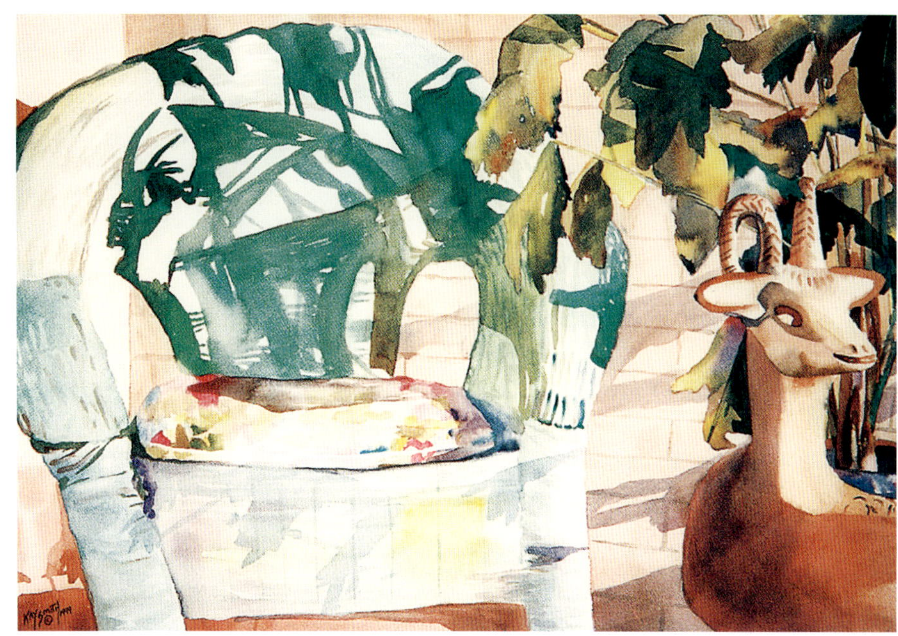

Blue Green Chair with Clay Goat **by Kay Smith,** ***15" x 22" (38cm x 56cm)***
The painting successfully contrasts the blue-green on the left against the red-oranges on the right. This is a good example of using a bisected color wheel.

RECIPE FOR SUCCESS
Dynamic color compositions arise when you contrast colors from the two sides of a bisected color wheel.

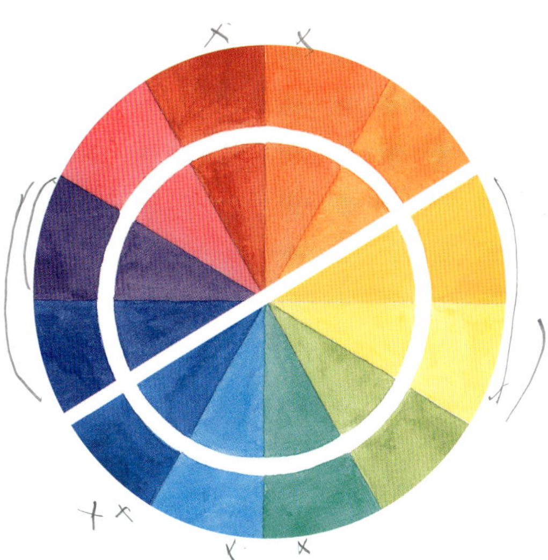

Diagram 1.13 The color wheel bisected along the blue/green, yellow/orange line.

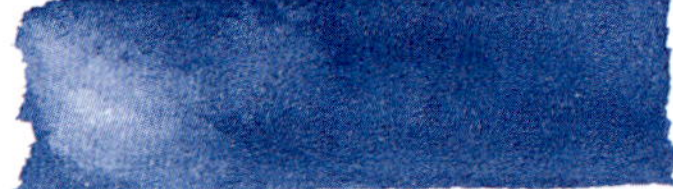
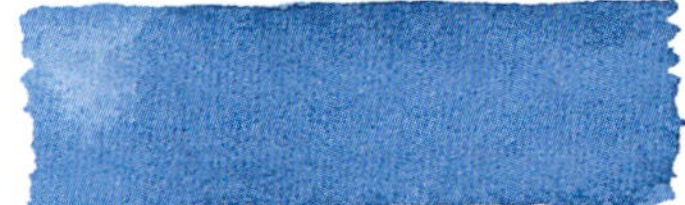
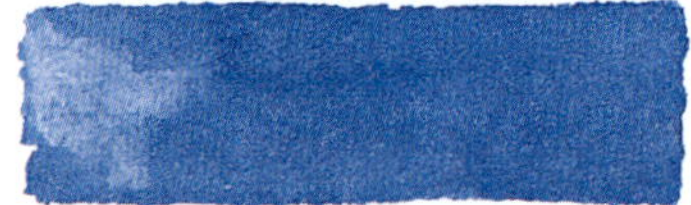

Diagram 1.14 I have used different blues on the color wheel. If you decide to substitute a color, choose one that is similar to a color already on the wheel.

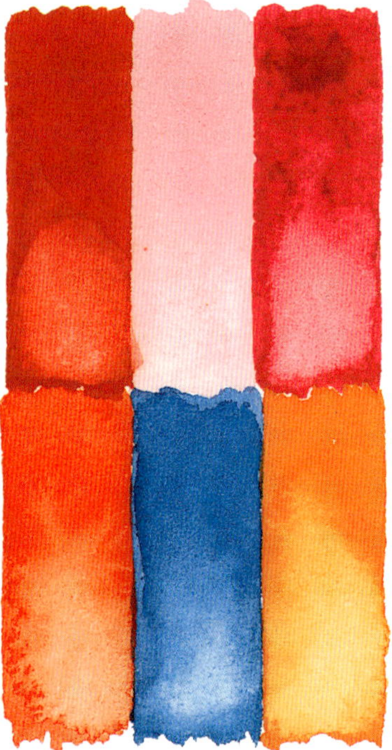

Diagram 1.15 The grouping of different oranges becomes more exciting when a small touch of blue is added. Small touches of different colors activate sections of a painting.

Choosing Your Own Palette

I think it is a good idea to use the twelve colors I have chosen at first. This way you can compare your own studies to my diagrams. There are a couple things you will wish to know when matching your colors to mine. Color names with the word "hue" are often confusing to artists. For example, there is a "cadmium red" and a "cadmium red hue." The word hue means different pigments are in the paint. However, the red from both tubes will usually look the same. Some paints might have a name such as "the bluest blue ever" that does not match any of my blues. Careful reading, though, will often discern small print that says the blue is a phthalo blue or an ultramarine blue. Then you know it will work (diagram 1.14). You can also paint swatches of your paints and choose the colors closest to the twelve I have illustrated. While it will not be exact, it should work fine for most of our exercises. Prepackaged paint sets are no guarantee that you will have bright saturated colors that span the spectrum, so I urge you to pay special attention to the colors included if you choose that route. You can paint small chips of your colors to match against the color wheel colors to see how they relate.

It is possible to mix almost every color we see with the hues of our twelve color palette. Occasionally, however, there will be a unique color that you just cannot get. Colors have particular characteristics and sometimes you need to switch one of the colors. For example, if you plan a large painting with a great deal of a color that is not on the color wheel, purchasing a tube of that color can save mixing time. I recommend temporarily substituting the new tube color with the one closest in hue on our color wheel.

Substituting one or two colors is not a problem. I have selected particular hues both for their vibrancy and their relationship to each other in forming a bright color wheel. You may prefer cadmium lemon yellow instead of cadmium yellow pale, or you may like the exact blueness found with a manganese as opposed to a cerulean. In deciding what color to substitute for a personal palette, choose a replacement color that is similar to the one on the circle you are replacing—do not substitute a blue for a red. Choose bright hues and watch your mixture colors; you want them bright rather than muddy or grey.

Whatever your subject, it is important to keep your whole palette of twelve hues available. Even if you are painting a blue ball under a blue sky against a blue ocean, you will want to have the whole range of colors ready to use. Omitting one or more on your palette causes mixing problems and problems seeing color options. I have had students who were painting pink drapery from a palette of red, white and black. They predetermined their colors because they thought the drapery would be made only of red with the addition of black and white. This limited their seeing and they missed the way the warm light made highlights appear yellow and shadows slightly violet. Maintaining a palette of twelve colors is not a problem with watercolor, because if the paints dry they are easily reconstituted with water.

I recommend artists don't start out by trying to reinvent a whole new color wheel by substituting many or all of the colors. If you ultimately wish to create one, you will want to carefully select full saturation hues that span the spectrum. Painting small chips of the paints you have, cutting them out, and arranging them into a circle is a good way to begin. You can also cut the chips from a paint swatch pamphlet some manufacturers print up and distribute at art stores. Either way, it is important to position an equal number of colors between your primary colors: red, blue, and yellow. In my color wheel, three mixture colors separate the red, blue, and yellow from one other. That is all advanced experimentation you might eventually wish to try. But first, let's jump right in and see how we can begin to give our paintings that incredible color and luminosity that I call the wow effect."

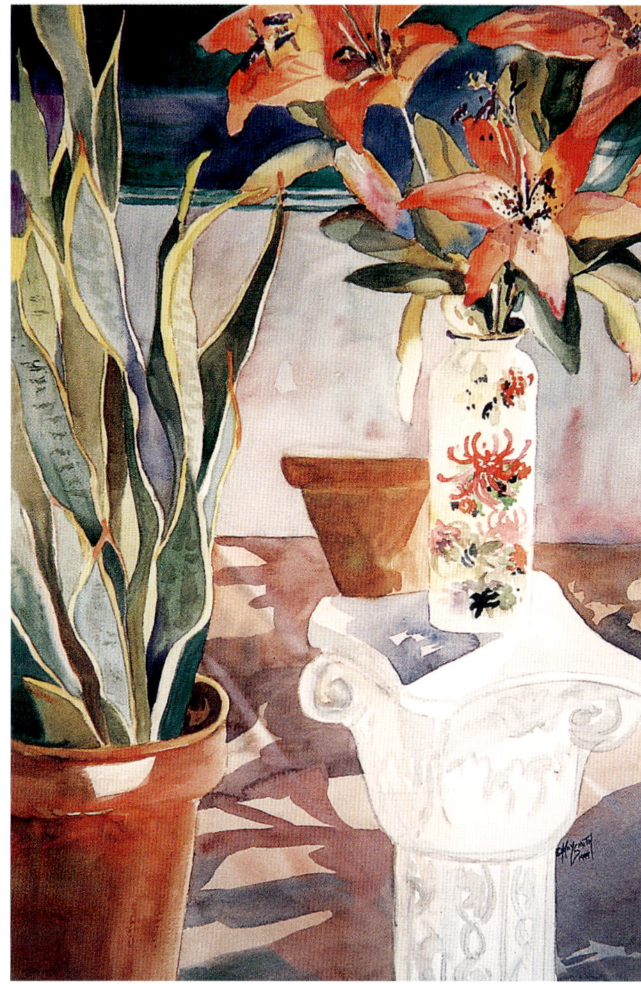

Tiger Lilies with Snake Plant **by Kay Smith, *22" x 15" (56cm x 38cm)***
Touches of unexpected colors appear everywhere here. The shadows are a variety of violets; touches of orange appear on the leaves. It is important to look for these hints of unexpected colors in your subject.

RECIPE FOR SUCCESS

Ready all twelve colors at the start of each painting session to help prevent predeterming the colors you will see.

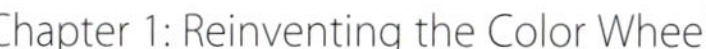

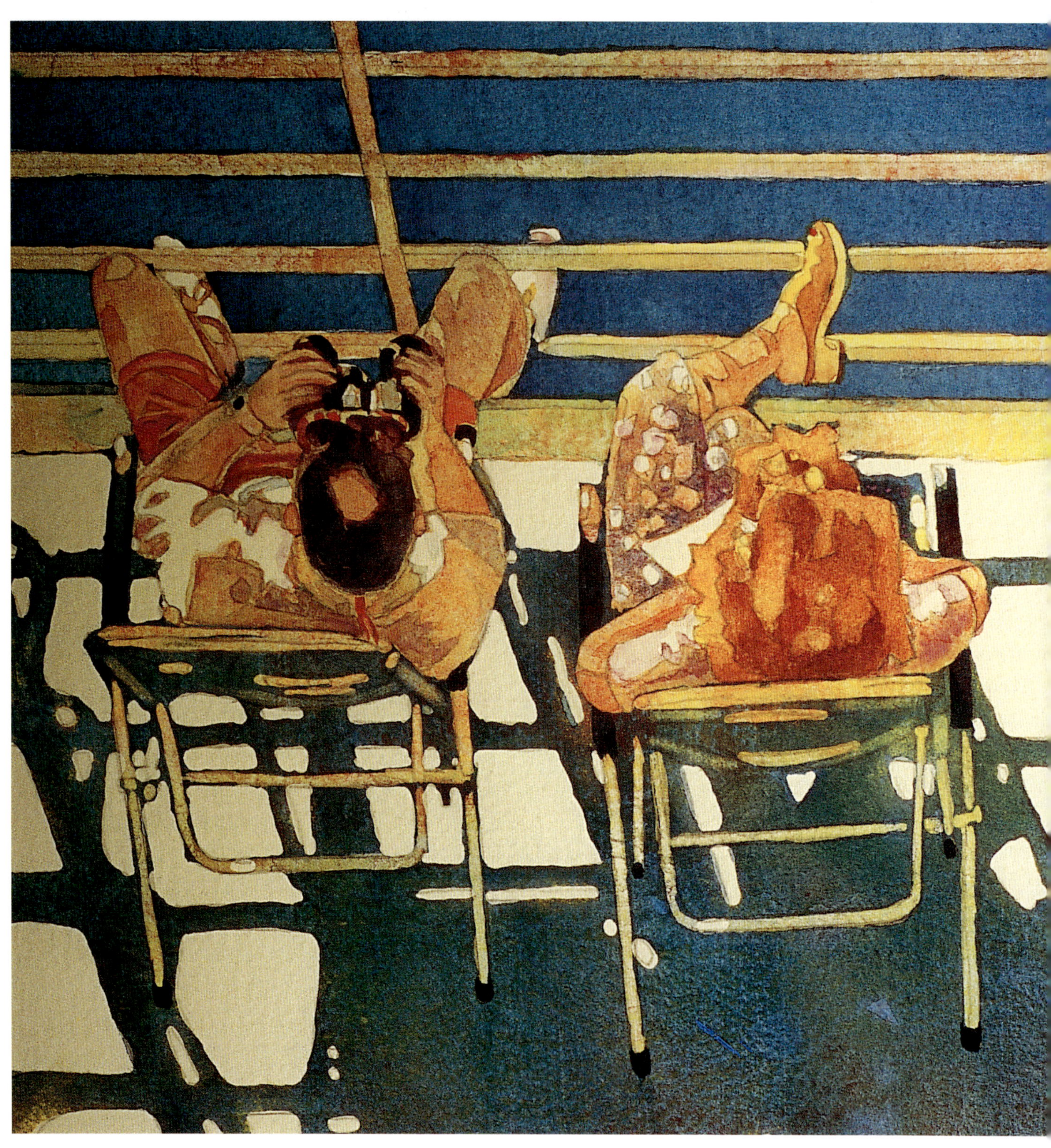

Opposite Attraction: Using Colors from the Opposite Sides of the Color Wheel

Complementary colors are sets of two colors that have a special relationship. They are found by drawing a line from any color on the color wheel through the center of the circle to the color on the other side. This opposite color is the complement of the first. There are three main sets of complements on the color wheel: red-green, blue-orange, and yellow-violet.

Altogether there are twelve sets of complements found using this color wheel. For example, a red-orange will be the complement of a blue-green. Complements next to each other provide an excitement that reminds me of the finale of Tchaikovsky's 1812 Overture, where the cannons are fired in time to the symphonic strains. It's almost impossible to resist such power. But complements mixed together result in subtle luminous greys. It's the special appeal of complements that they can perform such opposite functions so well.

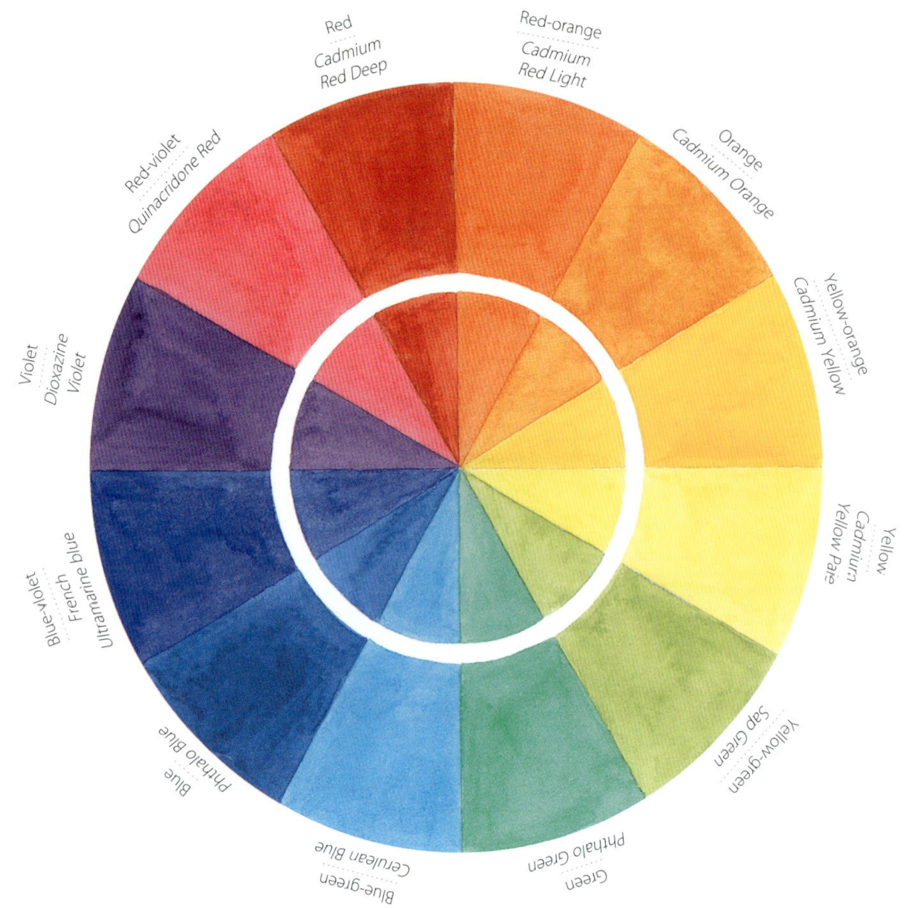

Diagram 2.1 Complements are found directly across from each other on the color wheel.

Complements are opposites that attract. In the real world, examples of complementary colors are found frequently. The striking complements found in flowers such as the viola or gazania and the inspiring complements of a blue sky with an orange sunset all attest to the power of complements used in close proximity. Artists who paint one color often feel they want to apply its complement in order to provide a more complete experience (diagram 2.2).

Diagram 2.2 Sets of the main primary colors at full saturation.

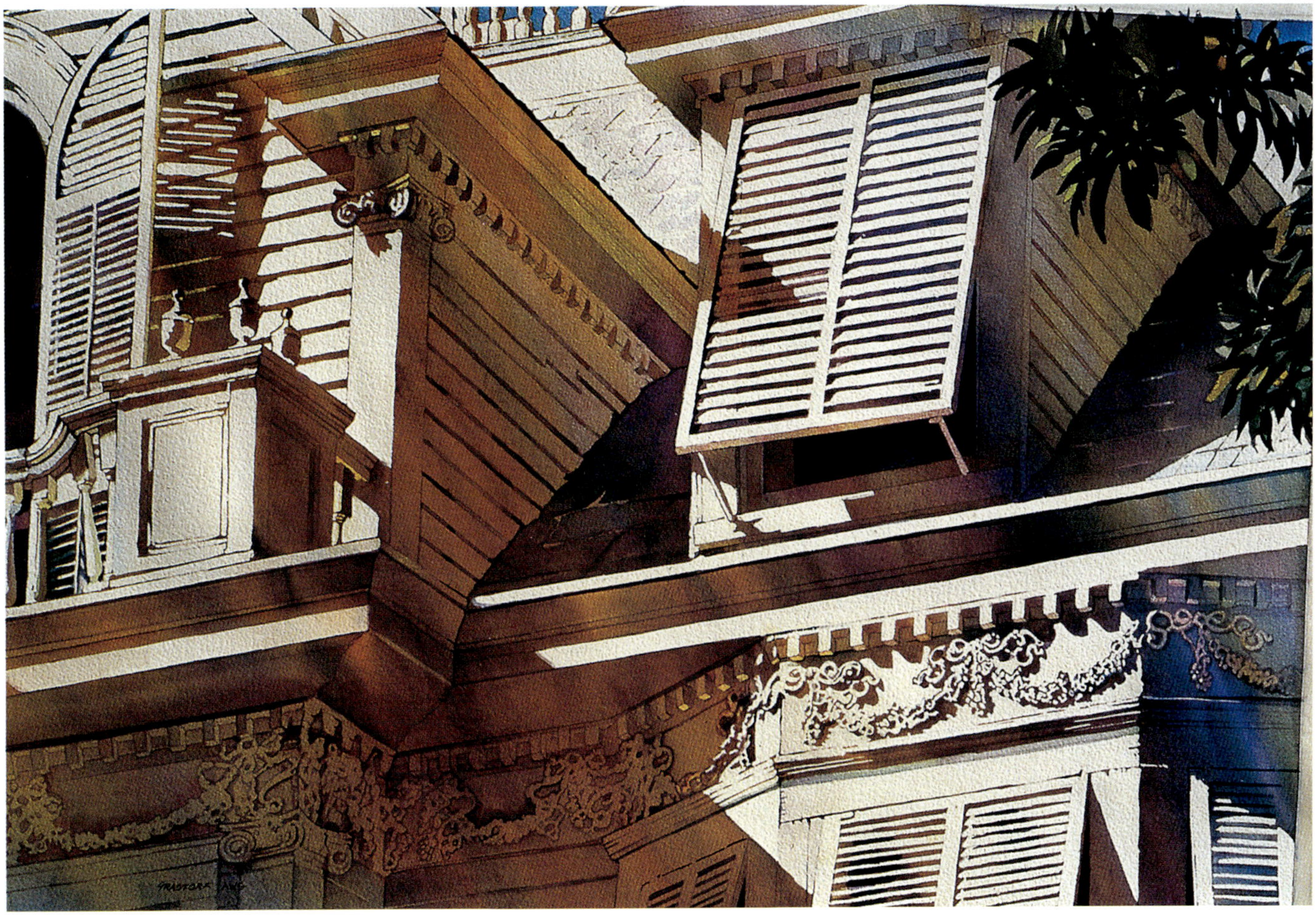

Key West House by Jean Grastorf, *30" x 40" (76cm x 102cm)*

The robust glow of this painting is secured through the complementary set orange and blue.

RECIPE FOR SUCCESS

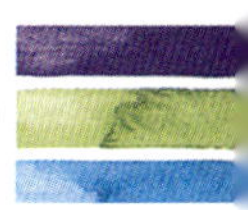

Place complementary colors next to each other for dazzling brightness.

Fully saturated complements produce a strong effect when placed next to each other. This can appear festive to some painters and garish to others. Yet, the colors described as garish might be described as harmonious by the same viewer when one or both of the colors is slightly greyed. Likewise, the addition of white or black to the complementary set will suggest a wide range of moods. When complements are presented with equal value they can become extremely ethereal and often uncannily bright (diagram 2.3).

Strangely enough, when such bright complementary colors are mixed together, the result is a greyish color. The two colors appear to cancel each other out. According to theory, their mixture should be a perfect grey; however, no two colors are perfect complements. A red, for example, may be slightly yellow or a green may be tinged with blue. Because of this, more often than not the mixtures are colored greys rather than a perfectly colorless grey (diagram 2.4).

The greys that are found by mixing complements are rich and can add brilliancy to a painting where black and white greys might fail.

Diagram 2.3 Complements of equal value that are placed next to each other can give bright and delicate effects.

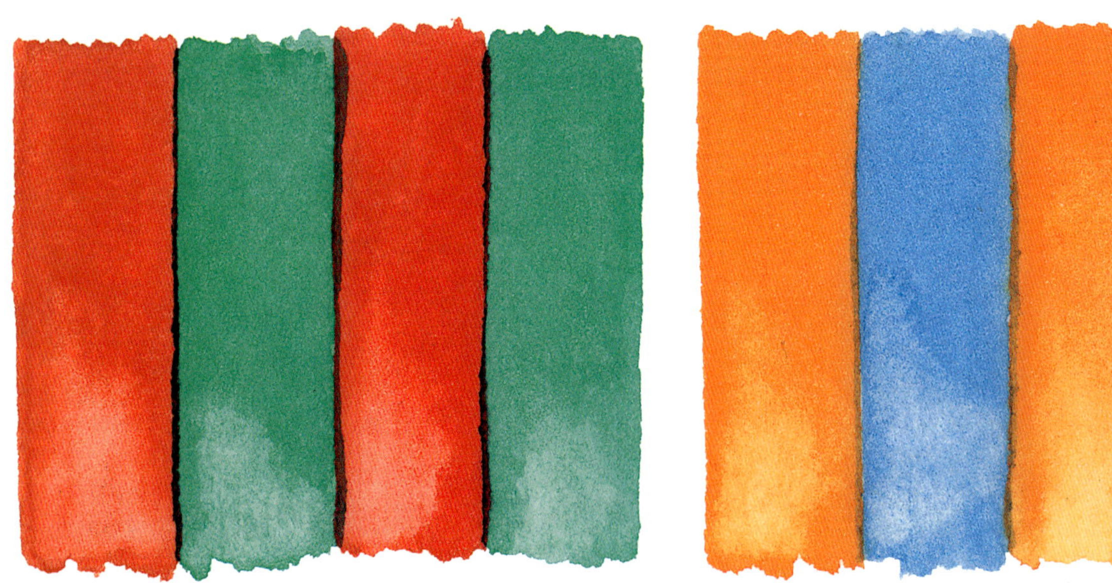

Red and Green

Blue and Orange

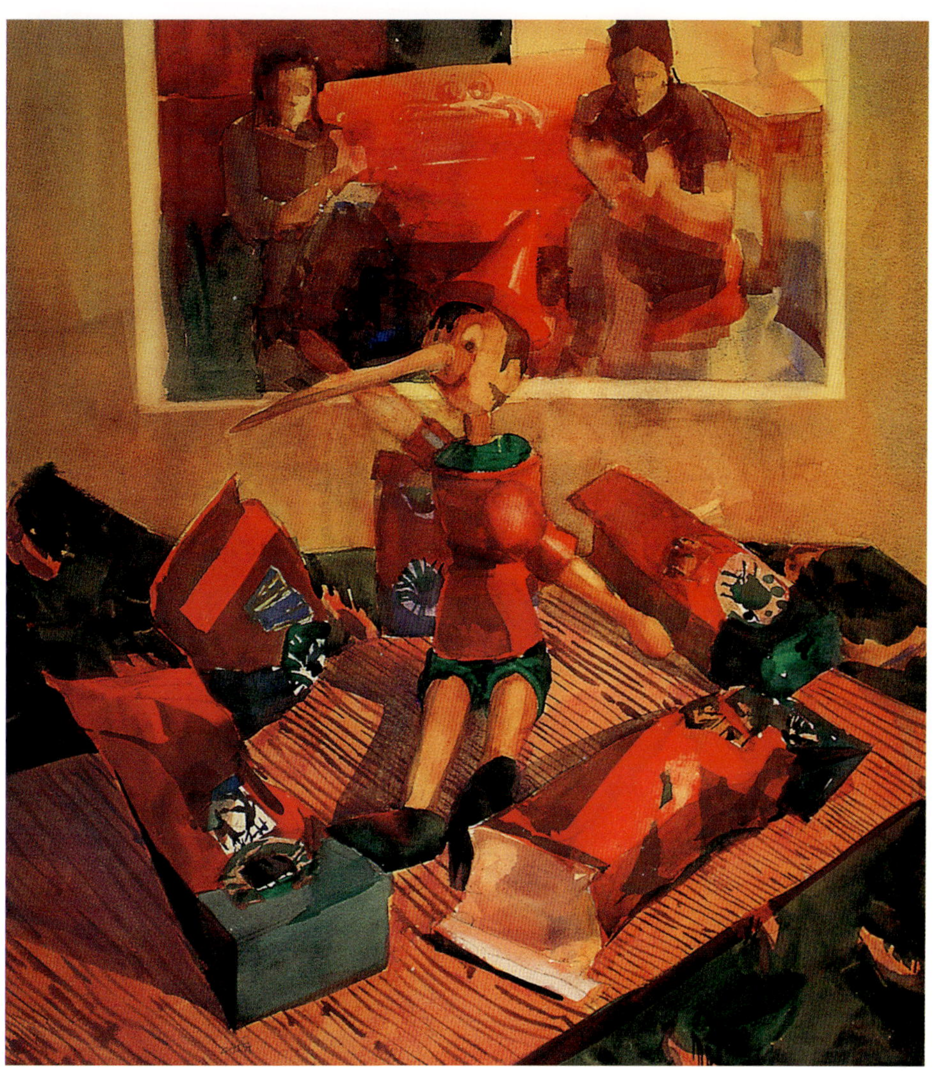

Caffeine Lies by Barbara Pitts, *32" x 29" (81cm x 74cm)*
This Pinocchio isn't telling a lie when he says fully saturated complements red and green have been placed next to each other, producing incredible vibrancy.

Yellow and Violet

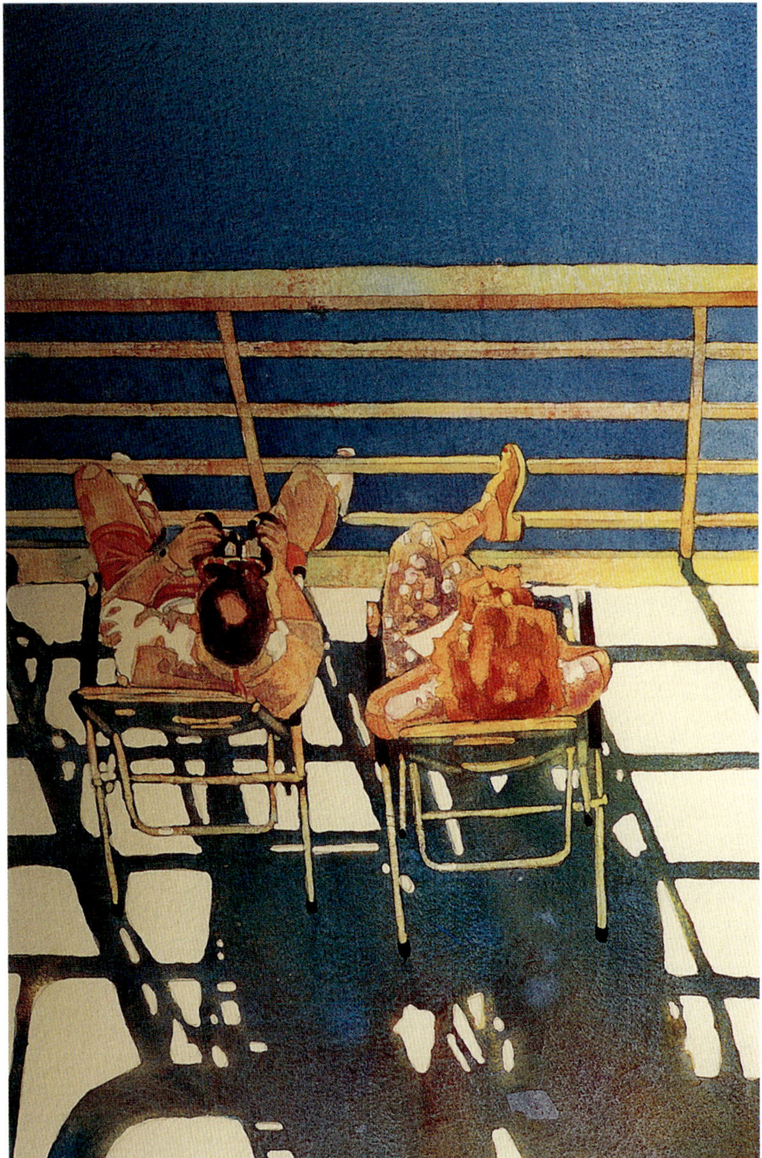

QE 2 Shadows by Jean Grastorf, *20" x 16" (51cm x 41cm)*
The blue-green sea is contrasted with a host of oranges, from yellow-orange to red-orange. The blue and orange are mixed together for the luminous grey shadows under the chairs. The importance of these luminous greys cannot be overstated.

Black and White

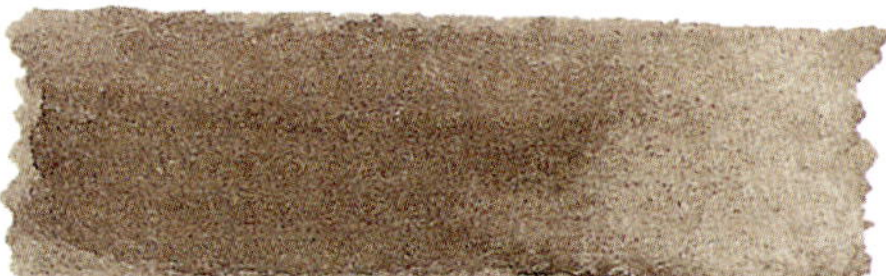

Yellow and Violet

Blue and Orange

Red and Green

Diagram 2.4 The grey on the top is made with black and white only. The more colorful greys are made using complementary colors.

Optical Complements

Around 1870, the physicist Ewald Hering addressed a peculiar problem regarding complementary colors. Artists and researchers knew that if they stared at a swatch of color for about forty seconds and then switched their eyes to a white surface, a ghostly color, called an afterimage color, would appear. This afterimage color would always be opposite from the first color stared at. This is also known as the optical complement. For example, staring at a red produced a greenish afterimage when the eyes were transferred to the white paper. What was unaccounted for was that a blue dot produced an afterimage of yellow instead of the known complement orange. It was also noticed that the afterimage color of a yellow swatch was blue. Hering and others went on to prove this effect is due to the way the human eye/brain system processes colors after the retina of the eye has received it. This process categorizes colors in terms of the opposites red/green, blue/yellow, and black/white. This means there are actually two sets of complements to consider, the paint mixture complements and the optical complements.

Paint Mixture Complements	Optical Mixture Complements
Red/Green	Red/Green
Blue/Orange	Blue/Yellow
Yellow/Violet	Black/White

Table 2.1 The primary colors of the two type of complements are compared above. The complement of blue is the key difference.

This oddity probably does not make a great deal of difference to painters who physically mix their watercolors together to make greys. In that case they will pay attention to the paint mixture complements. However, it makes a tremendous difference when the colors are painted as small separate pieces of unmixed colors. When applied as dots or thin lines, colors mingle together in the eye in what is called optical mixture. Optical mixture works differently than mixtures where the colors are physically mixed together before their application to the painting. Optical mixture in watercolors can often be found in areas where patterns or small elements such as leaves and sky show many small touches of color next to each other.

RECIPE FOR SUCCESS

Mix complementary colors together to form greys that are more radiant than those formed with only black and white.

The key part of optical mixture painters must be aware of is that when blue and yellow are applied in small dots, they tend to cancel each other out, and their optical mixture is more grey than green (diagram 2.5).

It is often said that when the French painter Georges Seurat wanted to paint grass, he would place tiny dots of blue and yellow next to each other that would mingle to a green that was greener than any green found in a tube of paint. Instead, such dots optically blend to a greyish color, which is one of the problems painters often encounter when painting grass or leaves. In fact, when painting grassy areas, Seurat would place a few dots of blue and a few dots of yellow, but also many, many dots of green.

Placing small dots of particular colors next to each other so they blend together in the eye is a good way to create lively areas of color (diagram 2.6). By placing the complements next to each other in such small dots, vibrant, pulsing greys can be achieved.

There is no one set of true complements between the paint complements and the optical complements. The key to success is knowing when to pay attention to which particular set, depending upon how the paint is applied.

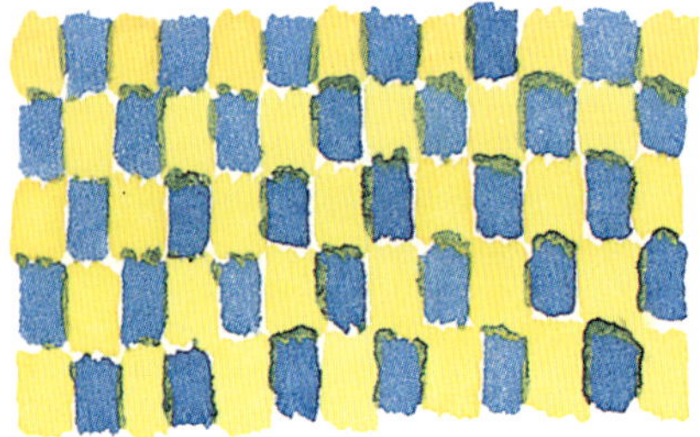

Diagram 2.5 From a short distance, the dots of blue and yellow blend to a greyish color rather than a saturated green.

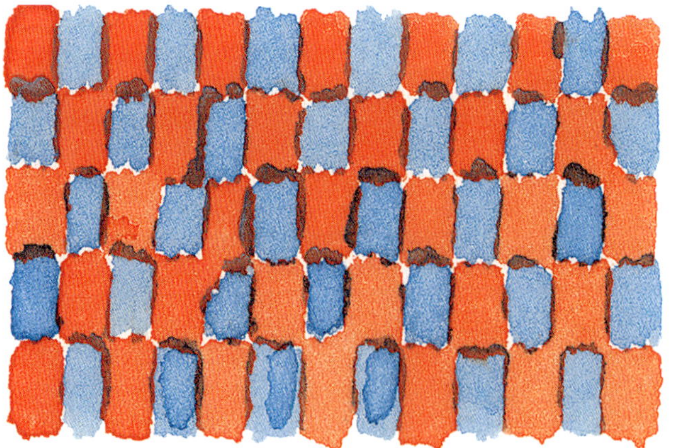

Diagram 2.6 Placing small dots of colors near each other in a watercolor, as in this example of red-orange and blue-green, is a good way to create optical mixtures that radiate a velvety light.

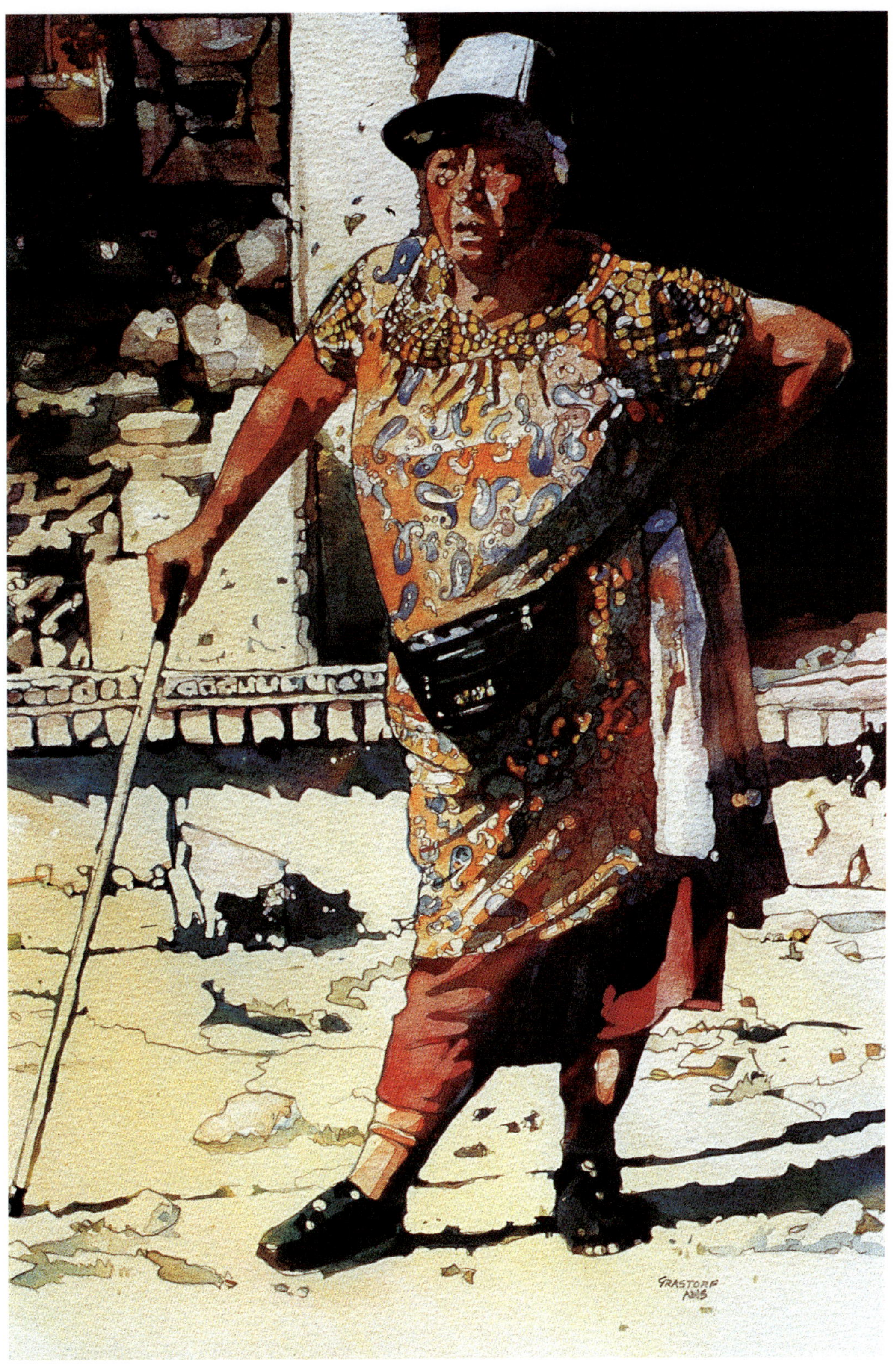

Chitzen Itza by Jean Grastorf, *25" x 20" (64cm x 51cm)*
The dazzling quality of the fabric is created with small pieces of blue and orange carefully applied as elements of the pattern.

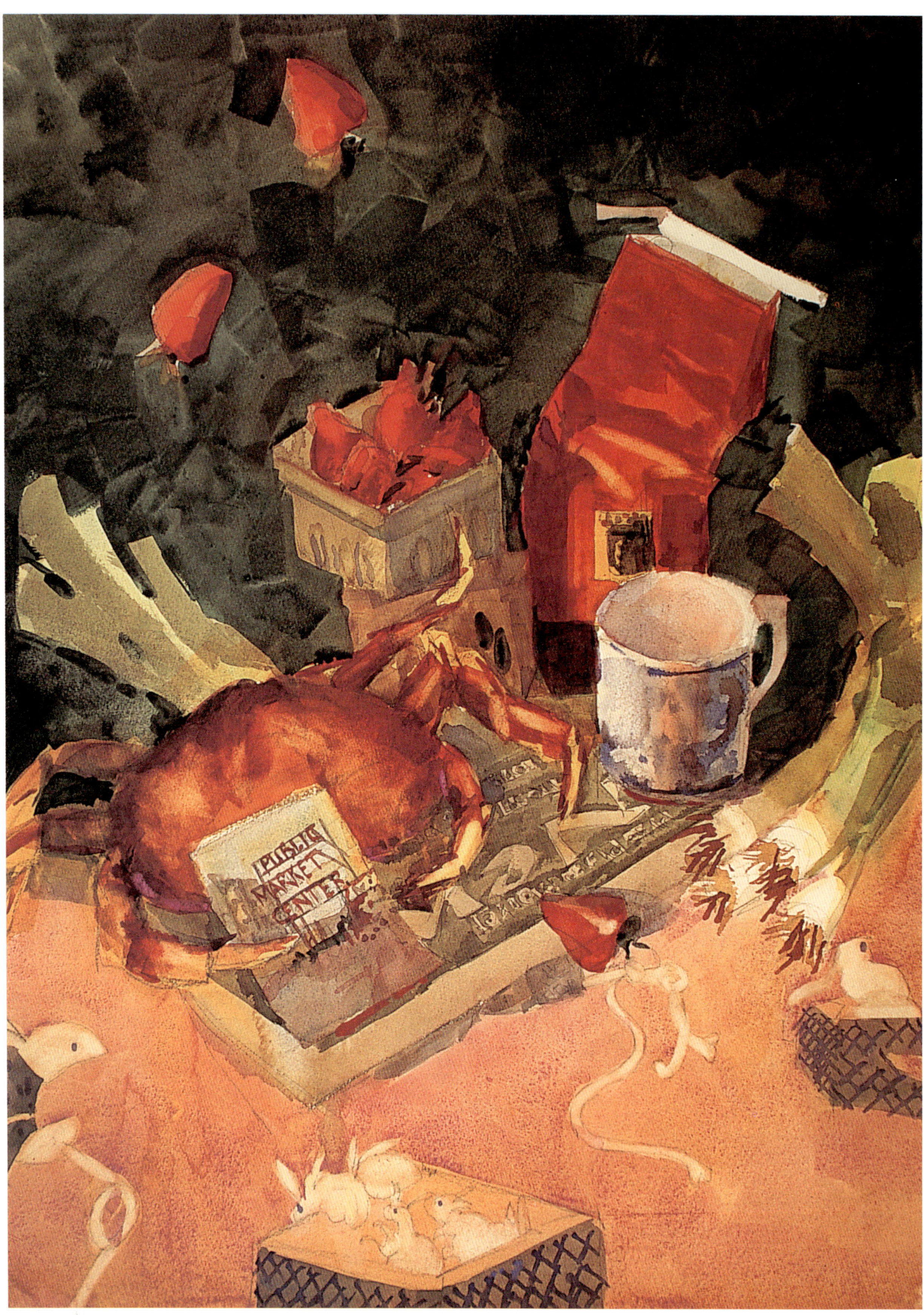
PUBLIC
MARKET
CENTER

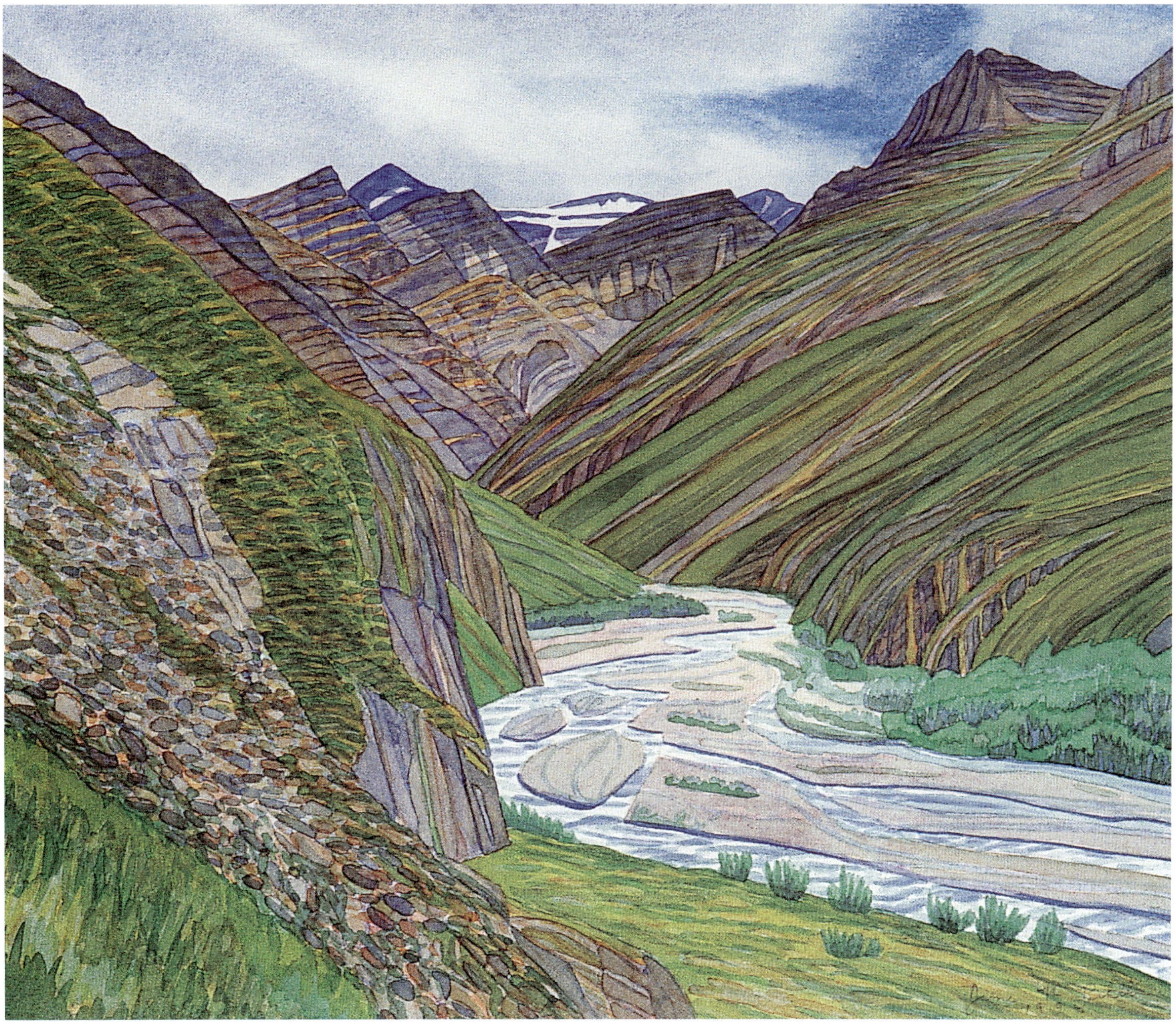

Marsh Fork Tributary by James Behlke, *17" x 21" (43cm x 53cm)*
The mountains and rocks are flecked with small dots and lines of colors for an uncommon sparkle that cannot be obtained with a flat applications of colors.

Left: ***A Beet Off*** **by Barbara Pitts,** ***28" x 22" (71cm x 56cm)***
The reds appears brighter than any color found in a tube because they are surrounded by greens. Note too how some of the complements have been altered in darkness and lightness.

RECIPE FOR SUCCESS

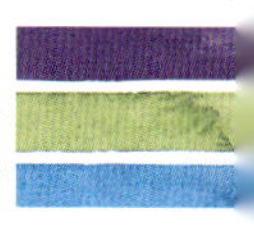

Consider juxtaposing small dots of complementary colors to produce subtle glows rather than painting an area one solid color.

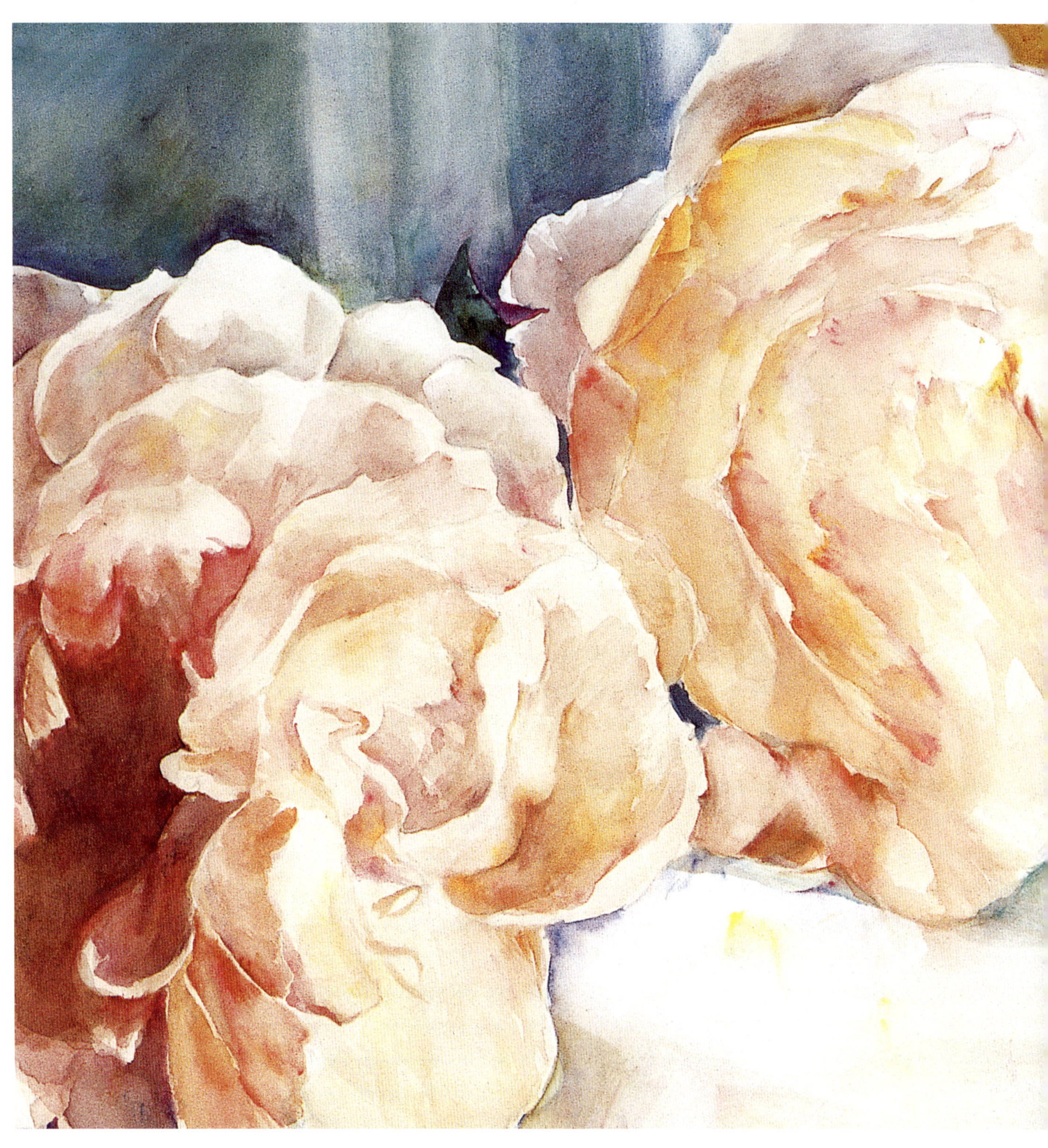

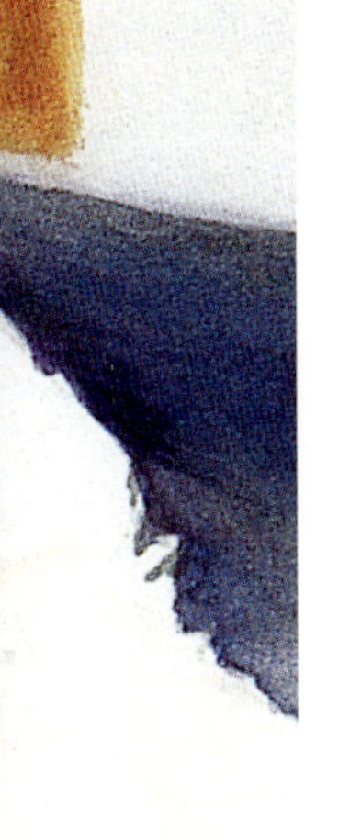

Creating Harmony with Three Hues:
Juxtaposing Color Triads

In a letter written in 1547, Benvenuto Cellini (1500–1571) voiced his opinion on the color usage of artists from the High Renaissance and mannerist periods of art. "I see all the other painters [apart from Michelangelo and Bronzino] wallowing in cornflowers and in a mishmash of colors fit only for fooling peasants." It certainly is a scathing condemnation of contemporary color usage. A grain of truth can be found in the comment, however. The colors the watercolorist chooses for painting can be compared to the framework of a house. Sensibly chosen colors give the painting structure and strength. The artist who chooses colors without any thought can quickly find himself or herself wallowing in an unmanaged and uncontrolled sty of jarring colors.

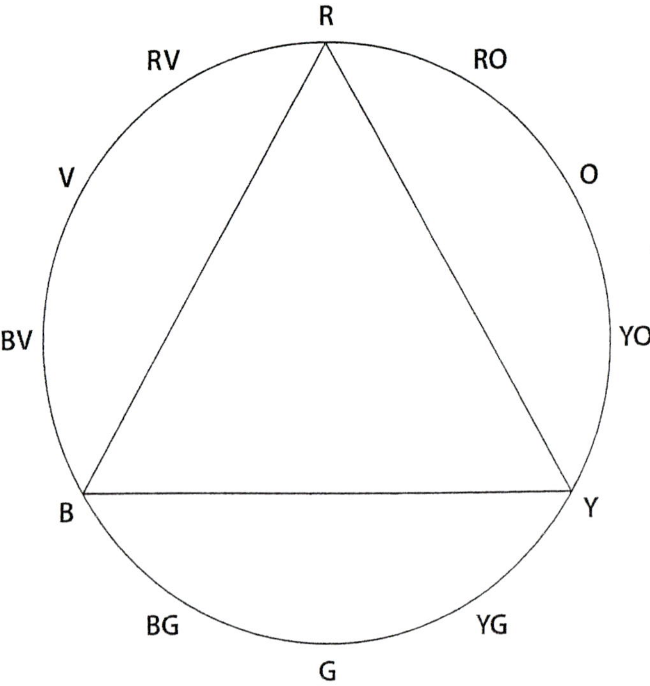

Diagram 3.1 An equilateral triangle placed within the color wheel points to the triad red, yellow, and blue.

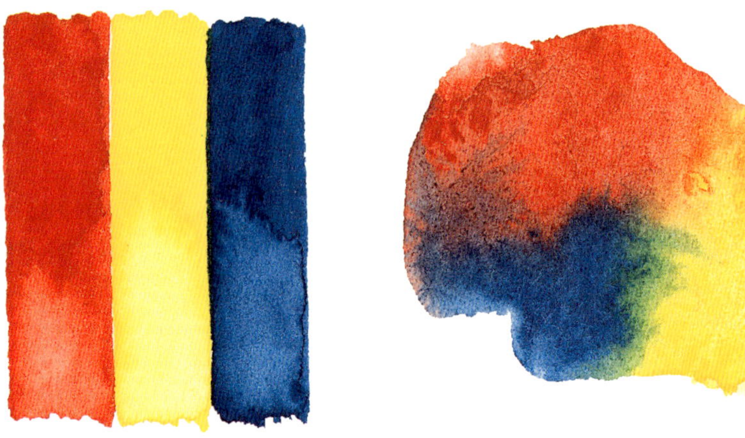

Diagram 3.2 Red, yellow, and blue triad.

The Primary Triad

Carefully chosen groups of three colors, known as triads, are particularly strong foundations upon which to build paintings. Triads are found by placing an equilateral triangle within the center of the twelve hue color wheel (diagram 3.1). The most commonly known triad found this way is made of red, yellow, and blue (diagram 3.2). Artists have long known these colors to be the primary colors of paint, or the three colors known to mix to all the other colors on the palette.

Theoretically this is true, but in reality it does not work that well because the primary colors are never perfect. A blue that has some red in it combined with a yellow will create a very muddy green, as many artists have discovered when trying to mix an ultramarine blue with a cadmium yellow to represent foliage. This is because both the ultramarine blue and the cadmium yellow contain some red. This red is the complement of the green that the blue and yellow are attempting to create, thus greying the final color. It is possible, however, to try a number of blues and yellows to find two that will mix to a more vibrant green.

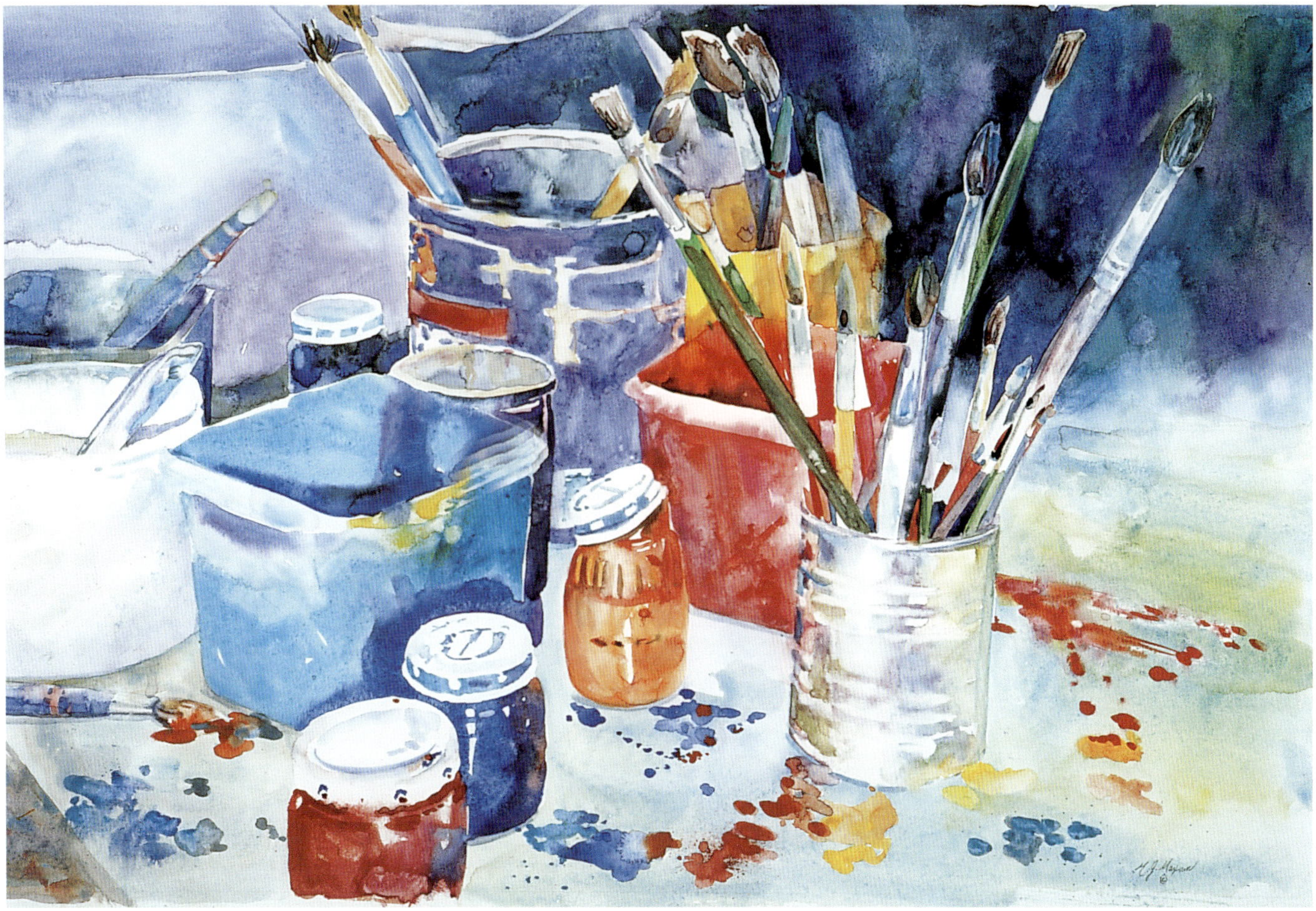

Art I Aftermath **by Mary J. Maxam,** ***18" x 24" (46cm x 61cm)***
The equilateral triad of red, yellow, and blue provides the foundation for this painting of the artist's tools.

The colors of the primary triad hold particular appeal because they are both bright and equidistant from each other on the color wheel. Three colors separate the red from the yellow and so on. This even distribution around the color wheel gives a sense of completeness for the viewer, much as regular intervals of musical tones can create harmony for the listener.

Some artists view the triad of primary colors red, yellow, and blue as the most important and most balanced and they use them as the foundation for their paintings. The Dutch painter Johannes Vermeer (1632–1675) was a master at building paintings around this triad.

RECIPE FOR SUCCESS

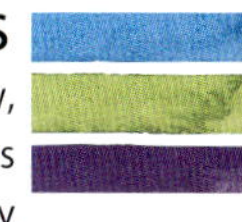

The primary colors of paint are red, yellow, and blue. They mix to the secondary colors orange, green, and violet. If the secondary color is dull, it is because one or both of the primary colors are slightly adulterated with the third primary.

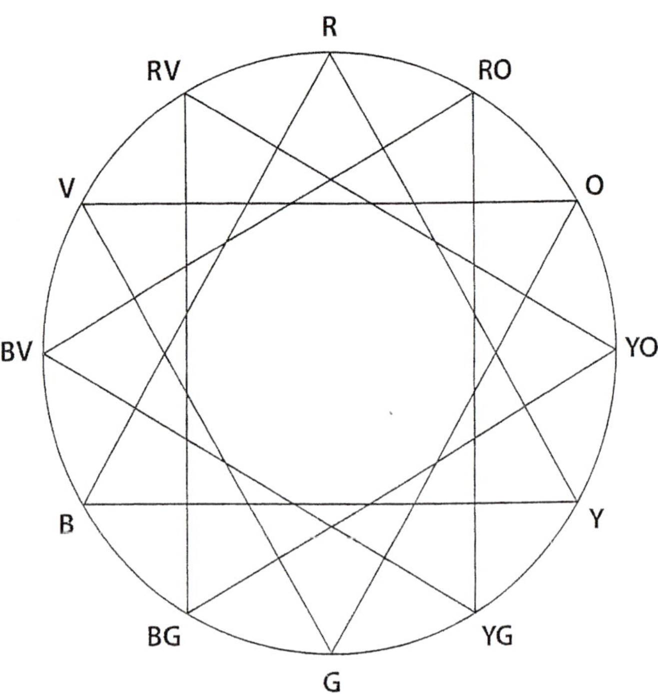

Diagram 3.3 The triangle may be rotated to point to other triads on the color wheel.

Expanding Triad Sets

Four sets of triads are found when the equilateral triangle is rotated.

Successful use of a triad in a watercolor does not mean the painting is constructed with only three colors, but it does mean the triad of colors plays a leading role. The triad of colors could occupy most of the area of the painting and be contrasted by fewer strokes of other colors. Or, as with the case of Vermeer, the painting may be constructed mostly with a greyer version of the triad and contrasted with more saturated triad colors to provide exciting focal points for the eye.

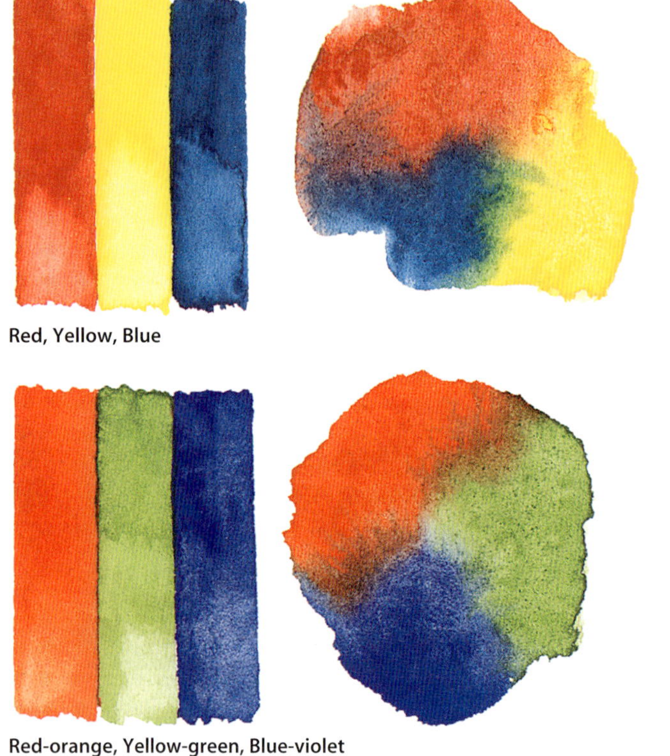

Red, Yellow, Blue

Red-orange, Yellow-green, Blue-violet

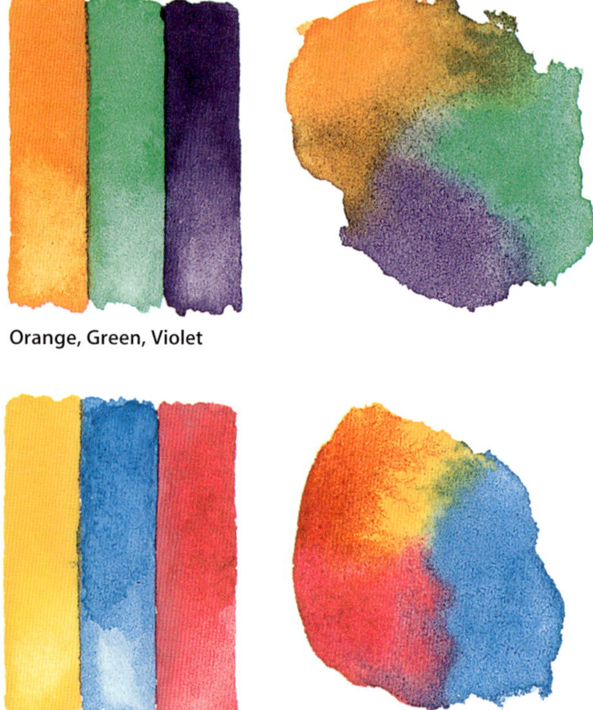

Orange, Green, Violet

Yellow-orange, Blue-green, Red-violet

Diagram 3.4 The tequilateral triads.

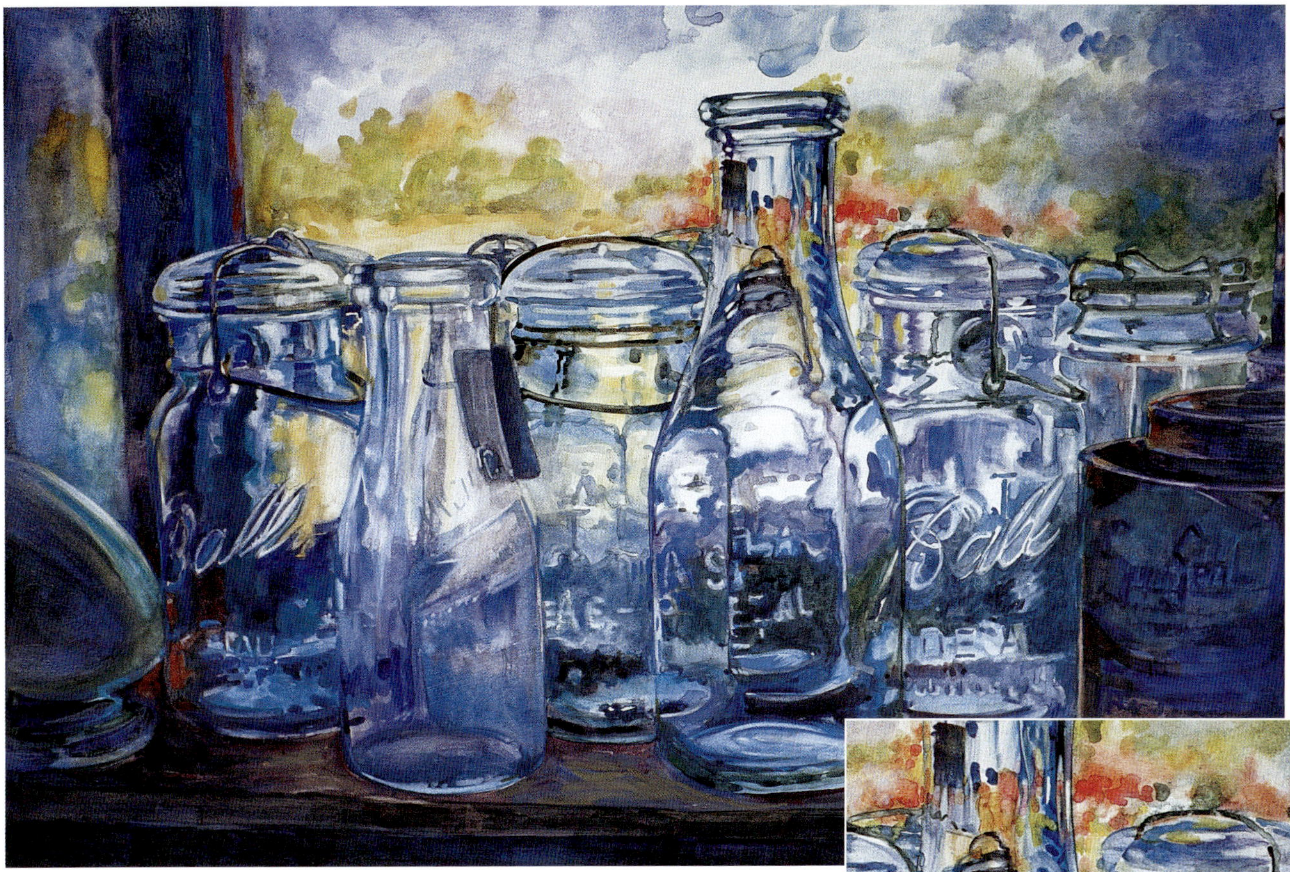

Ball Jars and Blue Glass by Mary J. Maxam, *20" x 30" (51cm x 76cm)*
The red-orange, yellow-green, and blue-violet triad provides a crisp transparency. The amounts of each color vary greatly, from an extensive use of the blue-violet to only the smallest touch of red-orange. Even the shelf the jars stand on is a mingling of these three colors.

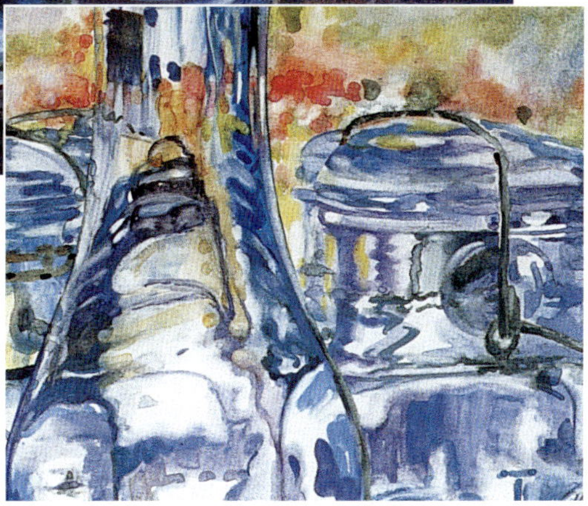

(Detail) The juxtaposing of the triad colors in a small area of the watercolor is a decisive point of interest and brings a sense of completeness.

RECIPE FOR SUCCESS

Desaturate, or grey, two of the triad colors while leaving the third at a full saturation for high contrast and energy without losing the harmonious nature of the combination.

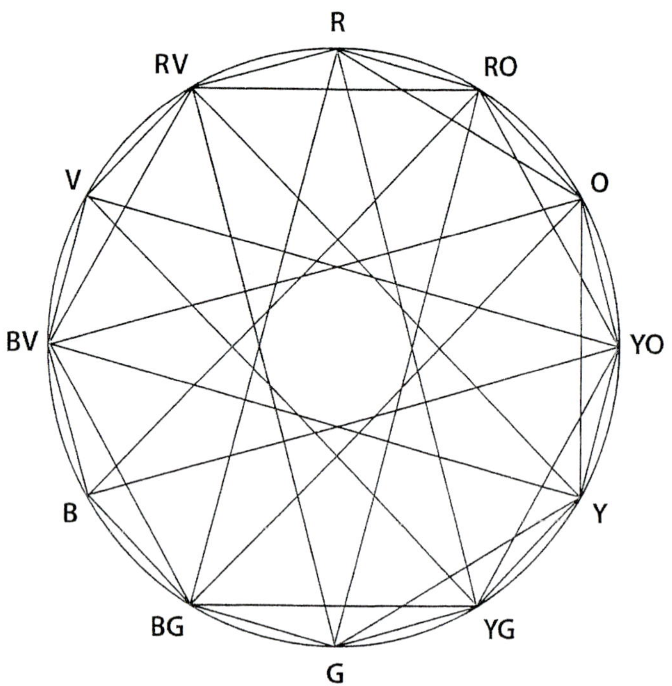

Diagram 3.5 The isosceles triangle points to twelve triads called split complementary triads.

When the shape of the triangle is altered from an equilateral triangle to a isosceles triangle (diagram 3.5), new triads are disclosed.

The isosceles triangle locates three colors—one color plus the two colors next to its complement. For this reason, it is called a split complementary triad (diagram 3.6). A split complement does not include the complement itself. Split complementary triads will offer unexpected color combinations that are nevertheless pleasing.

RECIPE FOR SUCCESS

In advance of the next chapter, where groups of four colors are discussed, add to your triad group the complement color that sits between the split complements. The triad of red, yellow-green, and blue-green would now include a fourth color, green. This can make an even more vibrant contrast as three similar colors intensify the one opposite color.

Diagram 3.6 Split complementary triads.

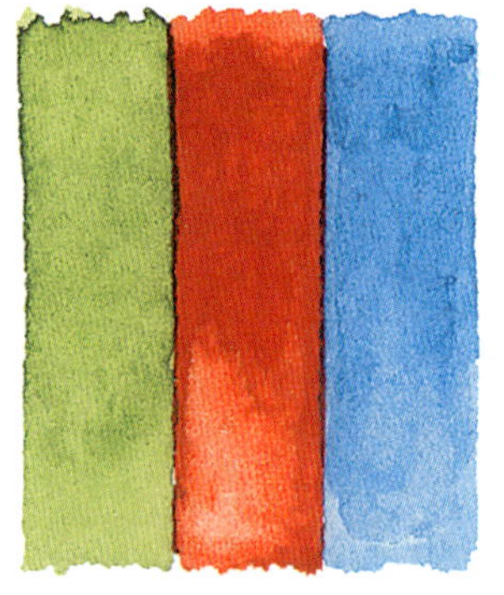

Yellow-green, Red, Blue-green

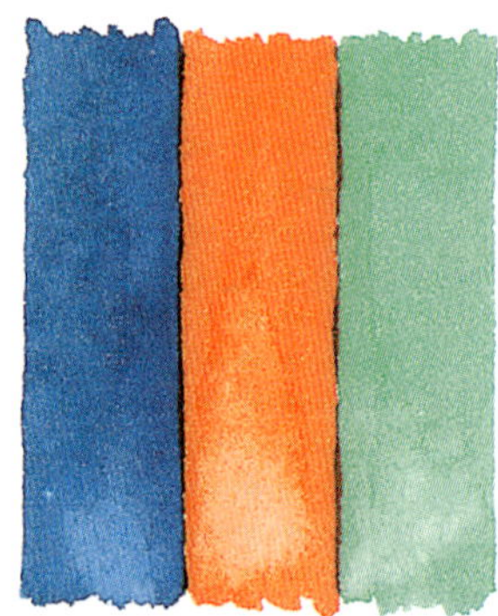

Blue, Red-orange, Green

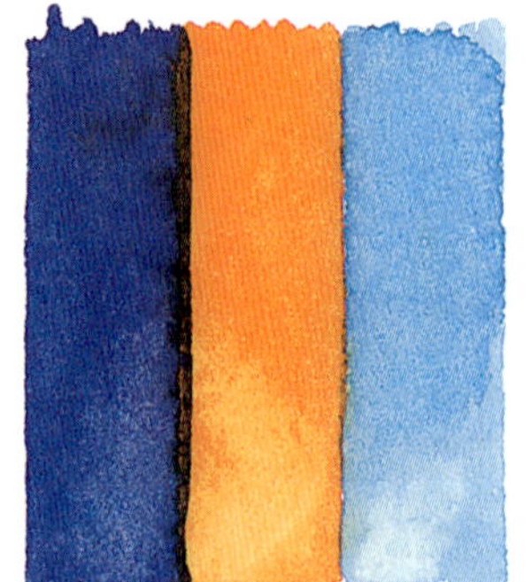

Blue-violet, Orange, Blue-green

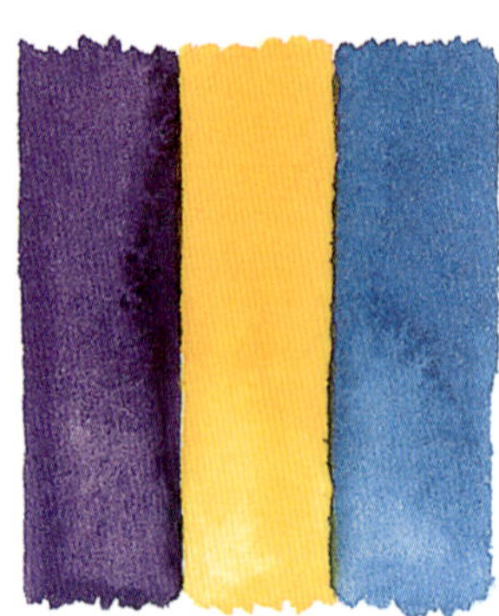

Violet, Yellow-orange, Blue

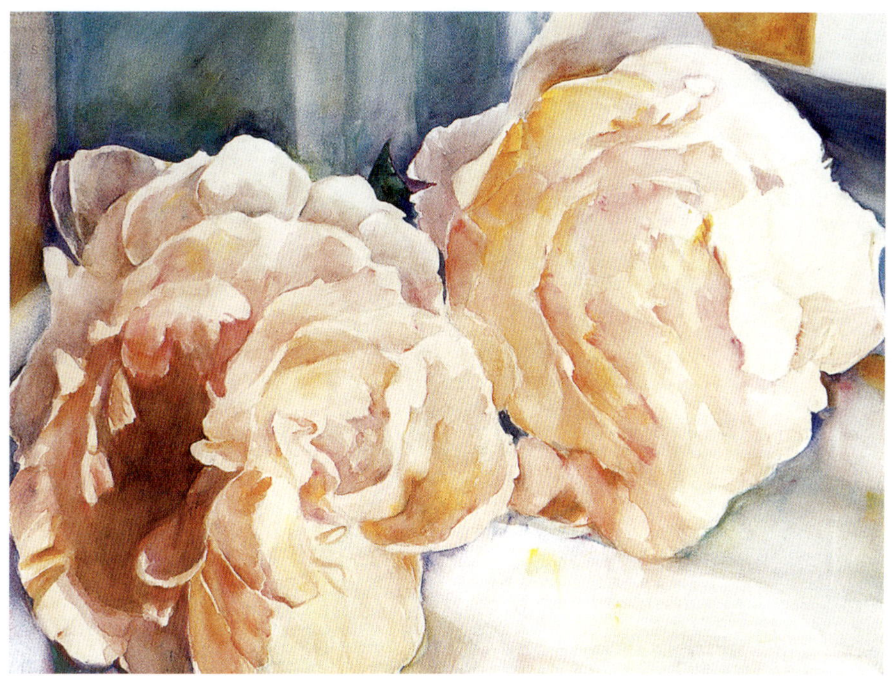

Peonies by Nancy Carey, *22" x 30" (56cm x 76cm)*
The flowing oranges and reds of the peonies shine clearly against the blue-green background in this deliberate use of a split complementary triad.

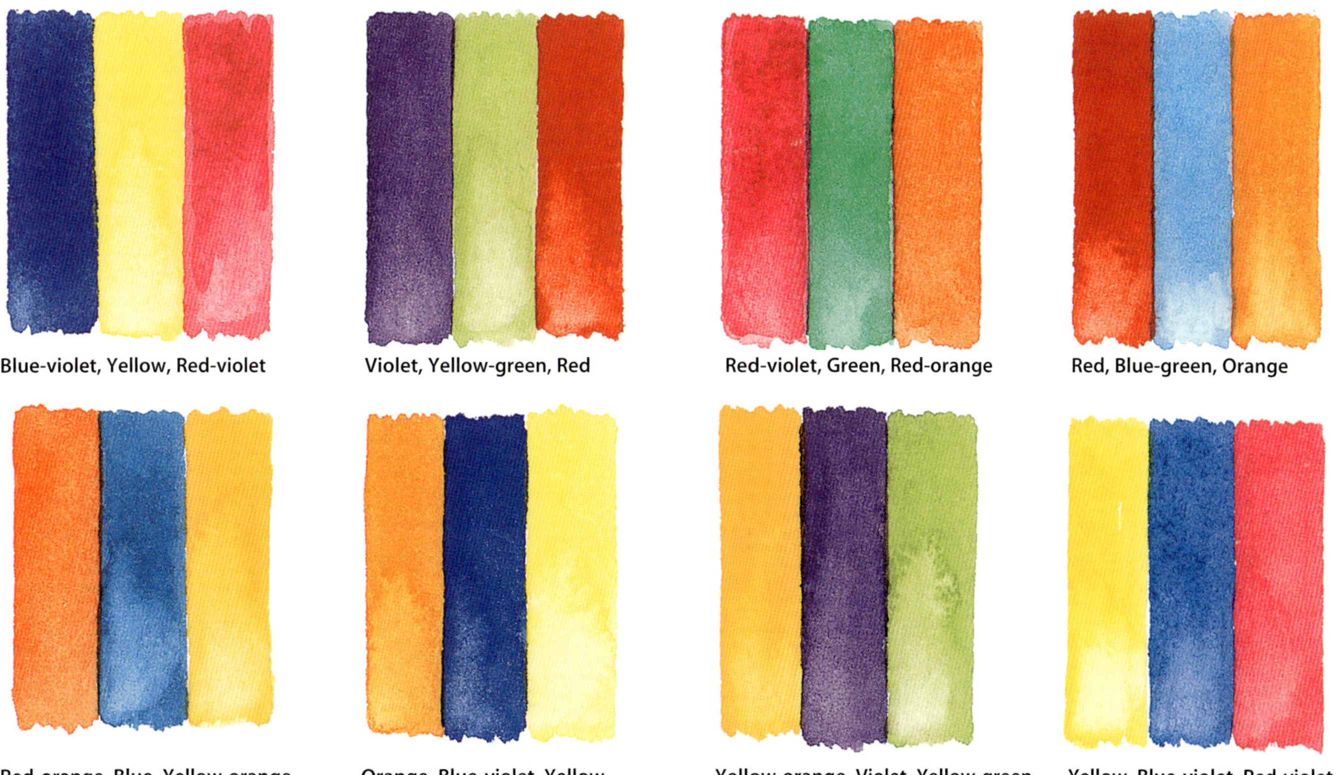

RECIPE FOR SUCCESS

When a car runs poorly, the entire car is not rebuilt, but rather a few small mechanisms are fixed. It is the same in painting. The difference between a mediocre watercolor and a great watercolor can often arise from a few simple adjustments in the colors or placement of colors.

Split complements do not have to be used straight out of the tube, but can be altered in value and saturation—just like complements (diagrams 3.7-3.8).

While full saturation triads can form a basis for a watercolor, altering one, two, or all three of the colors can provide many more variations that are both inspiring and original. It is often the small and unique color adjustments that give watercolors a sense of being made up of colors never seen before.

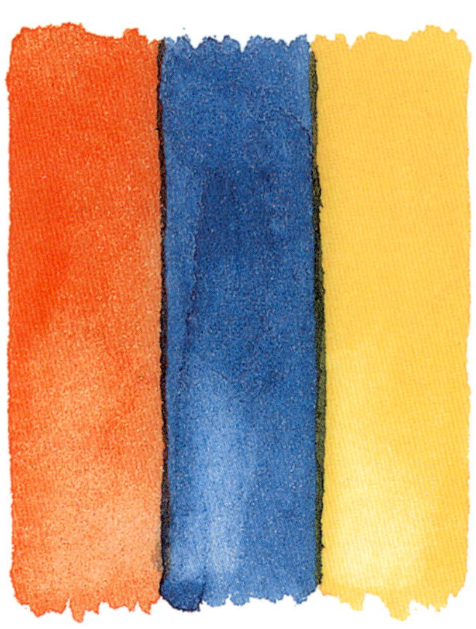

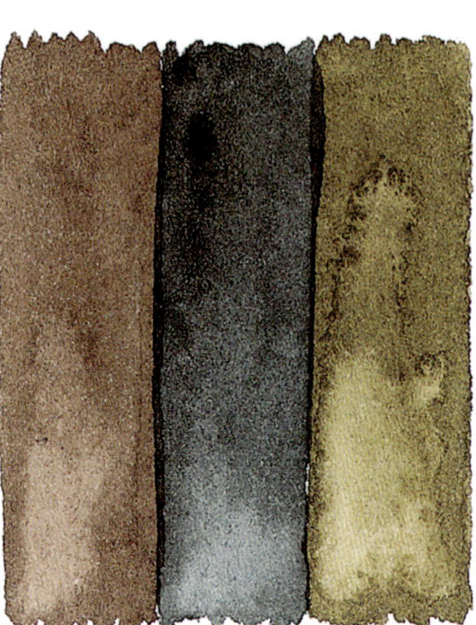

Diagram 3.7 This triad of red-orange, blue, and yellow is altered with the addition of black to create a group of harmonious but more subtle colors.

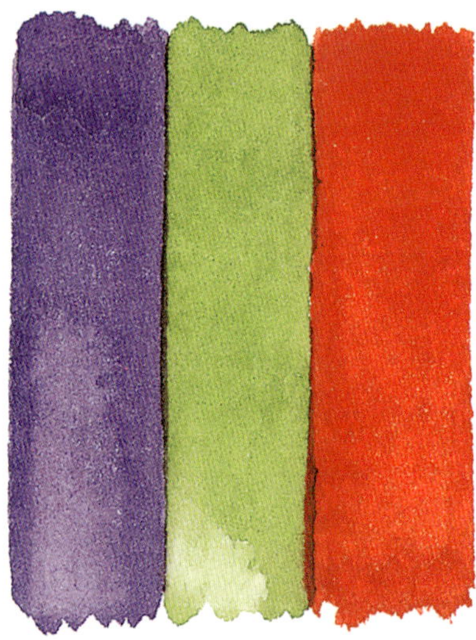

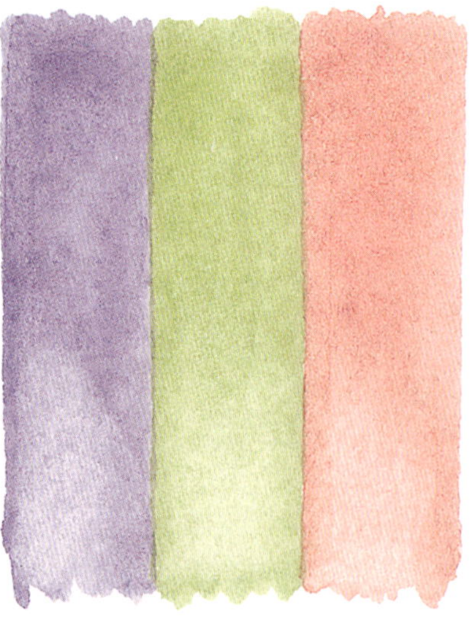

Diagram 3.8 Here the triad of violet, yellow-green, and red is lightened either with white or extra water to create harmonious pastel colors.

Left: ***Farmers Market Garlic*** **by Mary J. Maxam,** ***20" x 30" (51cm x 76cm)***
The split complementary triad orange, yellow, and blue-violet is hard at work here, although subtly used. The blue-violet is lightened, the yellow is desaturated to a greyer color, and the orange is darkened with black.

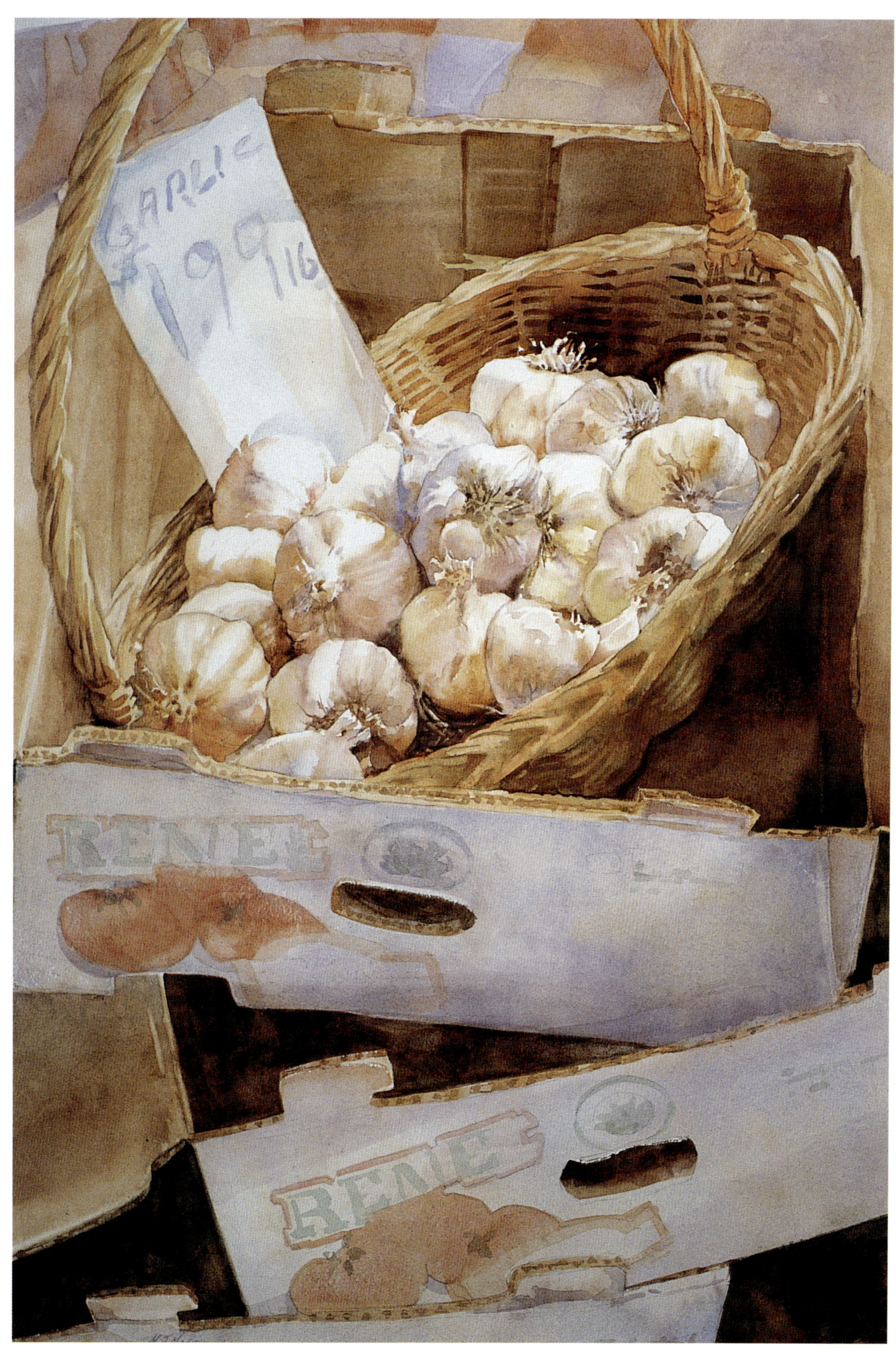
GARLIC
1.99
RENE
RENE

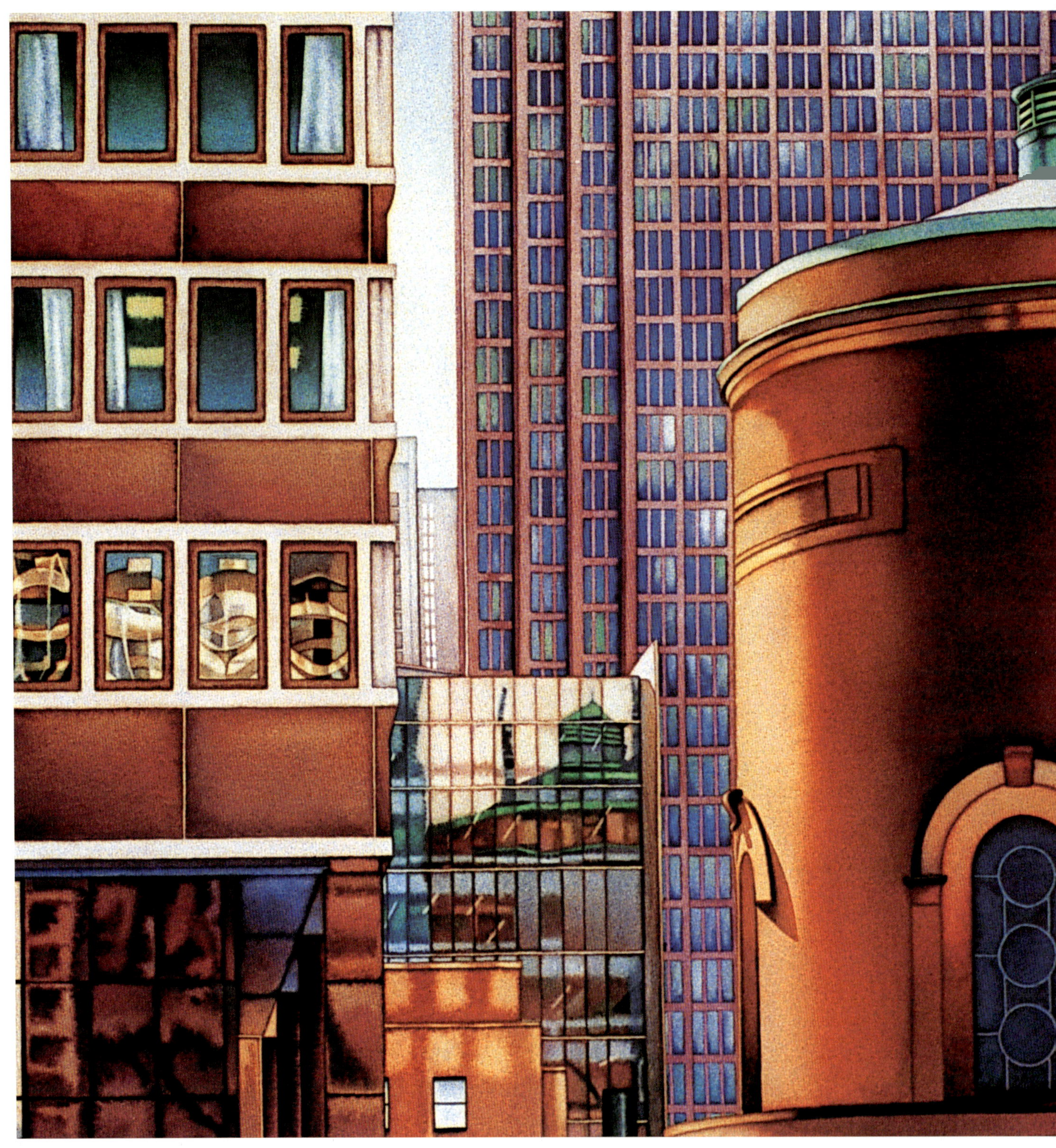

Limit Your Palette:
Tetrad Color Schemes

The jump from three colors to four colors is one small step for color and one giant leap in complexity. Practice has shown that when using four colors harmony can quickly make friends with chaos.

There are two approaches to pinpointing tetrads, or groups of four colors, that give structure and energy to a watercolor. The first is to find these colors based upon the way humans think about color, and the second is to once again place a regular polygon within the color wheel. The four colors of tetrads can provide very interesting combinations depending upon how the tetrad is constructed. One may revolve around a particular color to set a specific but stunning mood, while another may locate colors evenly around the color wheel for a more balanced foundation.

It's well worth the effort to explore the many variations of tetrads. They are a discriminating way to maintain the tension and excitement of a watercolor without the colors getting out of control.

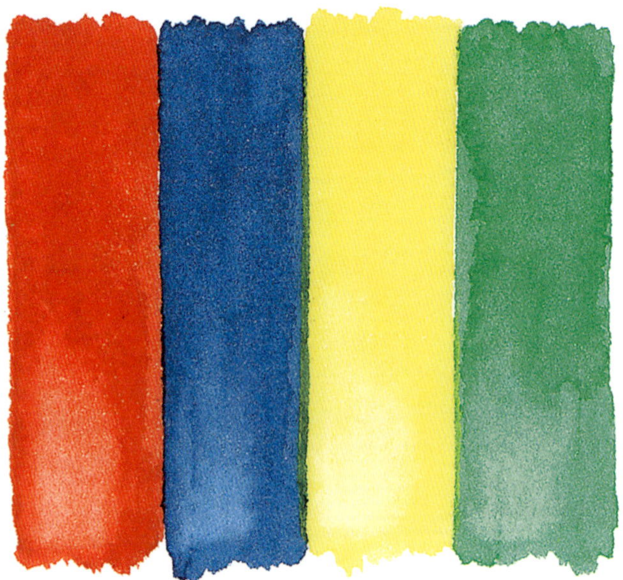

Diagram 4.1 **Red, Blue, Yellow, Green**

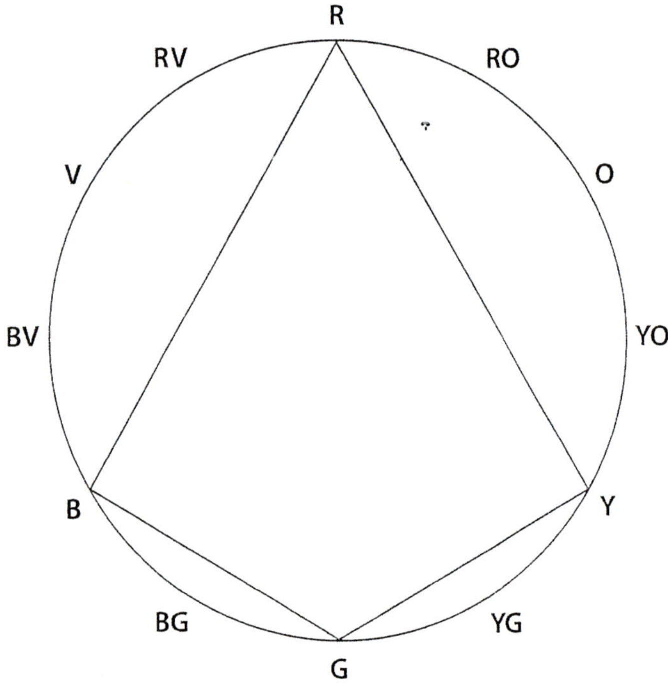

Diagram 4.2 **The red, yellow, green, and blue kite tetrad.**

Kite Tetrads

Research has shown that humans think about color experiences in terms of four distinct qualities. These are red, blue, yellow—the primaries typically associated with paint—along with the fourth color green (diagram 4.1). This concept springs from the ways humans tend to describe color sensations. It also has a physiological basis related to the way the eye/brain system codes colors, as described in Chapter two.

It is natural to describe color experiences using these four hues. For example, a picturesque summer landscape might bring to mind a blue sky, green grass and trees, red flowers, all suffused in a yellow sunlight. Four colors are used to describe distinct elements of the scene in a way that makes complete sense. Describing the same scene as a blue sky, yellow sunlight, red flowers, and a variety of mixtures of blue and yellow covering the ground and tops of the trees seems complicated if not absurd.

Although the tetrad of red, blue, yellow, and green is often thought of as an intuitively correct and very pleasing grouping, it does not span the color wheel in a balanced manner. Careful examination shows that these colors are anything but evenly distributed. Two of the colors of this tetrad are blue and yellow with the third color lying exactly in the middle of them, in this case green, with the final color red lying directly opposite to green. When the colors are connected, the polygon illustrating their relationship looks like an upside down kite (diagram 4.2), a figure that may be rotated around the interior of the color wheel to reveal twelve other kite tetrads (diagram 4.3).

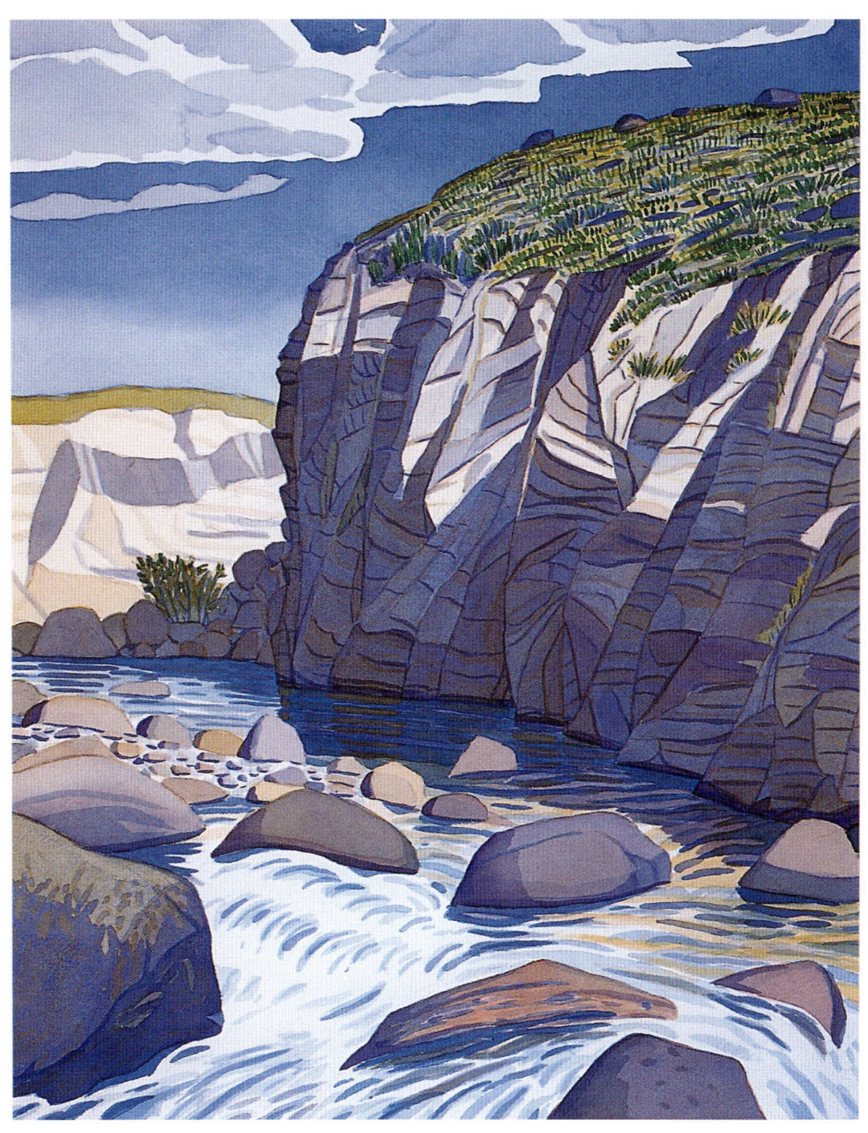

Grizzly Gorge **by James Behlke, *20" x 16" (51cm x 41cm)***
The kite tetrad of orange, green, blue, and violet is used here for this rich capturing of atmosphere. The violet is applied as a transparent glaze.

RECIPE FOR SUCCESS

Choosing a color tetrad before beginning a painting is a good way to ensure a complex but unified color structure.

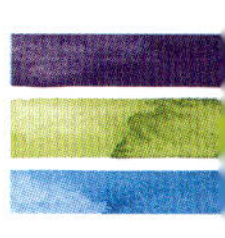

Diagram 4.3 Kite Tetrads.

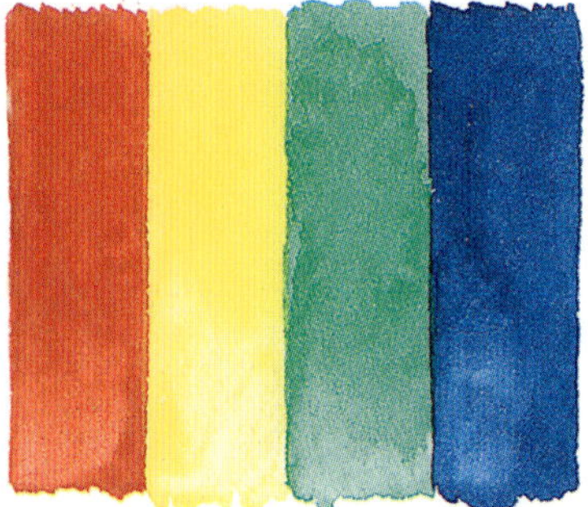

Red, Yellow, Green, Blue

Red-orange, Yellow-green, Blue-green, Blue-Violet

Orange, Green, Blue, Violet

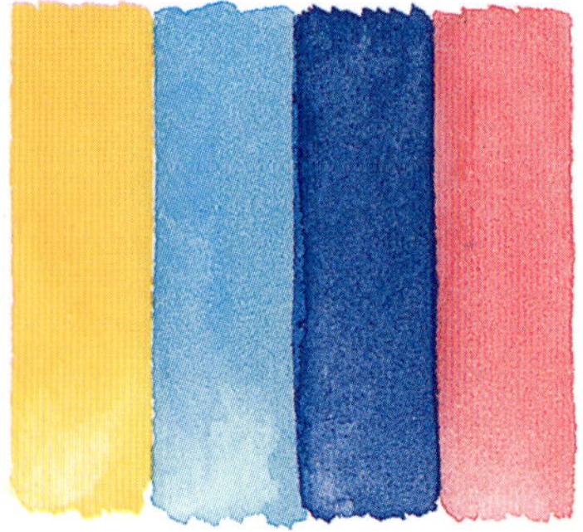

Yellow-orange, Blue-green, Blue-violet, Red-violet

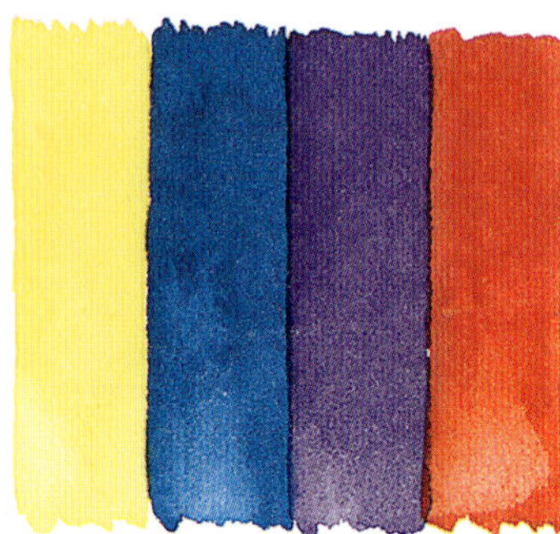

Yellow, Blue, Violet, Red

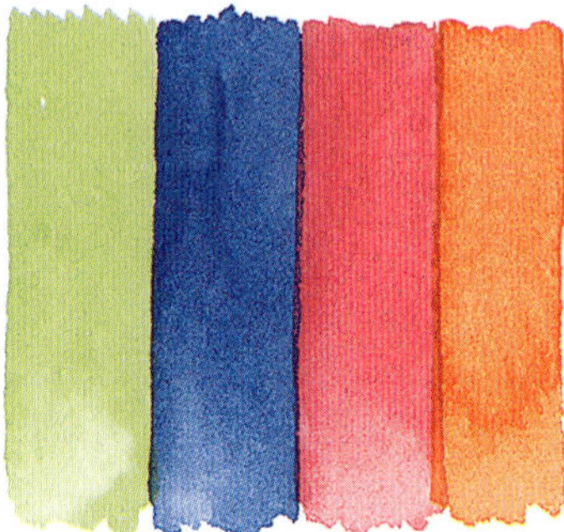

Yellow-green, Blue-violet, Red-violet, Red-orange

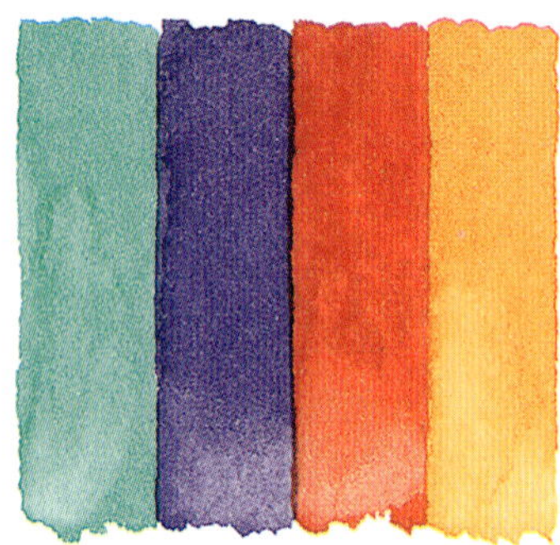

Green, Violet, Red, Orange

Blue-green, Red-violet, Red-orange, Yellow-orange

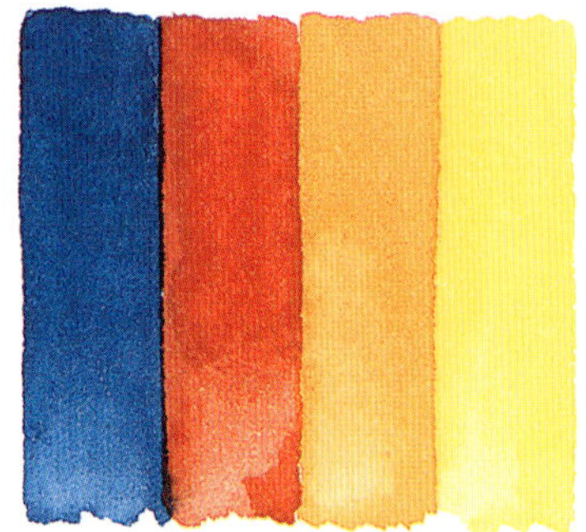

Blue, Red, Orange, Yellow

Blue-violet, Red-orange, Yellow-orange, Yellow-green

Violet, Orange, Yellow, Green

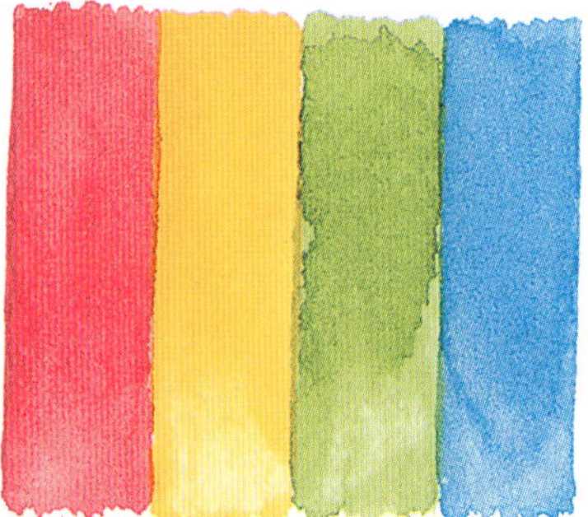

Red-violet, Yellow-orange, Yellow-green, Blue-green

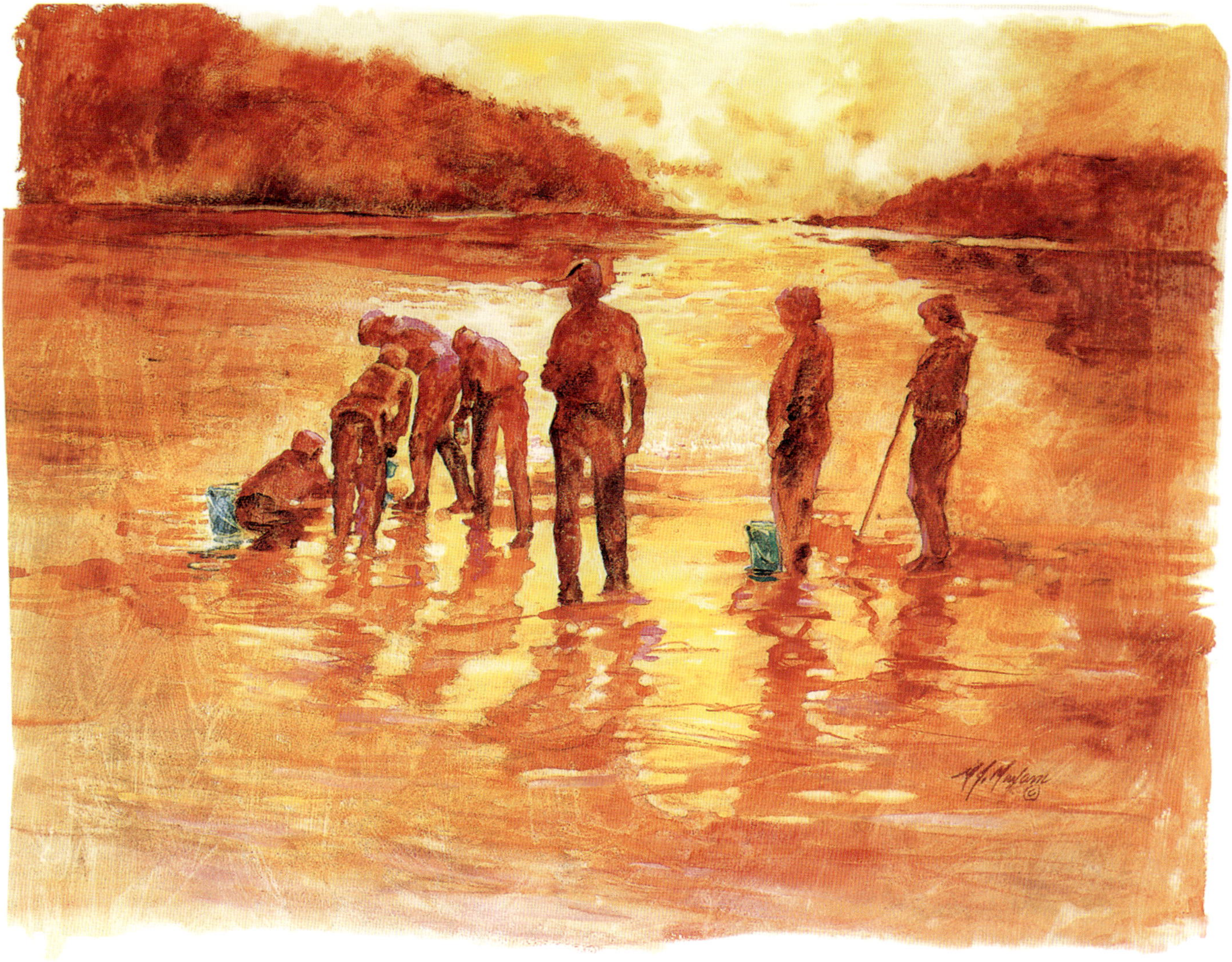

Beachcombers by Mary J. Maxam, *19" x 26" (48cm x 66cm)*
The rich warm light streaming over the ocean is created using the kite tetrad of blue-green, red-violet, red-orange, yellow-orange. The difference in the amount of area each color covers gives the painting an extra punch.

RECIPE FOR SUCCESS

Tetrads may suggest specific light conditions or emotions. Choosing a tetrad that prompts a similar light or emotion will often create an outstanding painting.

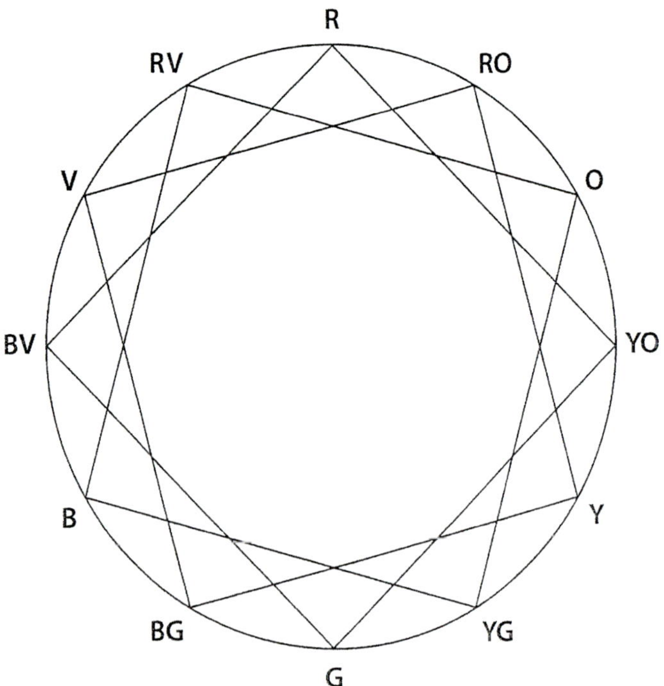

Diagram 4.4 The square tetrads.

Square Tetrads

A second way to discover tetrads is 'to place a square within the middle of the color wheel. This specifies three different tetrads.

Colors found by using a square are evenly separated from one another by two colors. Each tetrad also presents two groups of complementary colors. These complements work together to create an intense brightness while, simultaneously, the fact that they come from four equidistant areas of the color wheel allows them to appear balanced.

Diagram 4.5 The square tetrads.

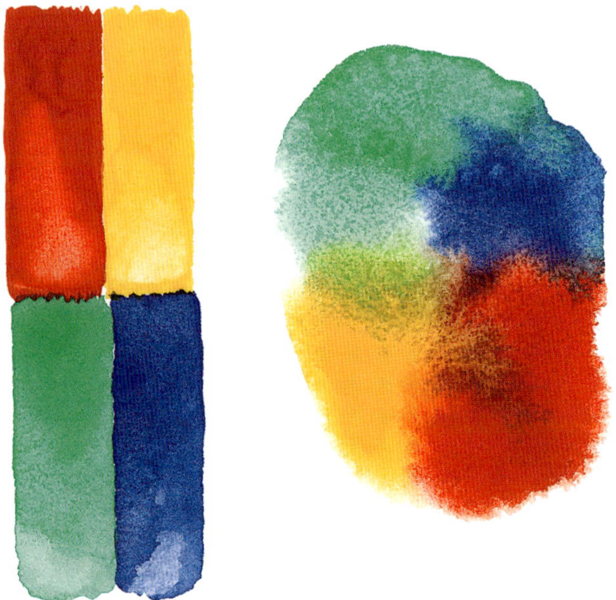

Red, Yellow-orange, Green, Blue-violet

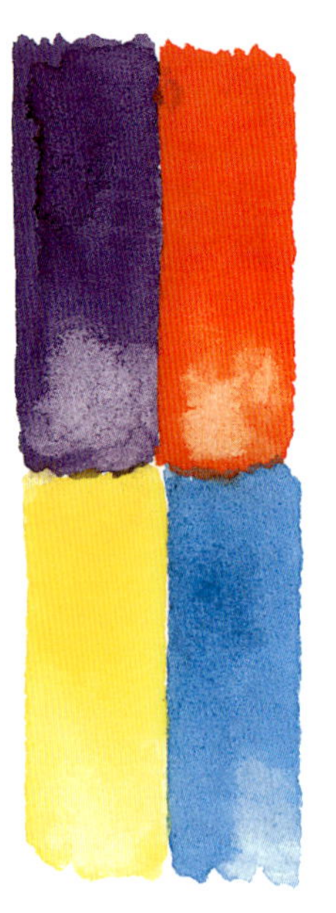

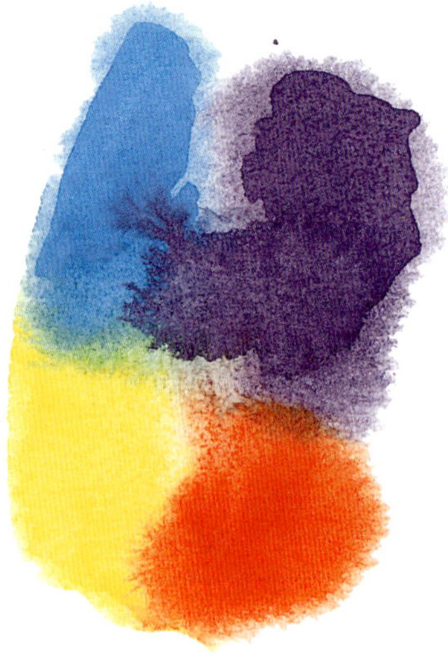

Violet, Red-orange, Yellow, Blue-green

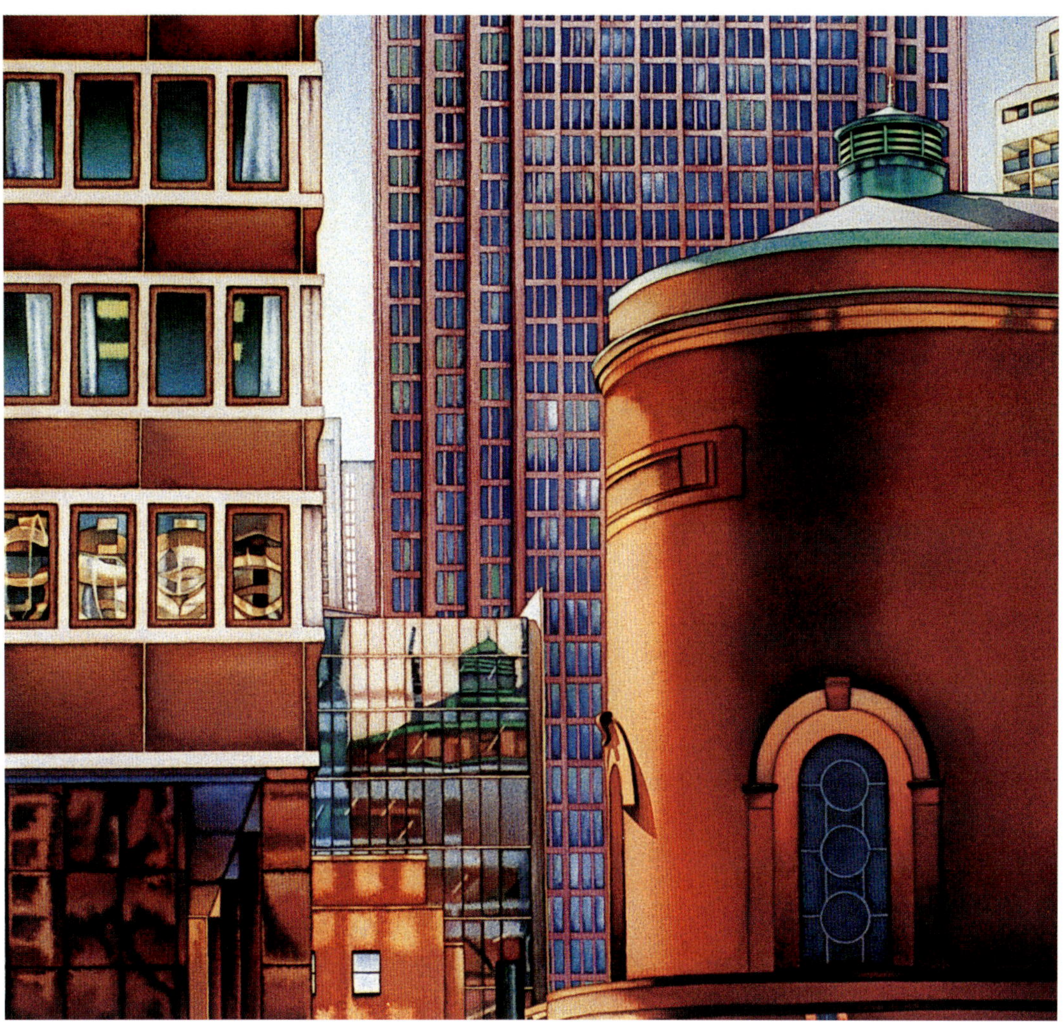

Windows96 by Ann DeLaurentis, *21" x 22" (53cm x 56cm)*
The basis for this painting is found in the square tetrad red-orange, yellow, blue-green, and violet. The yellow is used as contrast while the red-orange goes through many changes of value. The placement of small highlights of other colors builds toward greater complexity, based upon the strong tetrad foundation.

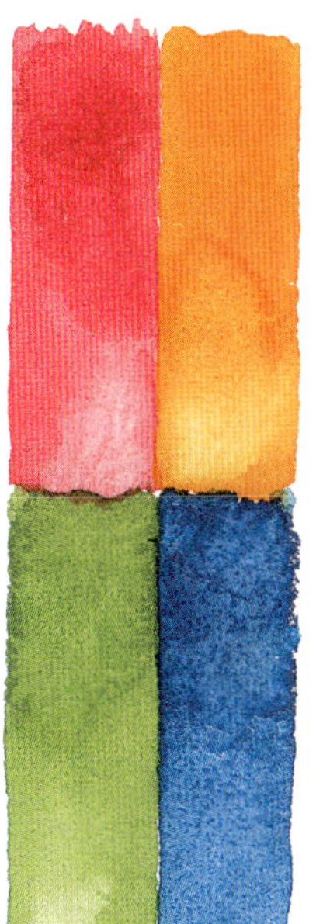

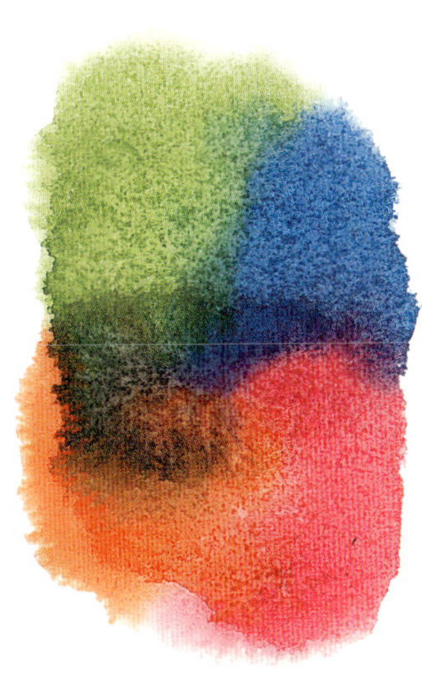

Red-violet, Orange, Yellow-green, Blue

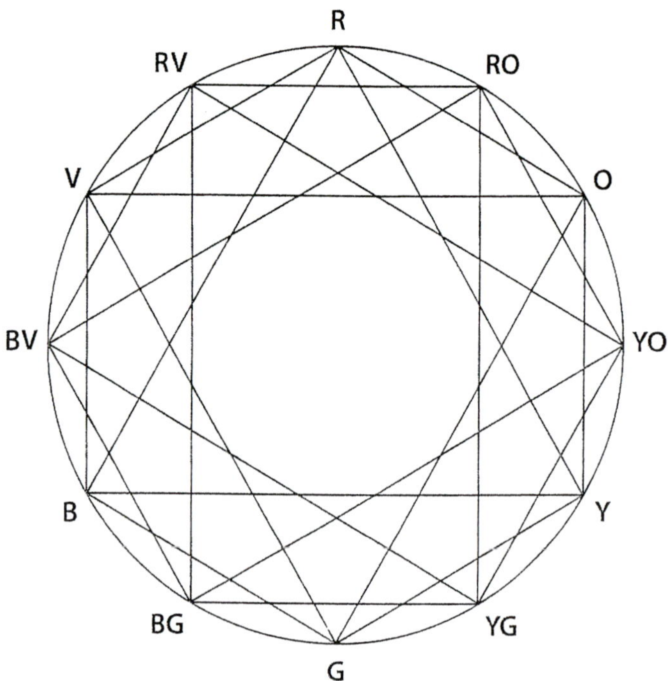

Diagram 4.6 The rectangle tetrads.

Rectangle Tetrads

A related hue scheme is found by placing a rectangle into the color wheel. In this case, two sets of tetrads contain two primary colors while two sets contain no primary colors.

The rectangular tetrad of red, orange, and blue, and green gives this painting its unique richness. Notice how the blue contrasts with the whole painting and how the background moves subtly from green to red. Compare this with the next painting, Antique Whites, to see the degree of flexibility found with tetrads.

Diagram 4.7 The rectangle tetrads.

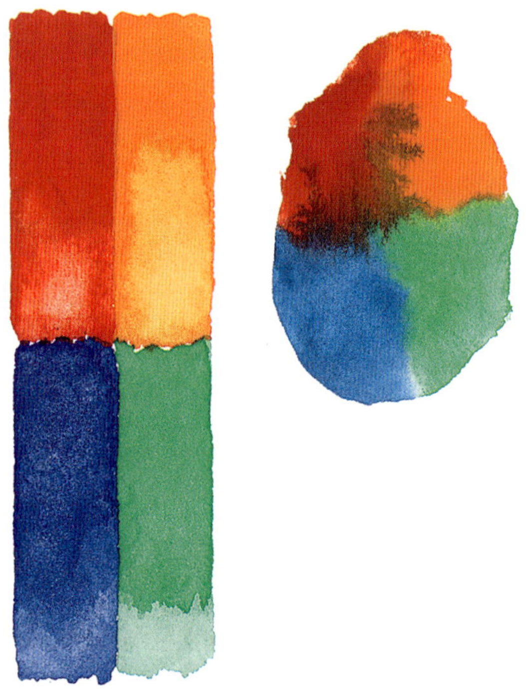

Red, Orange, Blue, Green

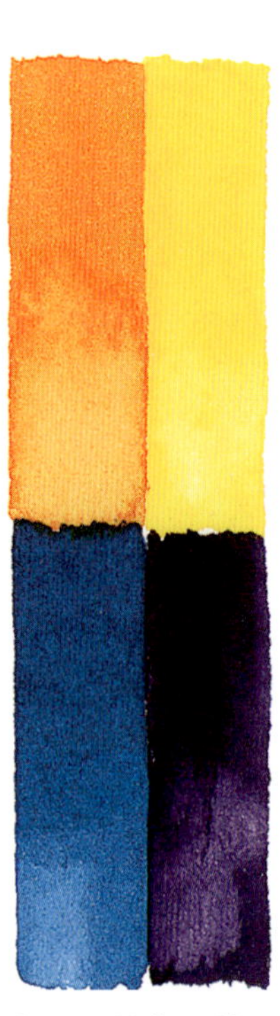

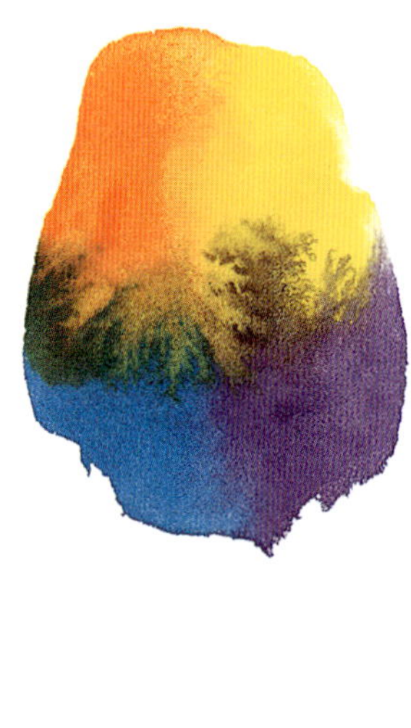

Orange, Yellow, Blue, Violet

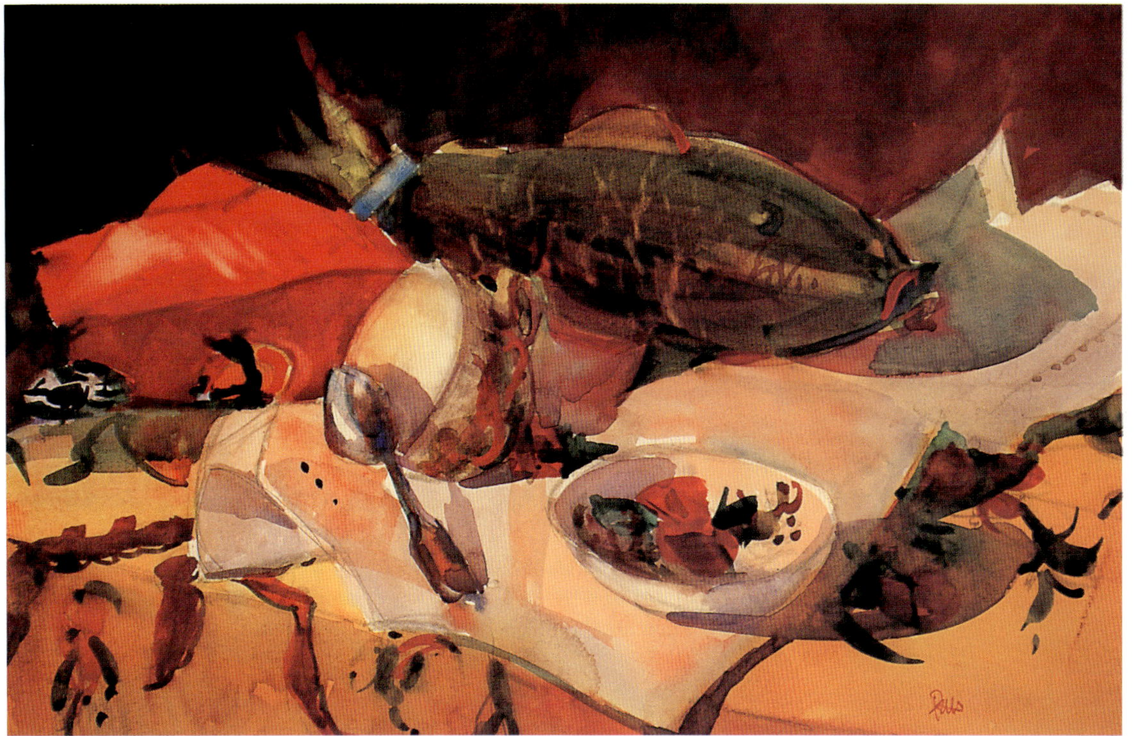

Low by Barbara M. Pitts, *11 ⅜" x17" (29cm x 43cm)*
The rectangular tetrad of red, orange, and blue, and green gives this painting its unique richness. Notice how the blue contrasts with the whole painting and how the background moves subtly from green to red. Compare this with the painting, *Antique Whites* on page 59 to see the degree of flexibility found with tetrads.

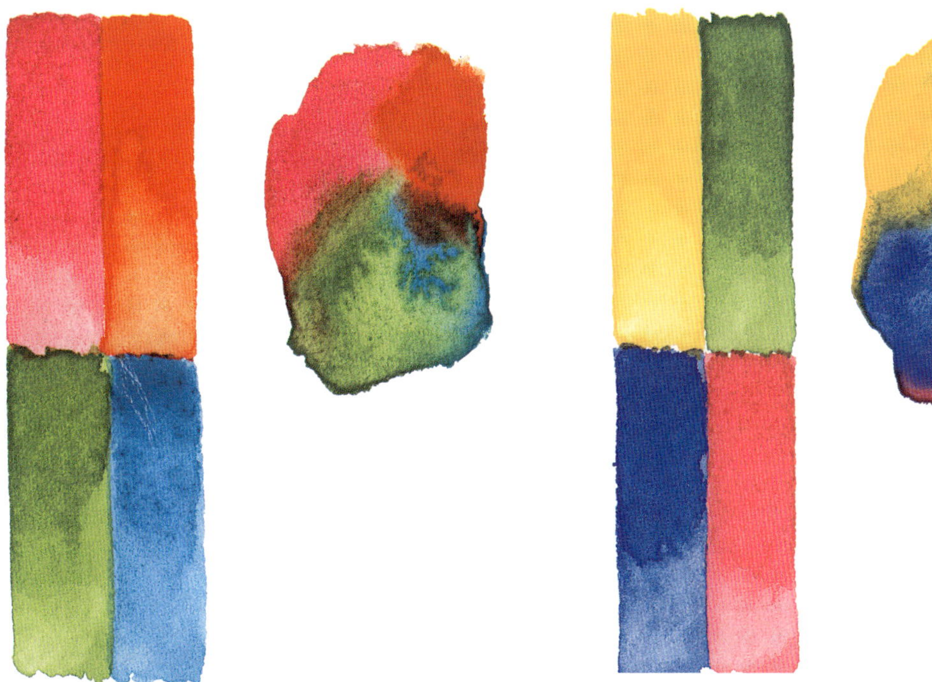

Red-violet, Red-orange, Yellow-green, Blue-green

Yellow-orange, Yellow-green, Blue-violet, Red-violet

There are a great deal of tetrads presented in this chapter and it is well worth the effort to devote some time to a conscious use of them in watercolors. The knowledge learned by such an effort will eventually become second nature, presenting useful ideas for difficult problems.

But for some, actively using the numerous groups of triads and tetrads looks a bit daunting. They do not all have to be tackled at once. Taking a few minutes once a month to do a study based on one particular set is a good start, or heading out to paint with only the four colors of a tetrad instead of the twelve can force artists to use them in innovative ways.

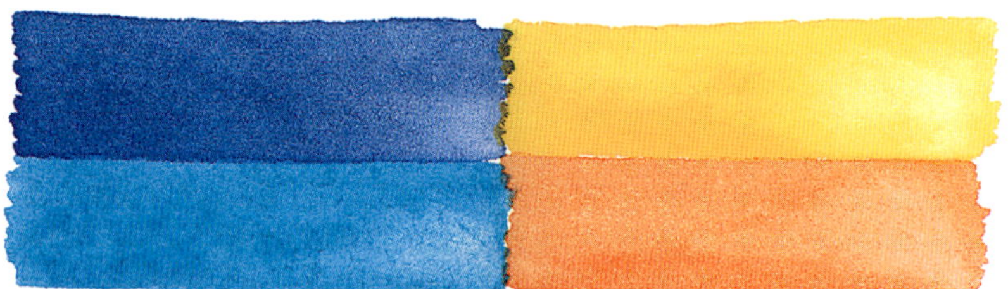

Blue-green, Blue-Violet, Red-orange, Yellow-orange

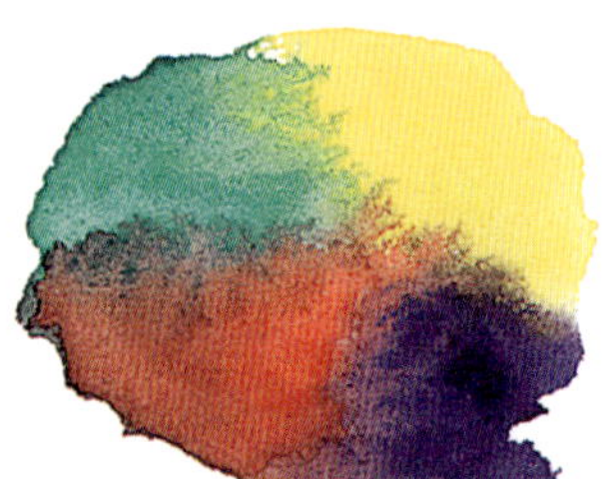

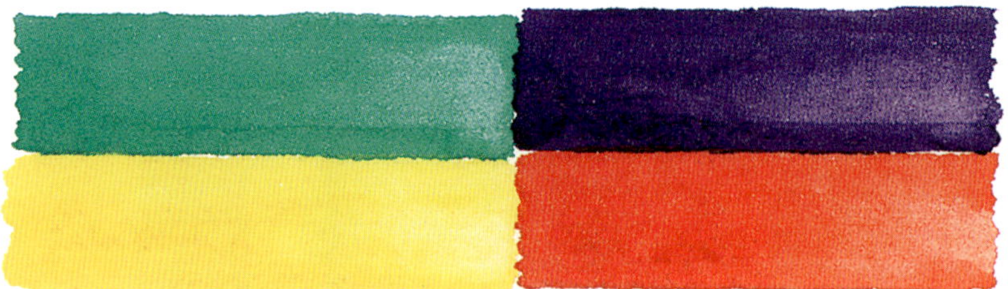

Yellow, Green, Red, Violet

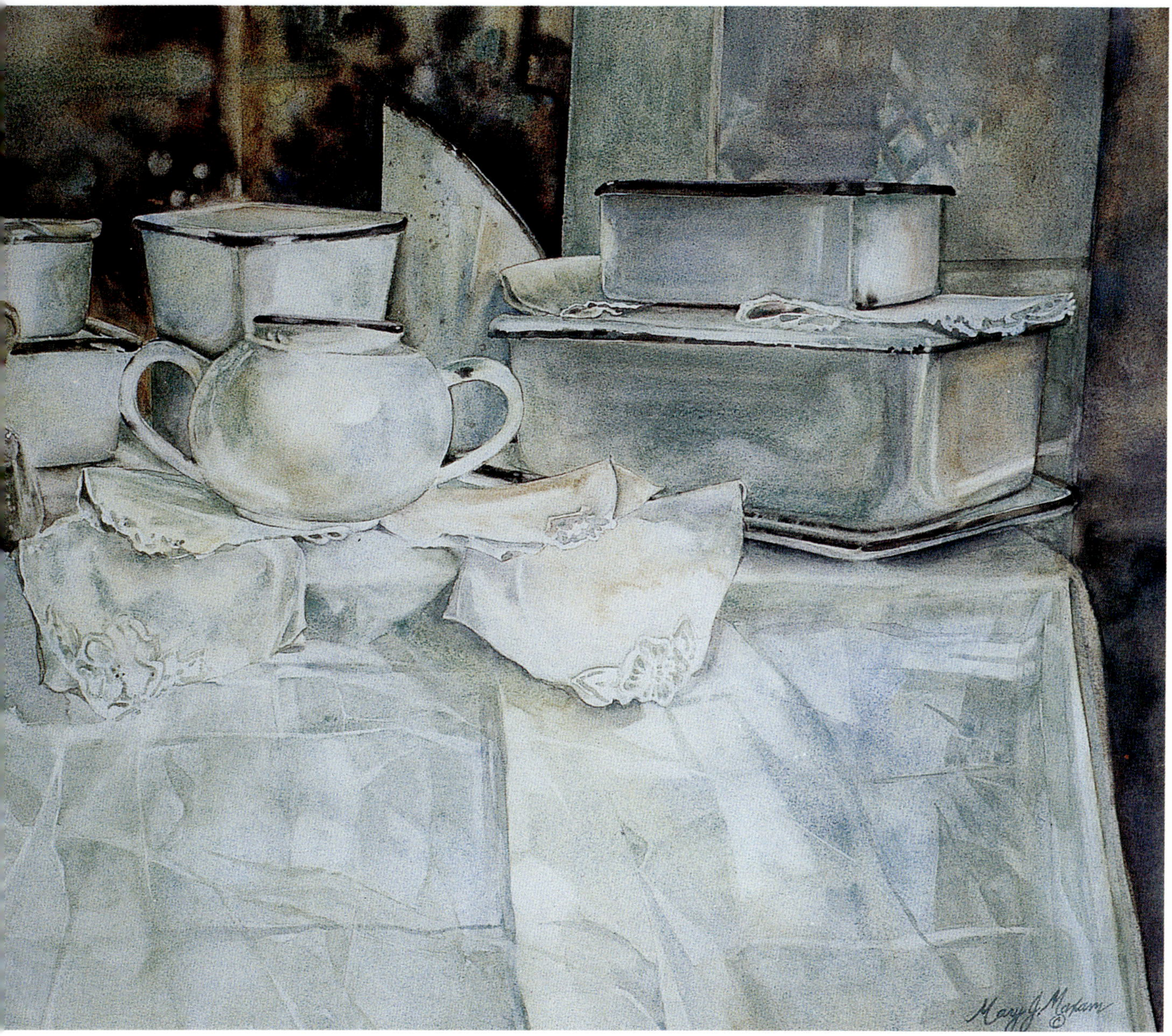

Antique Whites by Mary J. Maxam, *20" x30" (51cm x 76cm)*
Amazingly, this still life is also painted using the rectangular tetrad of red, orange, blue, and green. Each color is desaturated, lightened, or darkened.

RECIPE FOR SUCCESS

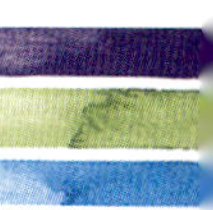

Choose or arrange a subject to paint that illustrates a specific tetrad. A conscious planning of the subject allows for a more intuitive yet controlled painting process.

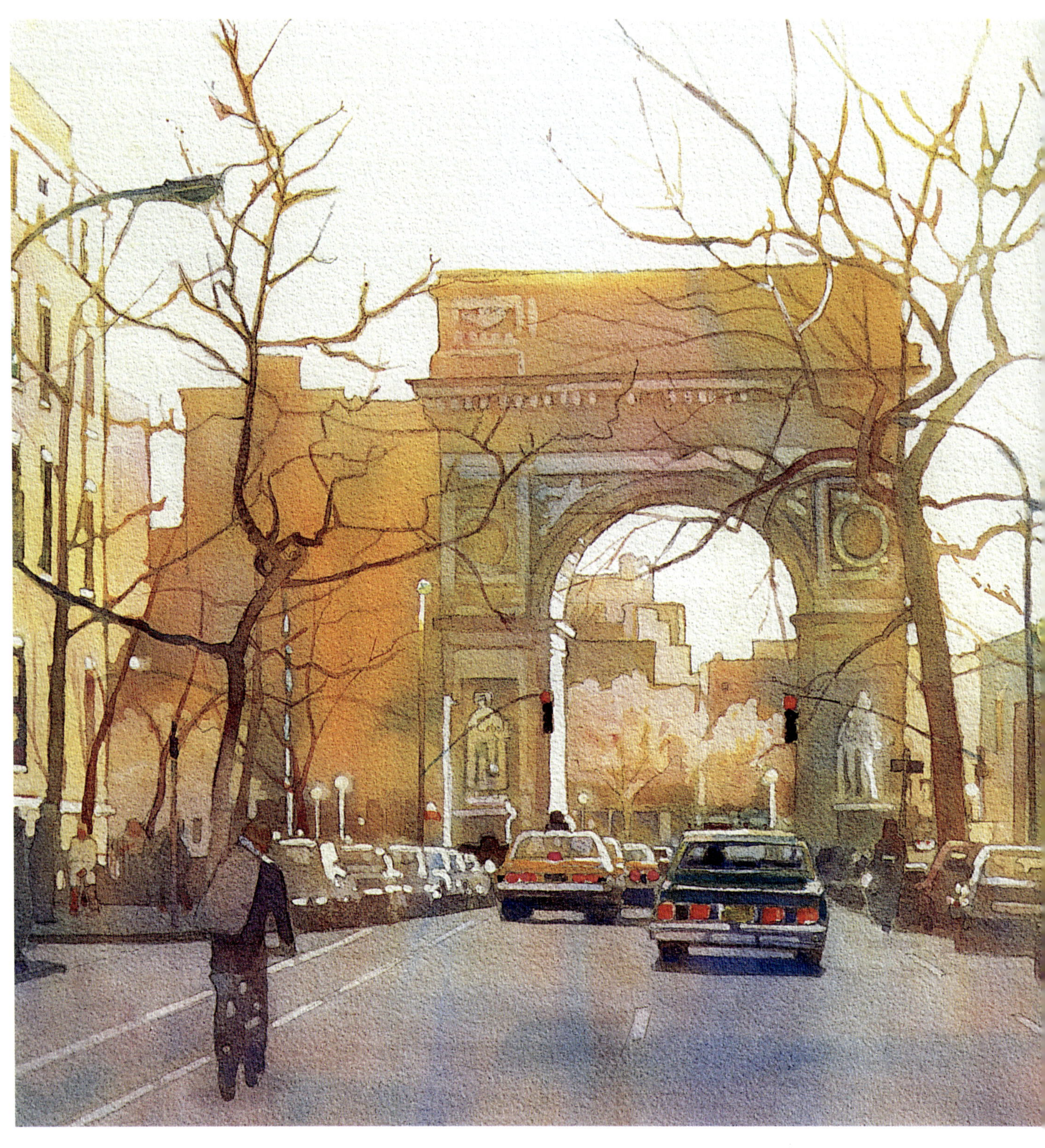

Toning Colors for Harmony and Glow

Color harmony is defined as the way two or more colors come together to form a pleasing arrangement or, as Leonardo da Vinci wrote, color can "give Grace to another." Artists choose their colors for different reasons and they often disagree about the colors that create harmony. Color combinations may appear harmonious to one artist, but not another. It is much like asking for opinions after a movie—some viewers may praise it while others express distaste.

Music is often used as an analogy to describe harmony in art because it is easy for us to hear whether notes form a melodious chord or a discordant one. Henri Matisse, whose second artistic passion was the violin, used a musical analogy to suggest that the goal of color was to create a "living harmony of colours, comparable to that of a musical composition." In 1713, Anthony Ashley Cooper, Third Earl of Shaftesbury, wrote in "An Essay of Painting," "The harmony of painting requires, that in whatever key the painter begins his piece, he should be sure to finish it in the same."

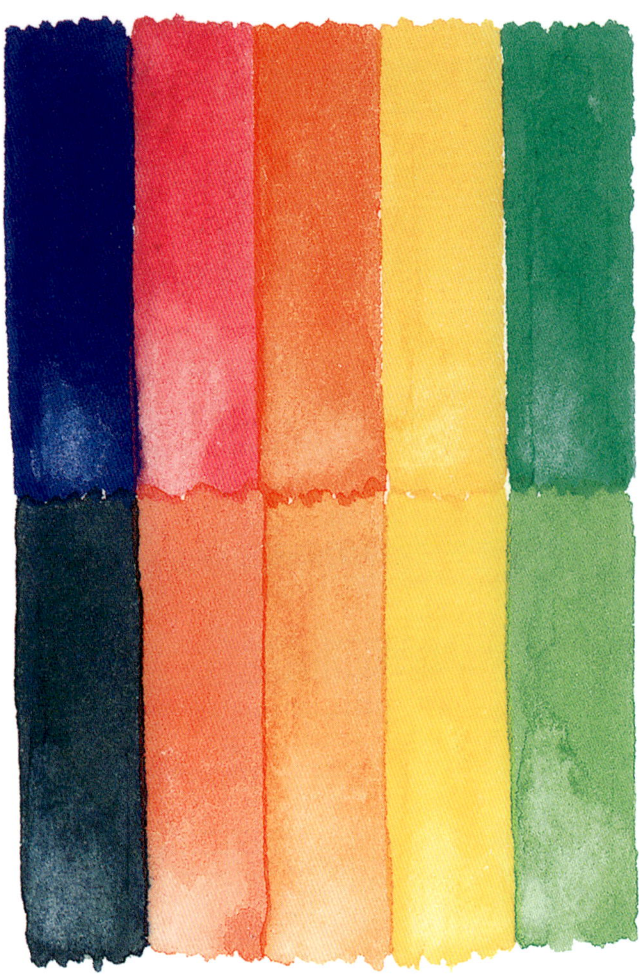

Diagram 5.1 Blue-violet, red-violet, red-orange, yellow-orange, and green are toned with yellow and appear underneath the original pure hues.

Single-Hue Toning

One way to get this harmony is to premix the few major colors of the motif. These are then precisely adjusted so the glow between them mimics the glow of the subject as closely as possible. It takes a bit of time, but it's well worth the effort because it tones the painting with a light similar to the one seen. If these main colors are correct, the painting may be worked on endlessly without disrupting the overall sensation.

In music, an overtone is a mysterious extra note that occurs when particular tones are heard together. The idea of one sound underlying all the notes is similar to the glow of some old master paintings that appear to be bathed in a golden undertone. In painting today, a predetermined toning is an excellent means to a harmonious end. For a landscape filled with a yellow light, it is obvious that the highlights will be yellow. But to increase

RECIPE FOR SUCCESS

Identify the three or four dominant colors in the motif, and mix these first.

the sense of a pervasive light, add a bit of yellow to each color of the painting. The blue will have a touch of yellow in it, the violet will have touch of yellow, and so on (diagram 5.1). Just as objects under a sunset sky all take on a slightly red-orange tinge, toning helps to keep the painting within color boundaries. The various colors of the painting, no matter how different, are locked together due to the small amount of toning color added to each. Even the whites or blacks should be toned. This daring solution sounds like a recipe for mud, but only a small trace of the toning color is added, not enough to dull the other colors.

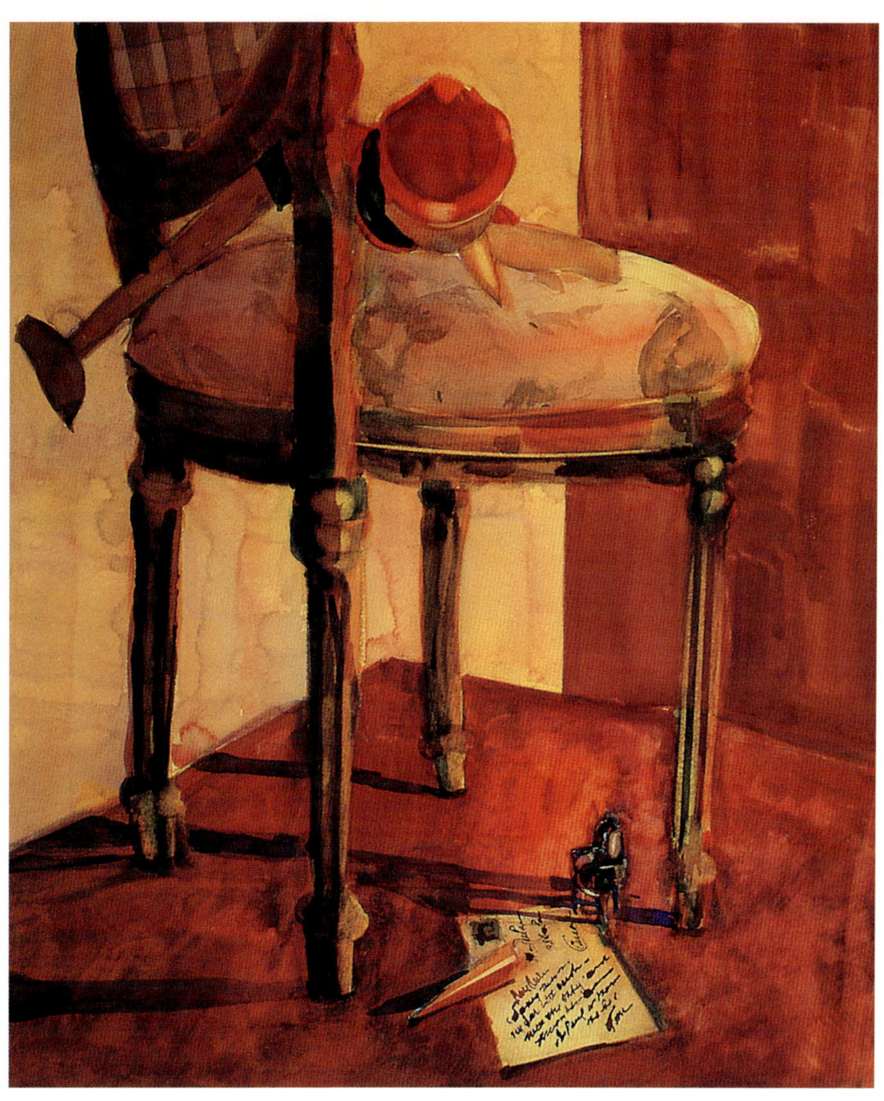

Looking at a Lie **by Barbara Pitts, *33" x 29 1/2" (84cm x 75cm)***
Toning nearly all the colors with yellow-orange provides a harmonious key for the painting. The small blue-violet shadows become very striking in such a context.

RECIPE FOR SUCCESS

Use mixture colors in most areas. Reserve pure colors for special touches.

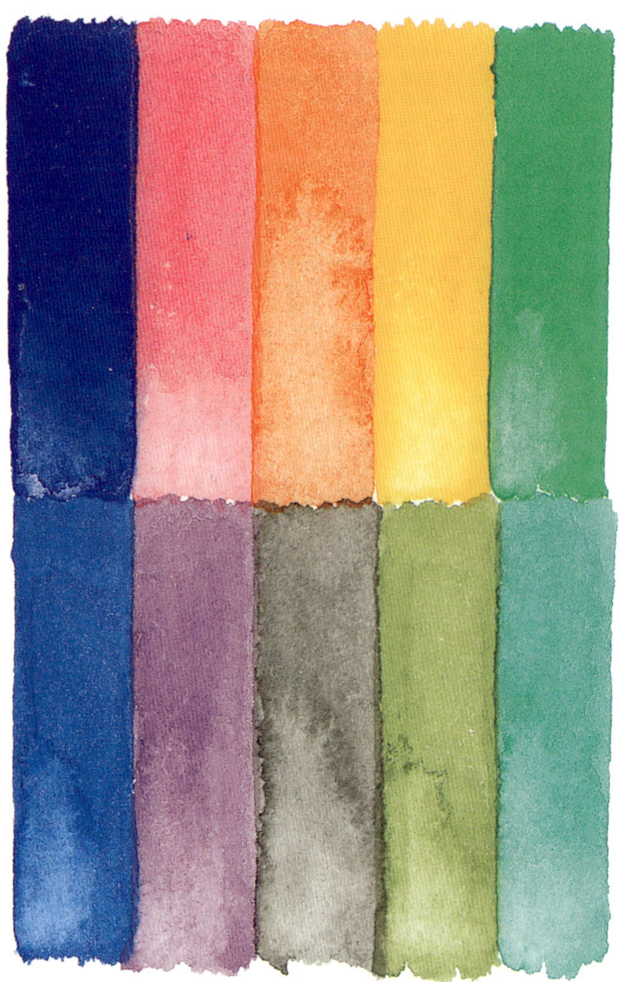

Diagram 5.2 Blue-violet, red-violet, red-orange, yellow-orange, and green are toned with blue and appear underneath the original pure hues.

The impressionist painters felt very strongly about toning color areas by adding touches of other hues (diagrams 5.2-5.4). They based this on their belief that light, being yellowish or bluish, would be reflected off from objects onto all other objects and even into the shadows. Later, scientists studying light and optics learned that this indeed takes place. For example, the impressionists would add spots of the yellow to the bluer and more violet shadow as a way of enhancing luminosity of the darker areas. This procedure of breaking up the color also helped to give unity to their work. The same unity occurs when colors are applied as flat separate areas that are toned by mixing a bit of one color into each.

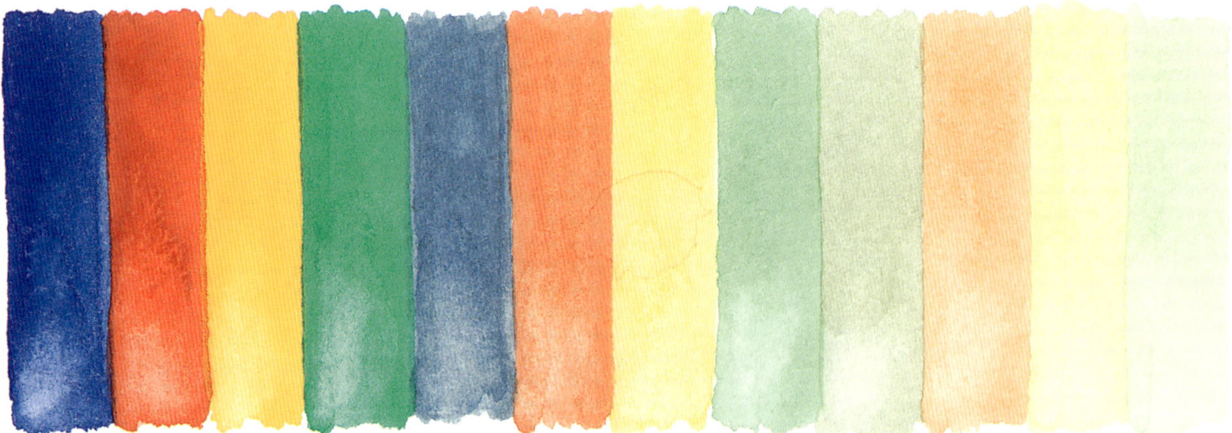

Diagram 5.3 The blue-violet, red, yellow-orange, and green are all toned with increasing amounts of yellow and white to show the effects of a bleaching sun.

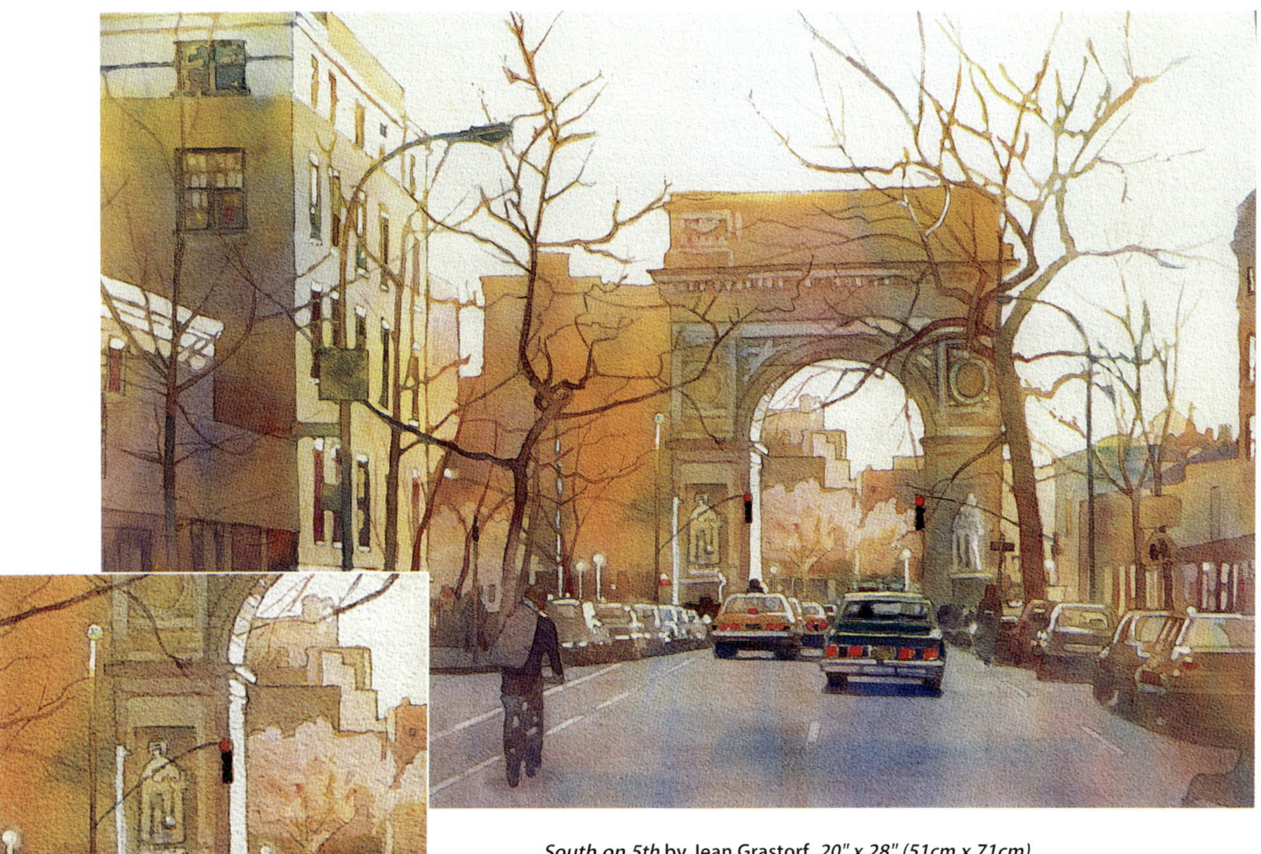

South on 5th by Jean Grastorf, *20" x 28" (51cm x 71cm)*
The city scene is striking because the colors are toned with yellow, giving the painting a sense of being drenched in sunlight.

(Detail) The spots of dark and light are critical contrasts to the pervasive yellow haze.

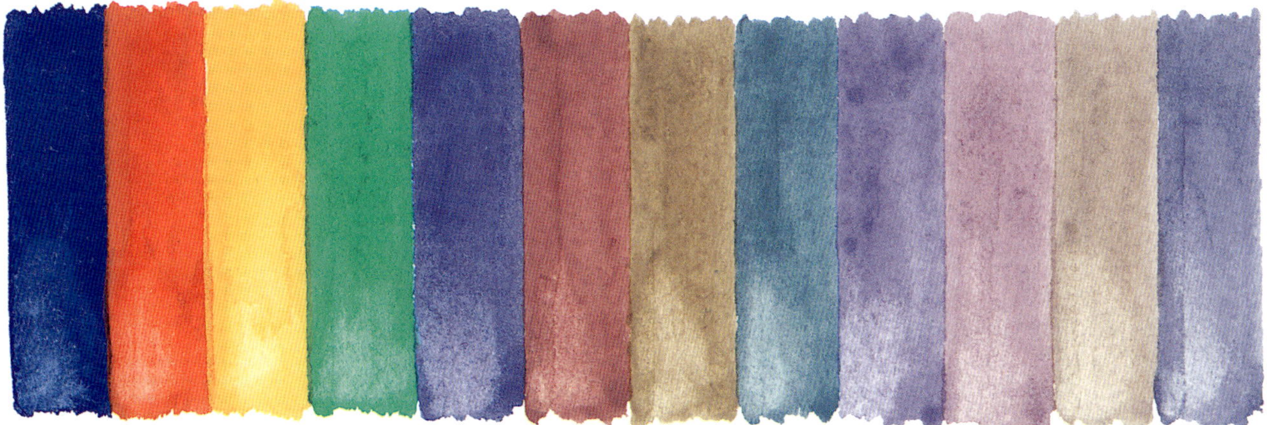

Diagram 5.4 The blue-violet, red, yellow-orange, and green are all toned with increasing amounts of violet and white to show the effects of distant shadows.

Toned Mixtures

Toned mixture colors are also found by combining colors that sit on both sides of one other color of the color wheel. For example, the colors on both sides of green, a blue-green and a yellow-green, are mixed together. An analysis of the colors shows that the mixture will contain two parts green, one part blue, and one part yellow. The green mixed by the blue and yellow is not as vibrant as the intense green of the color wheel, so the final mixture color is slightly duller than the original green (diagram 5.5).

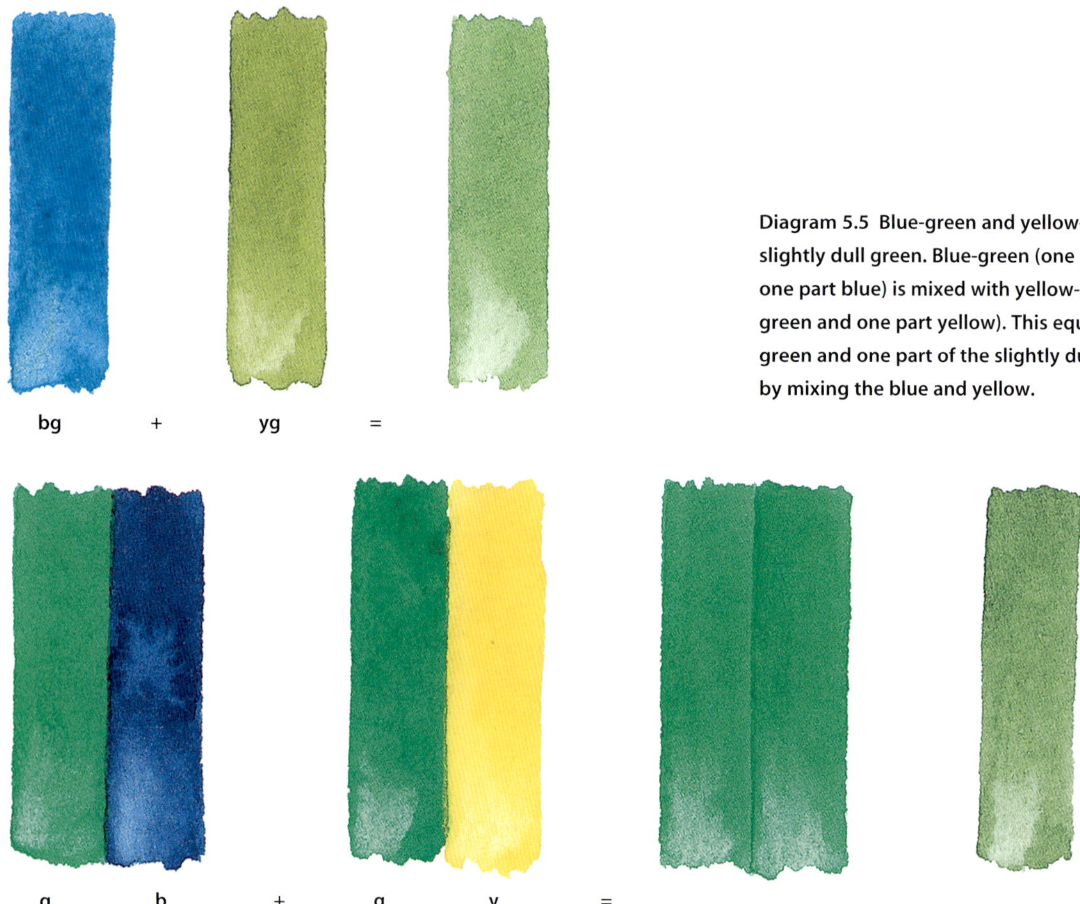

Diagram 5.5 Blue-green and yellow-green equal a slightly dull green. Blue-green (one part green and one part blue) is mixed with yellow-green (one part green and one part yellow). This equals two parts green and one part of the slightly dull green found by mixing the blue and yellow.

RECIPE FOR SUCCESS

Tone colors for harmony, and pay special attention to toning black and white, two colors that almost never appear as pure colors in the world

Another example is found by mixing the colors next to red, red-orange and red-violet. The colors of the mixture show two parts red, one part yellow, and one part violet. The yellow and violet tend to cancel each other out because they are complementary—the mixture becomes red mixed with a greyish color, or better described, a slightly desaturated red. It is interesting to note that the red has not been desaturated with a grey. The fact that red becomes a duller red with the addition of other colors is important because it creates what I call a chameleon color: It changes drastically depending what colors surround it. Near greens it appears very red, near other reds it appears greyish (diagram 5.6).

Viewers will find themselves peering closely at the work trying to decide exactly what color it is. Using these chameleon colors often helps to make a great painting.

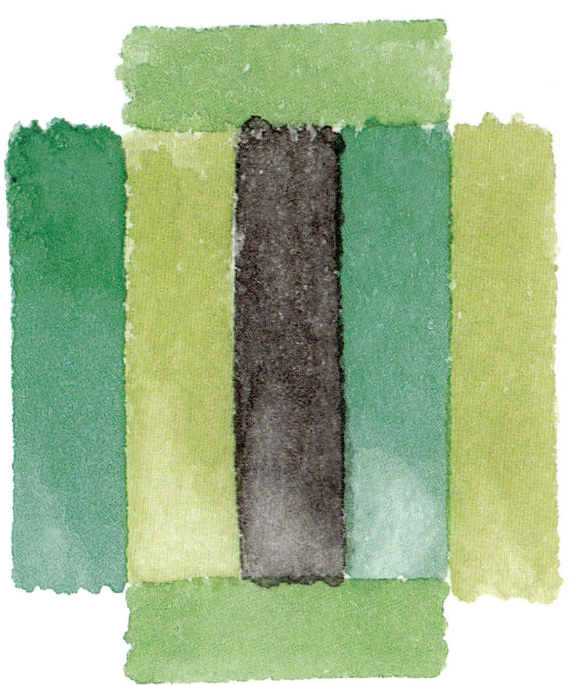

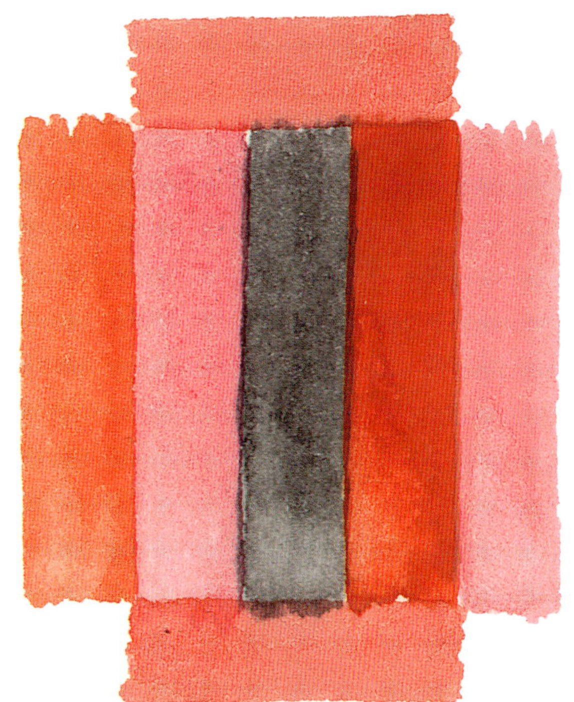

Diagram 5.6 This chameleon color looks slightly redder when surrounded by greens and slightly greener when surrounded by reds.

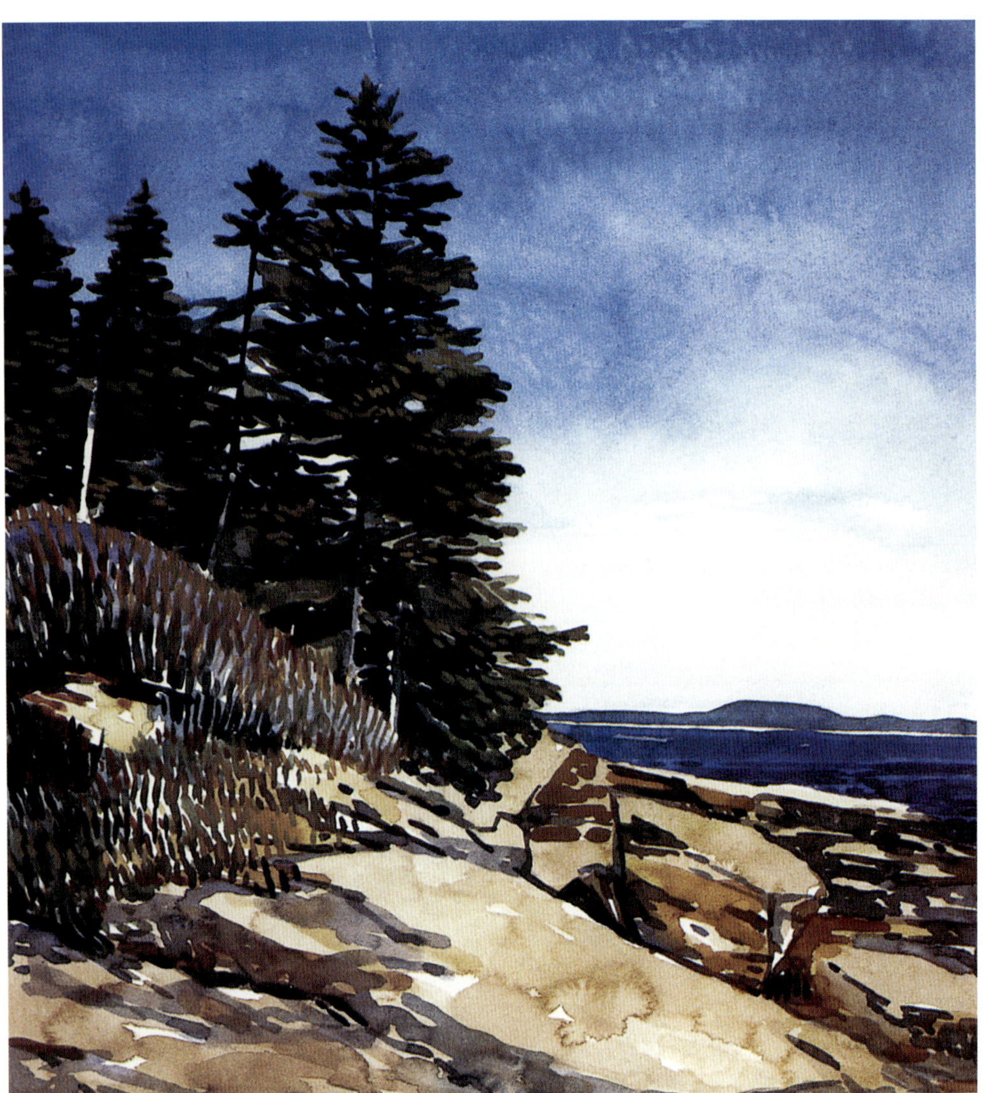

Study for *Lands End* by James Linehan *9" x 8" (23cm x 20cm)*
The grass and rocks are made of desaturated oranges and violets in various mixtures to form chameleon colors—beautiful, but difficult to define.

The next group of colors is found by again starting with one color on the color wheel, but this time mixing the colors two steps away. Moving two steps away from red in both directions locates orange and violet, whose mixture is difficult to imagine (diagrams 5.7-5.8). The result turns out to be a reddish color. This makes sense upon analyzing the components: orange is made of one part red, one part yellow and the violet is made of one part red, one part blue. Thus the mixture contains two parts red, one part yellow and one part blue. Since the blue and yellow mix to green, the components can be further reduced to two parts red and one part green. All this reducing may sound a bit like algebra, but analyzing this way can be a real aid to predicting color mixtures.

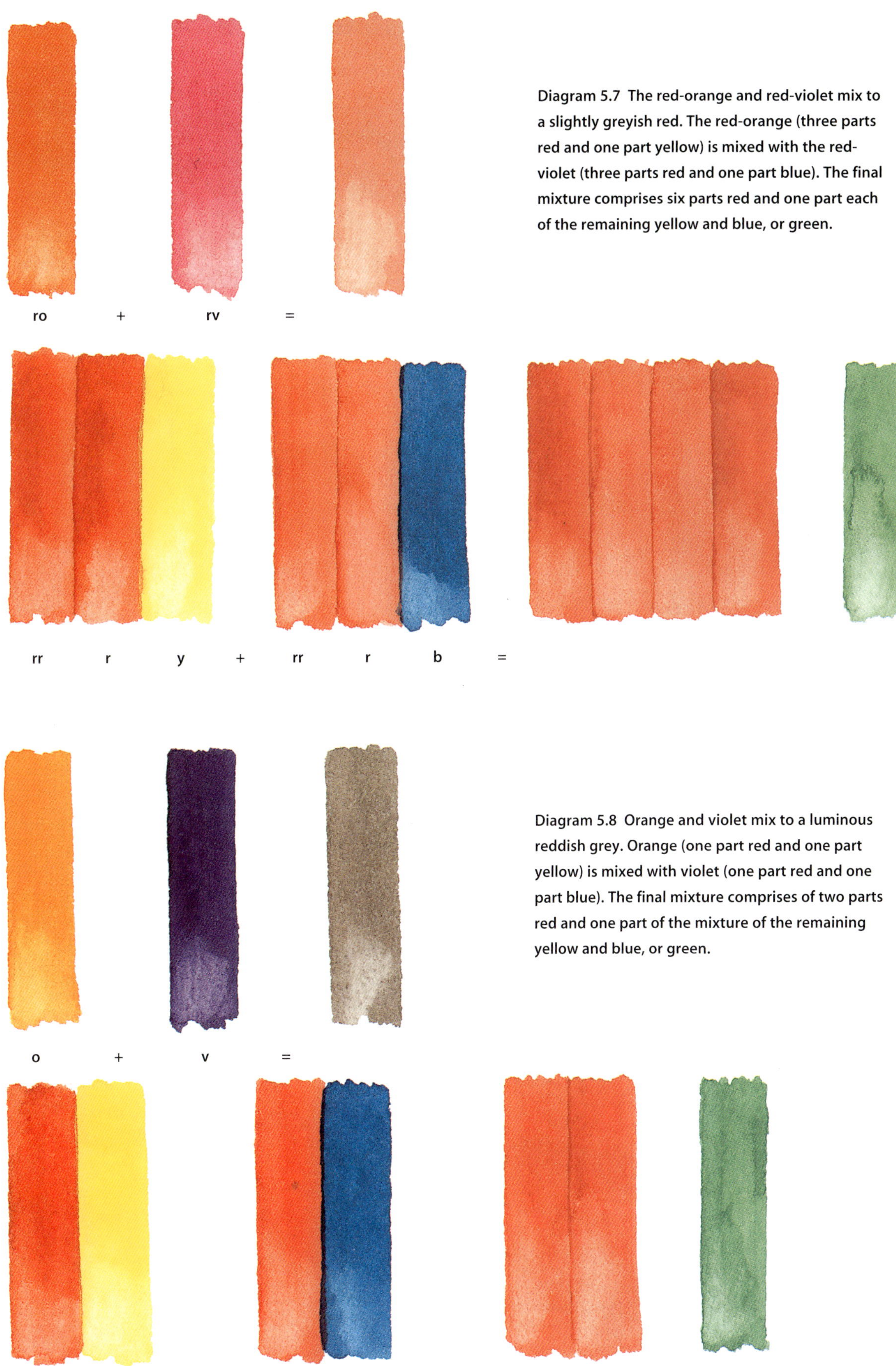

Diagram 5.7 The red-orange and red-violet mix to a slightly greyish red. The red-orange (three parts red and one part yellow) is mixed with the red-violet (three parts red and one part blue). The final mixture comprises six parts red and one part each of the remaining yellow and blue, or green.

Diagram 5.8 Orange and violet mix to a luminous reddish grey. Orange (one part red and one part yellow) is mixed with violet (one part red and one part blue). The final mixture comprises of two parts red and one part of the mixture of the remaining yellow and blue, or green.

Moving three steps away from the original color singles out complementary colors. These mix to toned greys (diagrams 5.9-5.12). The reason the greys are not perfectly colorless is because the complements are not perfect. A red may be slightly blue or yellow rather than a perfect red.

Browns are toned colors too (diagram 5.13-5.16). They are not found on the color wheel because they are of a darker value and often slightly desaturated. The first step

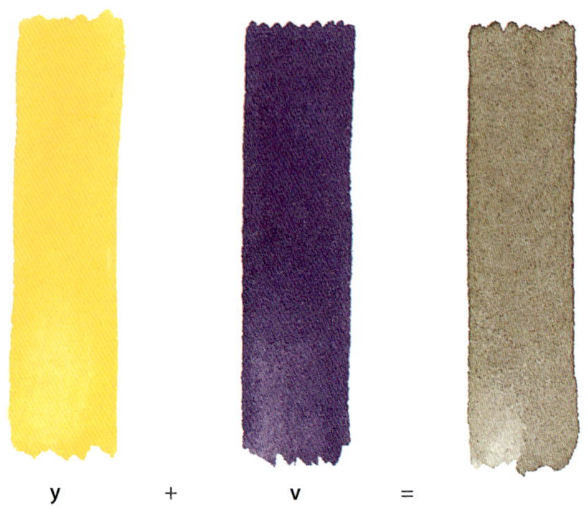

Diagram 5.9 The yellow and the violet are mixed to form a greyish color.

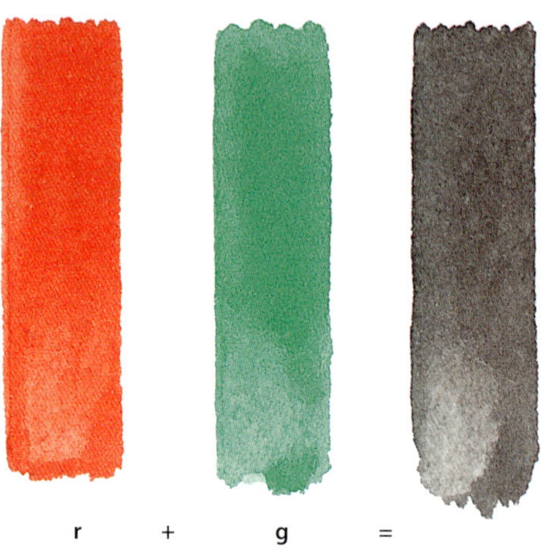

Diagram 5.10 The red and green are mixed to form a greyish color.

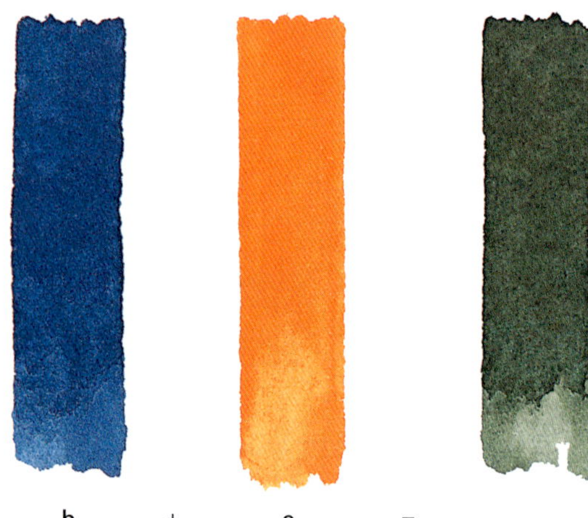

Diagram 5.11 The blue and the orange mix to a greenish grey.

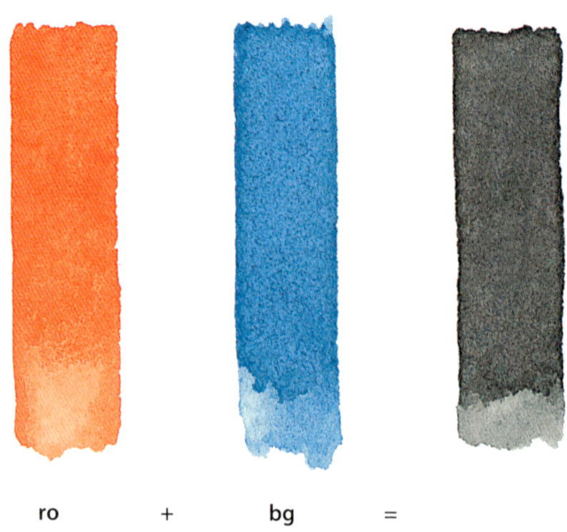

Diagram 5.12 The red-orange and the blue-green mix to a grey.

in mixing brown is to find out what color on the wheel appears to be closest to it. When placed near the red-orange, the brown gently resonates the same sort of hue. Because of this fact, making a good brown will necessitate starting with a red-orange. Now add black to this color to form a dark brown. Varieties of browns may also be found starting with oranges and yellow-oranges.

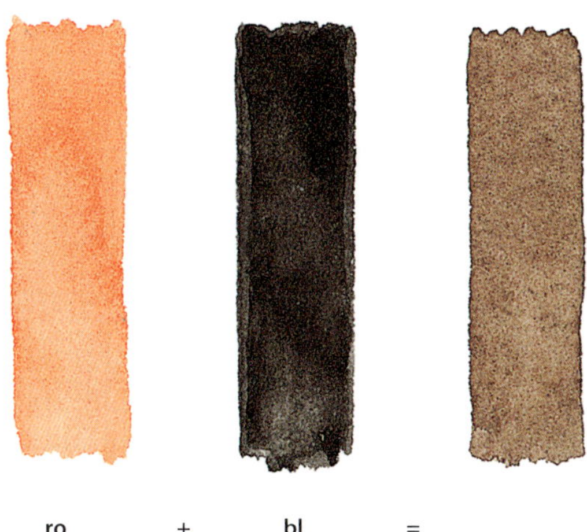

Diagram 5.13 The red-orange mixed with black forms a dark brown.

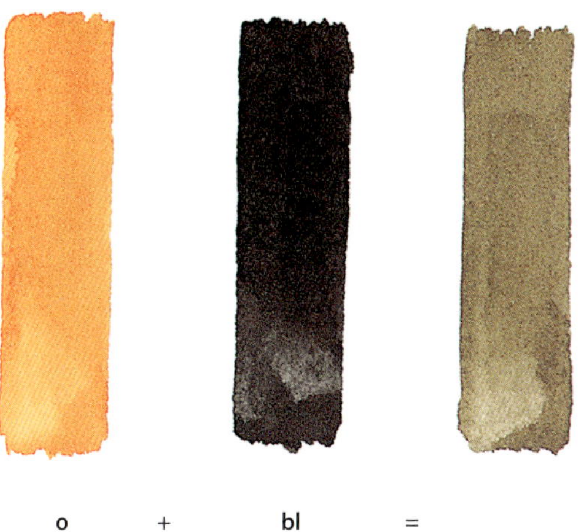

Diagram 5.14 The orange mixed with black forms a light brown.

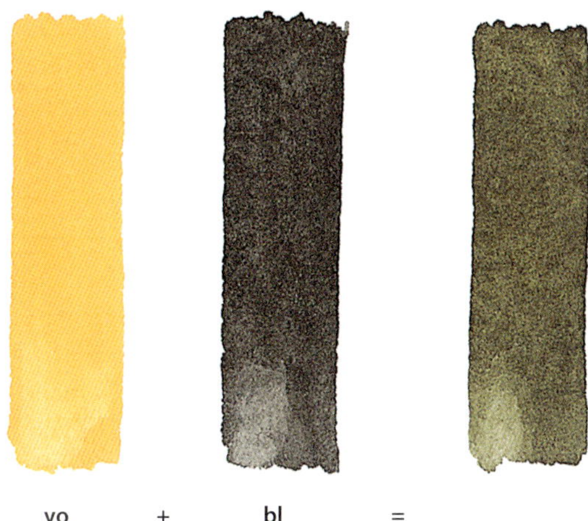

Diagram 5.15 The yellow mixed with black forms a greenish brown.

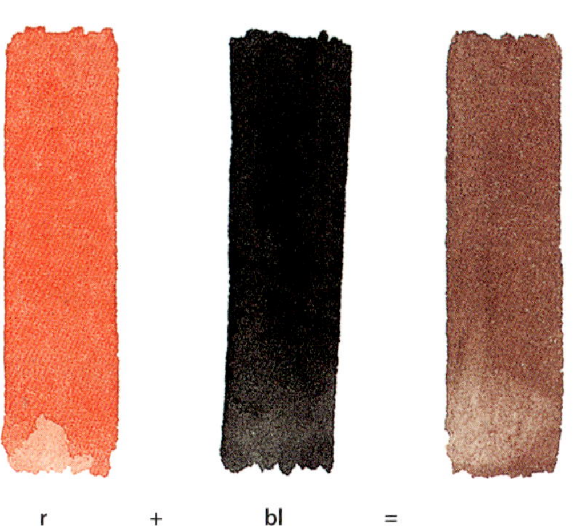

Diagram 5.16 The red mixed with black forms a reddish brown.

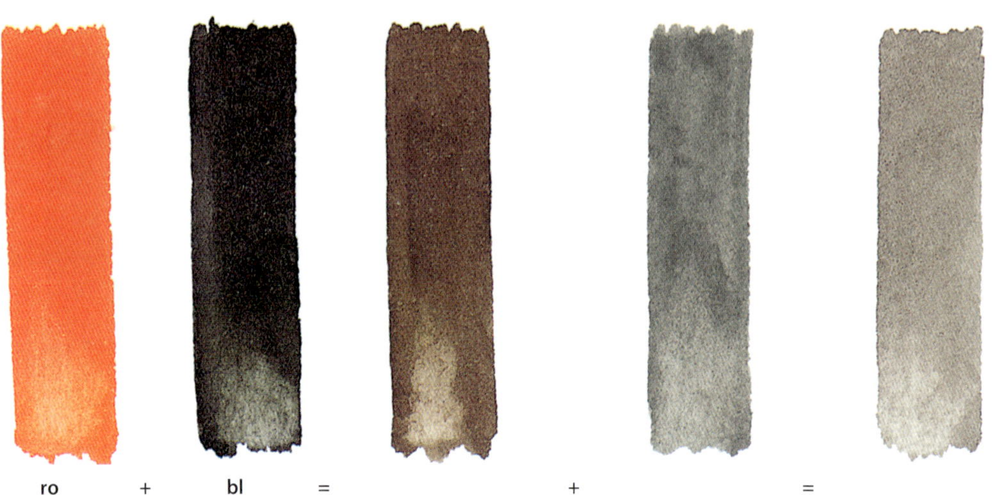

Diagram 5.17 Browns may also be further adjusted by desaturating them with grey. The red-orange mixed with black forms a brown. This brown is mixed with a grey to form a greyish brown.

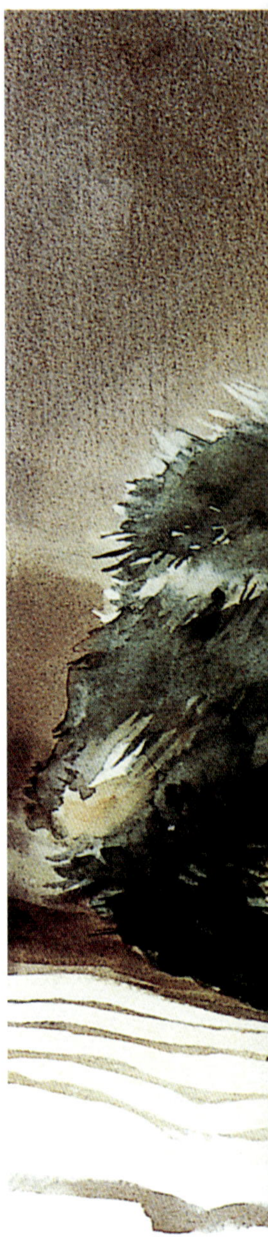

The fact that complements are not perfect colors means the jumps between the colors are not perfectly equidistant either; a red may sit slightly closer to the red-orange than the red-violet. This means some nice toned browns and greys can be obtained by mixing a color not with its complement, but with the color next to its complement— for example, green mixed with a red-orange rather than a red (diagram 5.17).

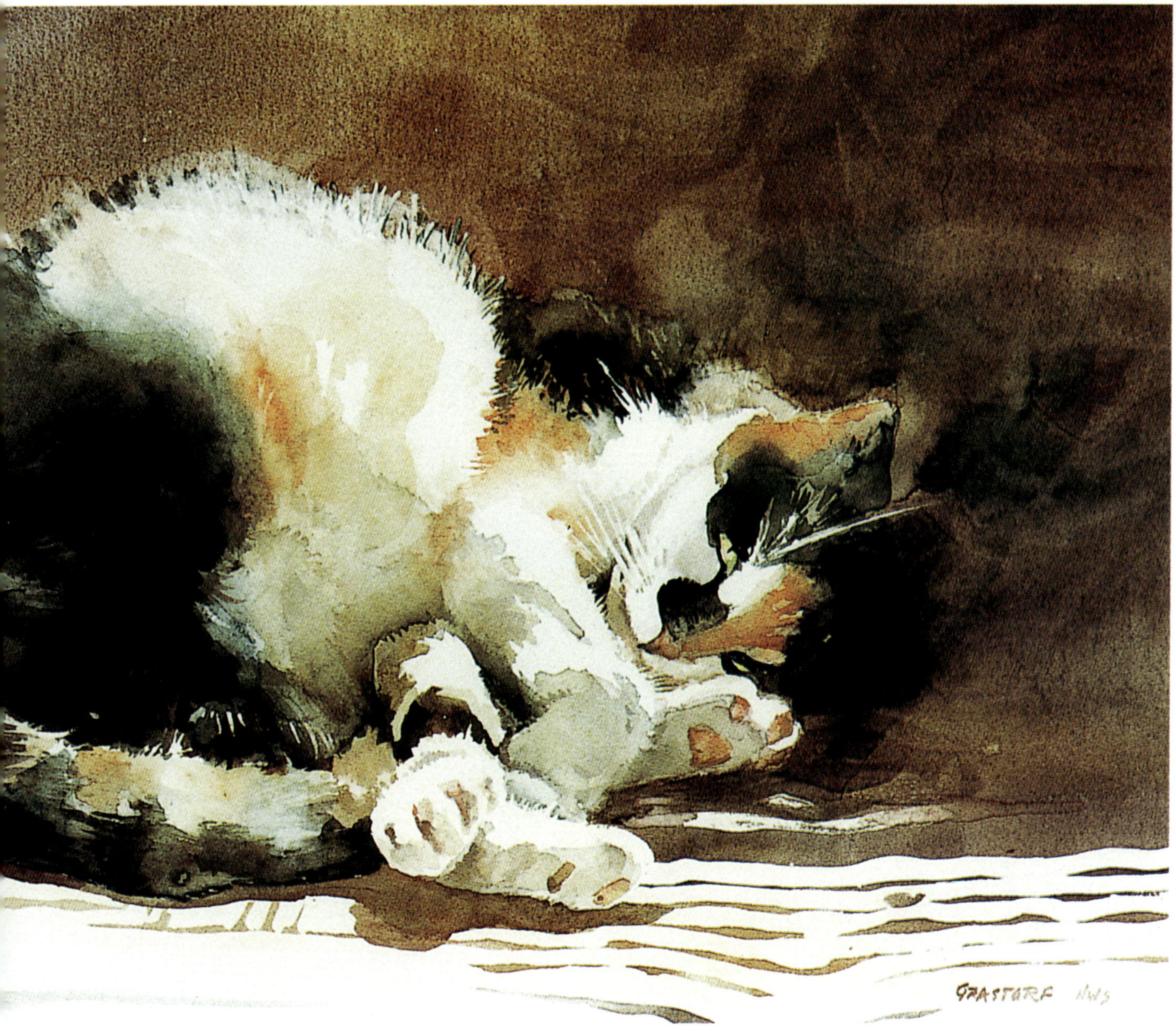

Calico by Jean Grastorf, *18" x 24" (46cm x 61cm)*
A calico boasts a variety of colors, and so does this charming portrait of a sleeping cat created with a variety of desaturated red-oranges and oranges.

RECIPE FOR SUCCESS

Browns are red-oranges and oranges toned with black. These browns may be further adjusted by adding grey.

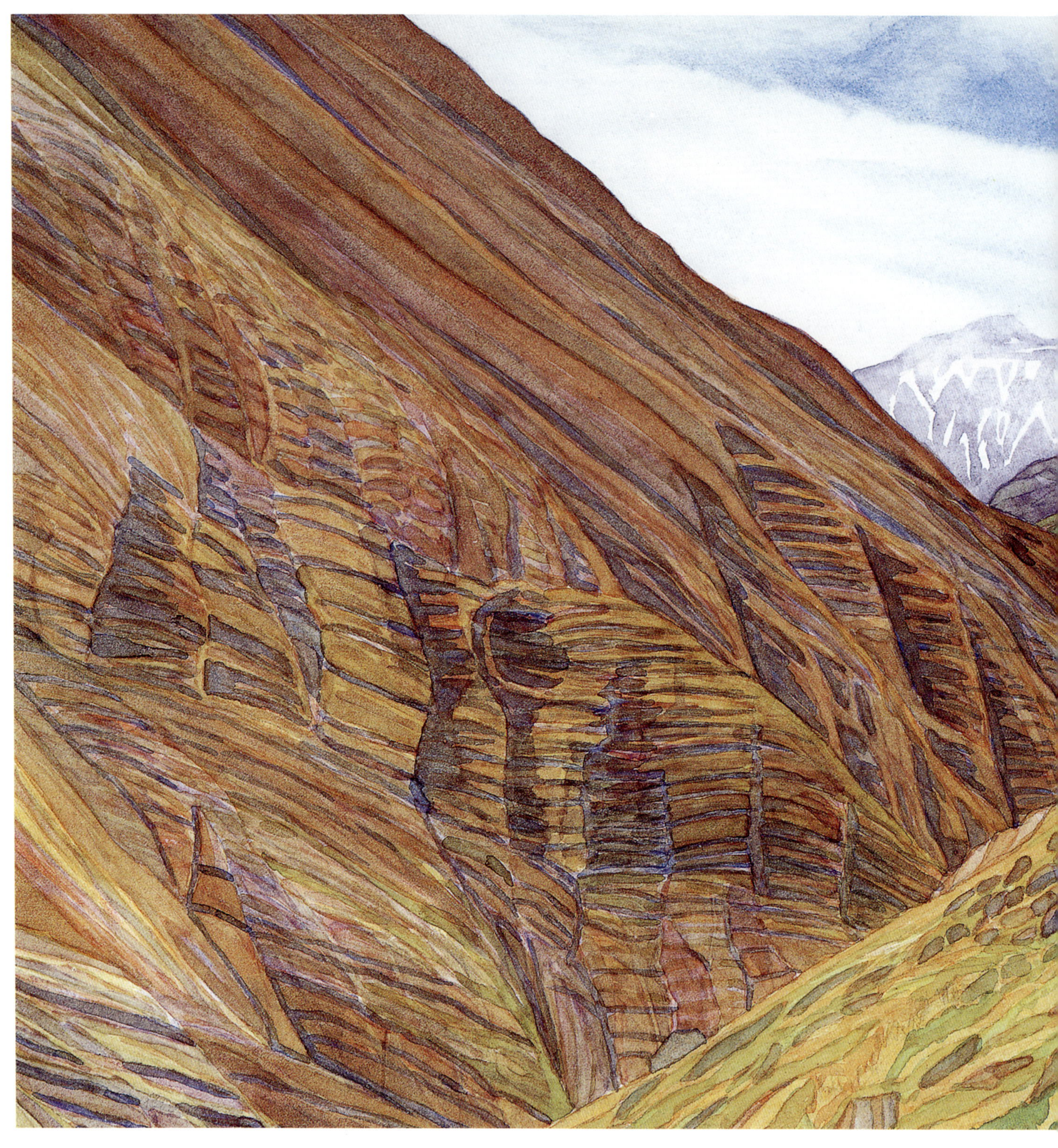

6

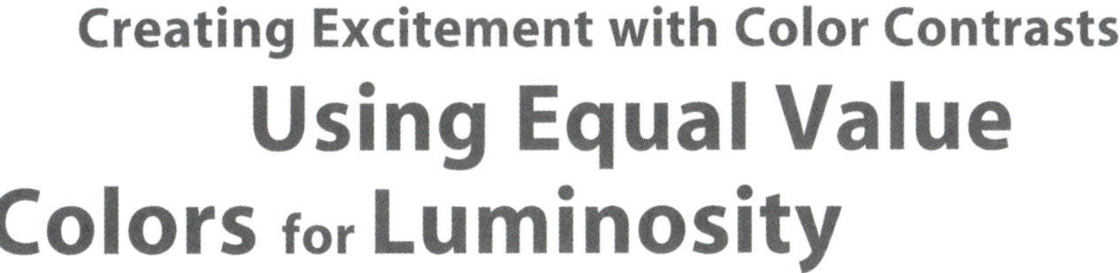

Creating Excitement with Color Contrasts:

Using Equal Value Colors for Luminosity

Contrasts are the spice of painting. They occur whenever two different elements are placed near each other, such as small marks near large marks, curvilinear lines next to straight lines, dry brush next to washes. Colors have their own contrasts that can and should be used in paintings.

Without color contrast, the painting is dull and lifeless, while with it the painting demands notice. It is impossible to walk by a good contrast without stopping to look more closely and wonder how the artist is able to arrest attention so completely. Contrast in a painting is so important that without it, many of the other color fundamentals presented in this book will fall flat. Combining the fundamentals with one or more of four contrasts will almost guarantee success.

A contrast of hue is often a natural occurrence for a painter who uses different colors. Creating a hue contrast by allowing more than one color to come in contact with another in a painting requires little thought, but the contrast of hues does not in itself make the painting good. In fact, the reckless contrasting of many hues is perhaps the most common mistake artists make. A better plan is to choose them according to the structures provided in this book and to combine hue contrasts with one of the other types of contrasts listed below.

Value contrast will pump up a painting with its strong variations of light and dark. Watercolors that exhibit a strong value contrast catch our eye; the watercolors of John Singer Sargent (1856-1925), Winslow Homer (1836-1910), and Andrew Wyeth (b. 1917), are good examples of how the white of the unpainted paper can provide sparkling contrast next to painted areas. But careful use of contrasting values is significantly more complex than putting one dark color near a light color.

For example, I'm sitting by a window, and it is a very bright day outside. This makes the interior of the room appear quite dark. If I wish to paint this lighting condition, I have three problems before me, and each one of those problems suggests a separate painting. The first is to represent the strong effects of a bright sun outside, the second to depict the difference between the bright exterior and the darker interior, and the third to capture the murky interior light. These problems are full of interest—just

Diagram 6.1 Sequence of achromatic (colorless) values is called a grey scale.

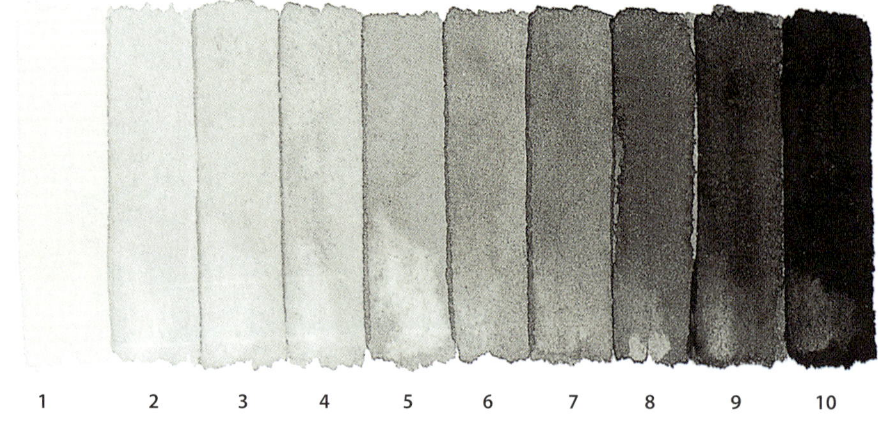

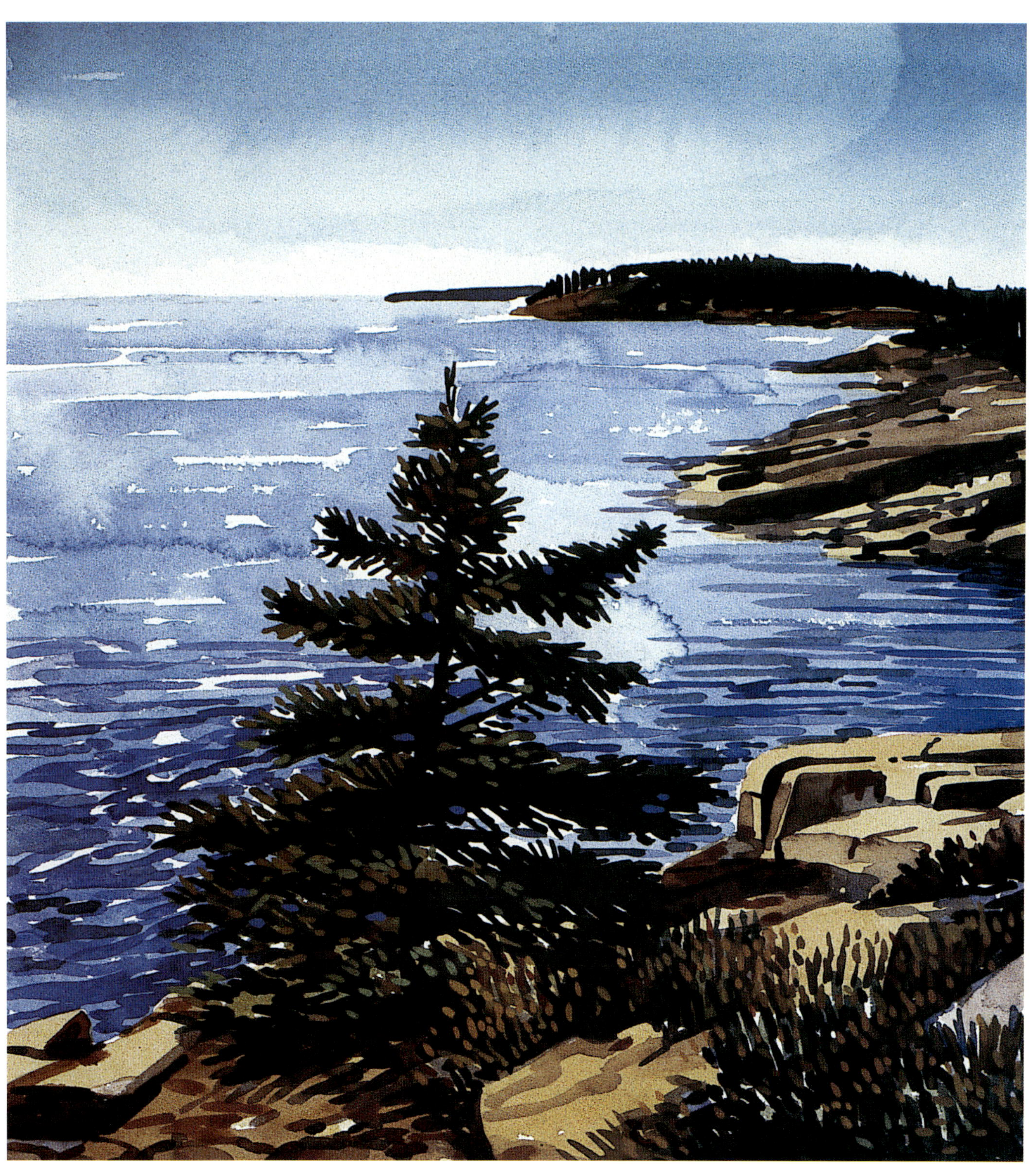

Study for *Ragged Spruce* by James Linehan *9" x 8" (23cm x 20cm)*
Crisp, bright light is created by using different values of colors in high contrast. Some of the brightest areas of the painting are adjacent to the darkest areas.

thinking about them makes me want to grab a paint brush and start right in!

A scale of ten different greys will assist in figuring out how to paint these lighting conditions. The white-grey on the left of the scale will gradually step up to a black-grey on the right. The greys are each assigned a number for reference.

The high contrast of the light outside means using a great deal of colors in the grey scale range of 1 to 3, especially where the sunlight is bouncing off objects. These greys would be the relative values of colors that can be matched against them. For instance, a grey in the light range will correspond to a full-strength yellow or a blue-violet thinned with water or tinted with the addition of white (diagram 6.2). The strong shadows would be colors matched against the values in the 8 to 10 range.

Painting the interior space will be the reverse process. Most of the colors will now be darker, matched to the 5 to 7 range, with a few highlights of the lighter colors in the 2 range and maybe a couple darks from the 9 range (diagram 6.3). I recommend reserving the absolute darkest dark and lightest light of the palette for later in the painting in case they are needed to add some final zing to the work.

A painting depicting a view through a window to the outside will be the trickiest, and recalling how the first two problems were solved in terms of value will help. This suggests painting the outside

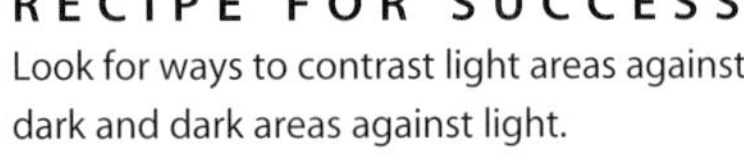

RECIPE FOR SUCCESS

Look for ways to contrast light areas against dark and dark areas against light.

Diagram 6.2 The range of values used to create a bright outdoor scene.

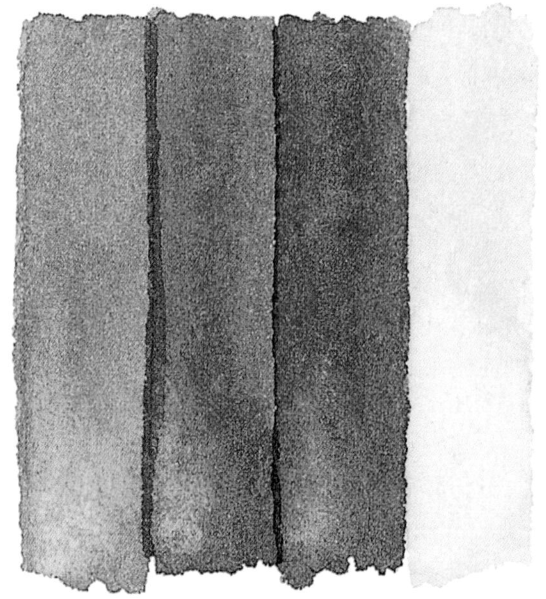

Diagram 6.3 The range of values used to create a darker interior scene.

scene with light value colors and the interior with the medium darker colors. However, sometimes this still won't replicate the existing brilliance. In that case, artistic license must be used to adjust colors to match the intensity of what one sees. The inside wall next to the window appears somewhat dark at first, but when squinting at the same scene, the wall appears very dark. In order to mimic the high contrast that exists, the colors inside may all have to be darkened a bit more than they really are and the ones outside may have to be lightened a bit more than they really are. The goal is to use contrasts to give the same impression as what is seen, and fudging colors a bit to nail that down is absolutely fine.

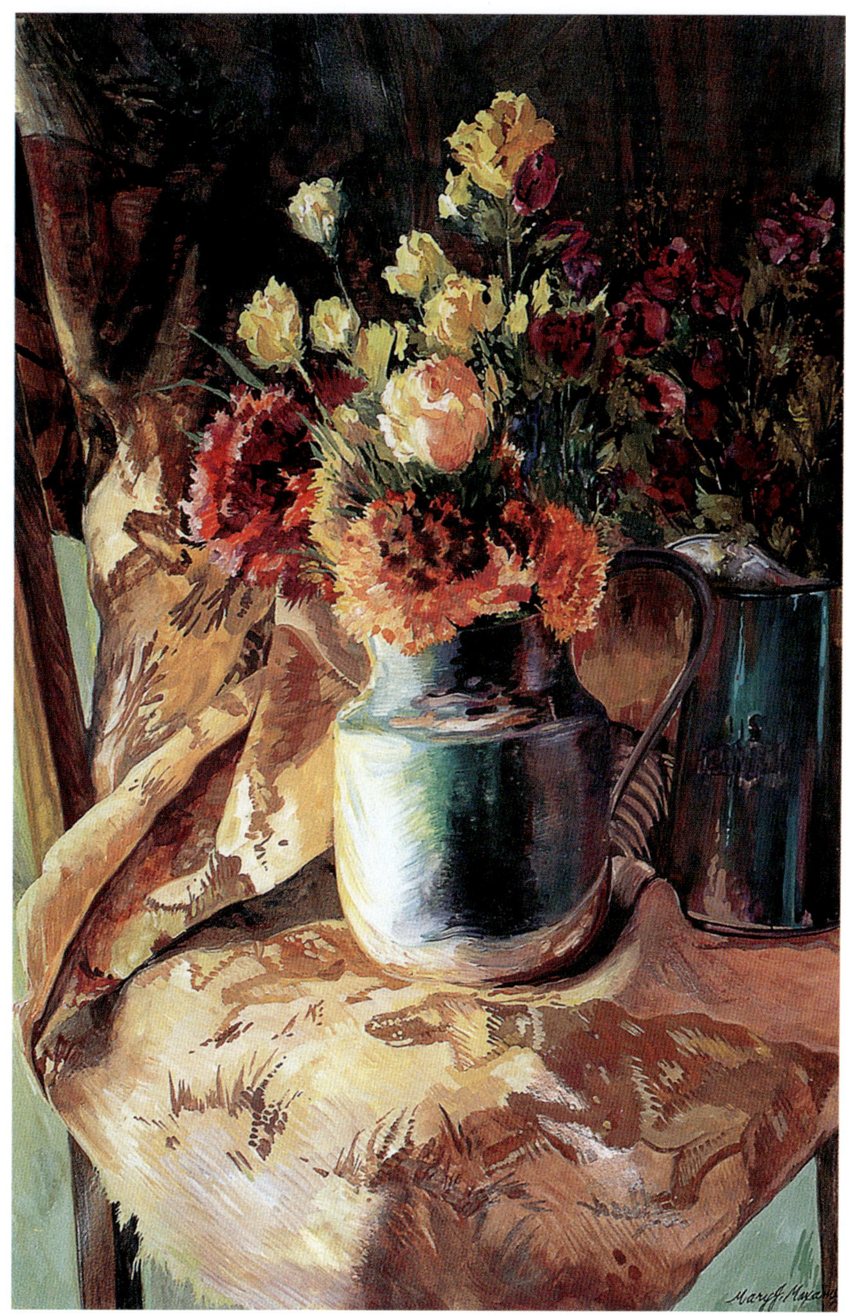

Hunter Bouquet **by Mary J. Maxam,**
28" x 20" (71cm x 51cm)
If the bright highlights are covered, the remaining colors are relatively dark in value. These darker colors suggest the interior studio space and provide a foil for the objects hit with light.

Diagram 6.4 Make a black and white card to assist with judging the values in a motif. This can then be placed near a still life or held up to compare the values of a landscape. Often something that seems to be white is discovered to be grey when compared to the white of the card.

RECIPE FOR SUCCESS

The main color contrasts are:

- Contrast of Hue
- Contrast of Value
- Contrast of Saturation
- Contrast of Extension

If the painting seems a bit bland, or not as vibrant as the motif, check that the contrasts are in order. A handy trick is to create a small 3″ x 1 1/2″ (8cm x 4cm) card from white paper. One half is kept white and the other half is painted black (diagram 6.4).

No matter what the subject look for ways to tweak the values so darker areas come into contact with lighter areas. It's an old trick used by old masters, but it sure does work. One example would be a background that subtly moves from light to dark in opposition to the darks and lights of the portrait.

Contrast in Saturation

It is a rare artist who chooses only full saturation colors throughout a painting because such a grouping can appear garish. The antidote to this ostentation, and the mainstay of many great paintings, is desaturated colors. These colored greys form a bridge supporting the few touches of brighter colors, darker colors, and lighter colors. The most typical solution is to choose colors that are somewhat grey and contrast them with more saturated colors. The opposite solution, using mostly bright colors with a few touches of greyed colors, can also be effective although it produces a completely different energy.

Contrast in Extension

The final contrast is one of extension. Without thought, people do this on a daily basis when they dress. A green dress is juxtaposed against a small colorful scarf; a dark blue suit is contrasted against a brightly colored tie. In each instance, a larger color area is placed near a small area of another color. In painting, one color is extended over a large amount of space and another color is extended over a very small area of the

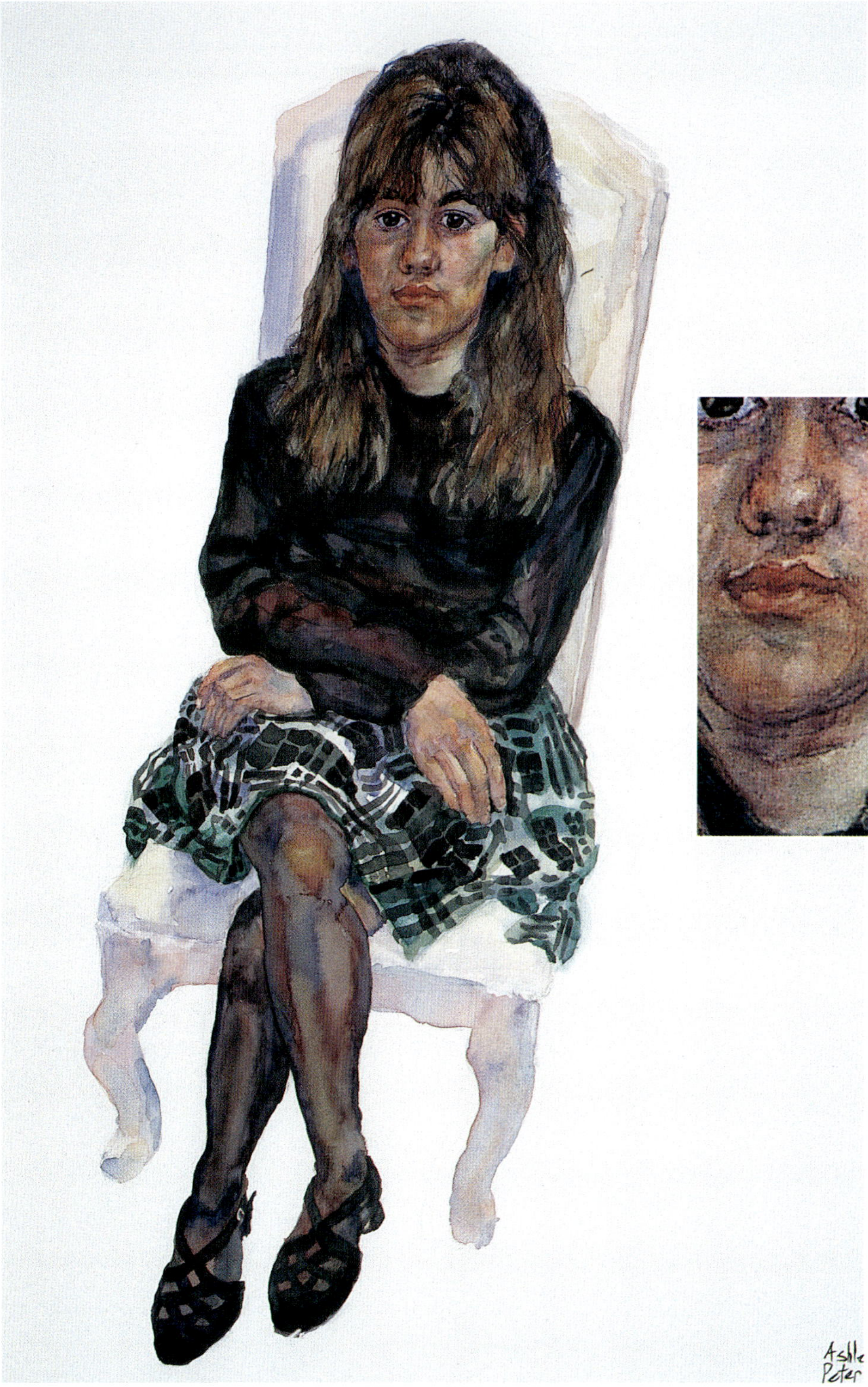

Sarah by Ashley Peter,
22" x 30" (56cm x 76cm)
Many of the colors in this portrait are desaturated colors that contrast against the more saturated hands, face, and pattern on the dress.

(Detail) The many different colors of the face blend into a coherent skin tone. The artist uses colors of near equal value and analogous colors to enhance this assimilation.

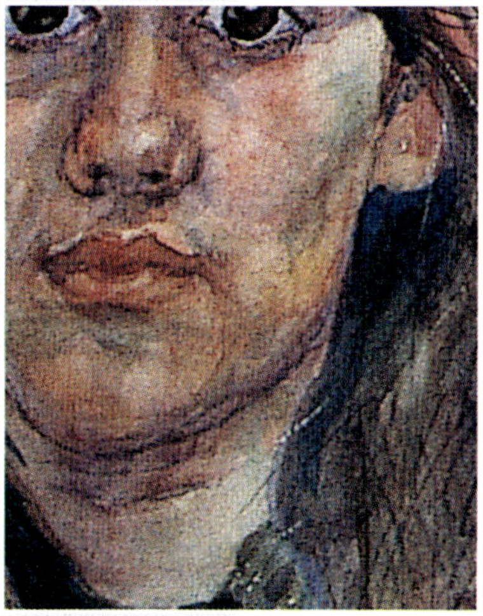

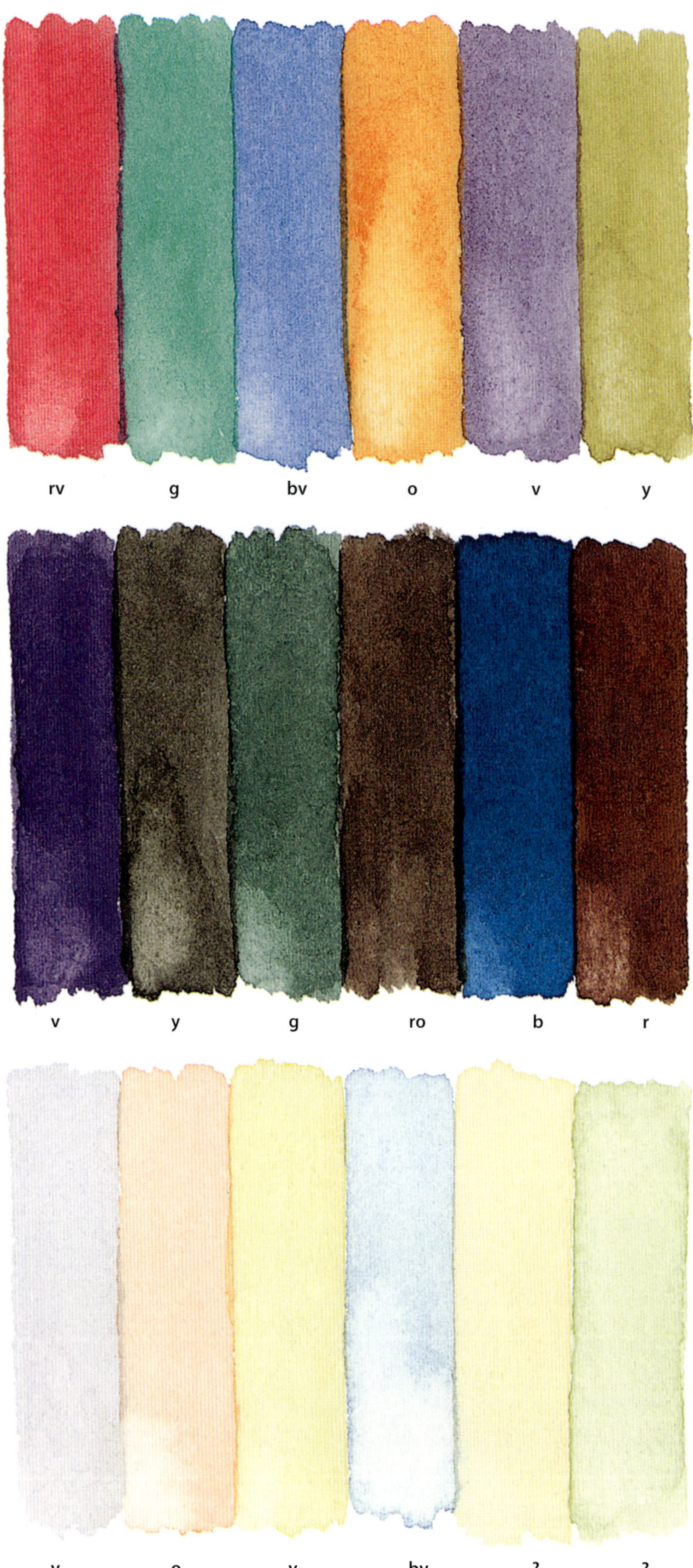

Diagram 6.5 The red-violet, green, blue-violet, orange, violet, and yellow are of near equal value in the middle value range, the dark value range, and the light value range.

work. The size difference of the colors forces them to be seen together, one reinforces the other; if you remove the small color, the large color no longer retains its robustness.

One human tendency is to make things similar: similar size chunks of colors, similar amount of space on all sides of portrait, similar amounts of darks and lights. The more an artist consciously sets up contrasts that show the differences between colors and color sizes, the better the painting becomes. When everything is uniform in a painting, it's a bit like walking into the stereo department of a store—a hundred different tunes are all competing for attention, but not one stands out.

Assimilation

The opposite of contrast is called assimilation. When colors blend together they assimilate. A color will assimilate when its hue, value, or saturation (or all three) are close to another color. This lack of contrast is also of importance to painting. For example, when painting a portrait, one can contrast the shadow and light, one

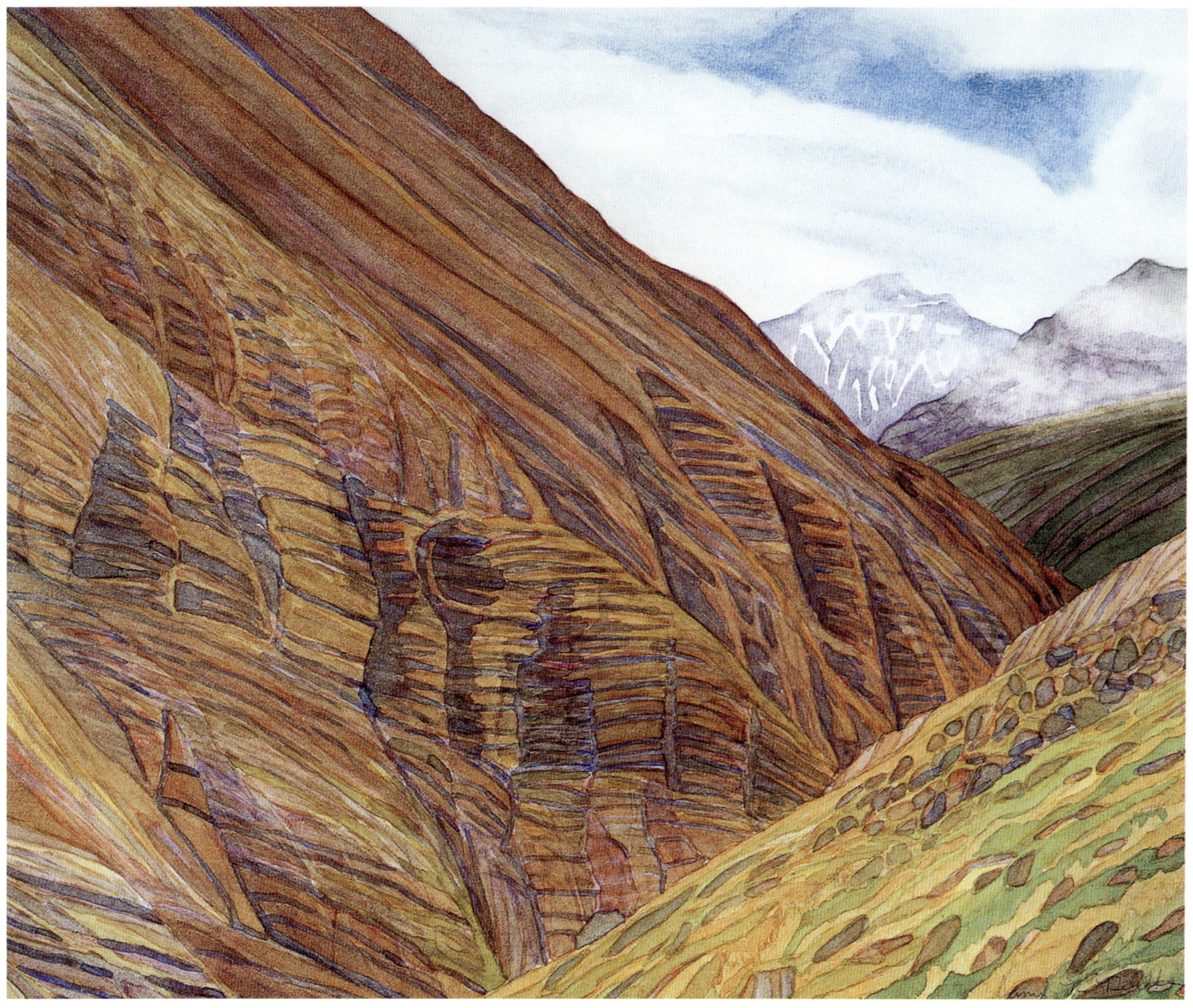

Arctic Canyon **by James Behlke,** ***17" x 21" (43cm x 53cm)***
The colors of the sloping walls assimilate because they are of almost equal value. They possess a vibrancy that is greater than if the areas were painted with solid blocks of a single color.

can contrast the bright sparkle of the eyes against the softness of the hair. But what makes the rest of the face hold together and contrast against the eyes is the way a large number of skin tones assimilate. They blend together and form a large similarly colored unit.

Most areas of color in a painting that do not exhibit strong light and shadow differences are constructed by changes in color rather than by changes in value. Look for, find, and paint backgrounds and objects more with colors that assimilate rather than with shifts created by adding black and white. The overuse of black and white in such areas cause these to lose vitality and become dull. This dullness can also occur when the paints are watered down too much, a technique often used in lieu of adding white.

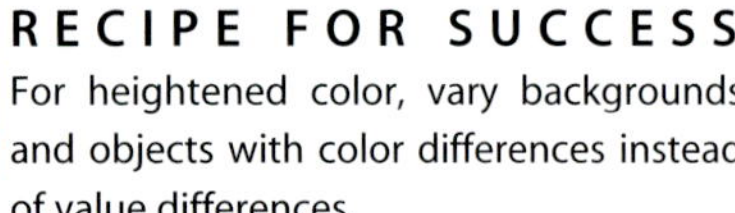

RECIPE FOR SUCCESS

For heightened color, vary backgrounds and objects with color differences instead of value differences.

Modulating a background or object with assimilation can also rely on colors close to each other on the color wheel. A red, red-orange, and yellow-orange can be mingled in one area but still give an overall impression of red. Even more colors can be added to an area and still assimilate as long as the values and saturation are carefully kept the same for each color. A bad habit is to paint parts of the painting with what is called local color—one flat color covering the whole object or background. This is a pretty easy habit to break by using colors that assimilate.

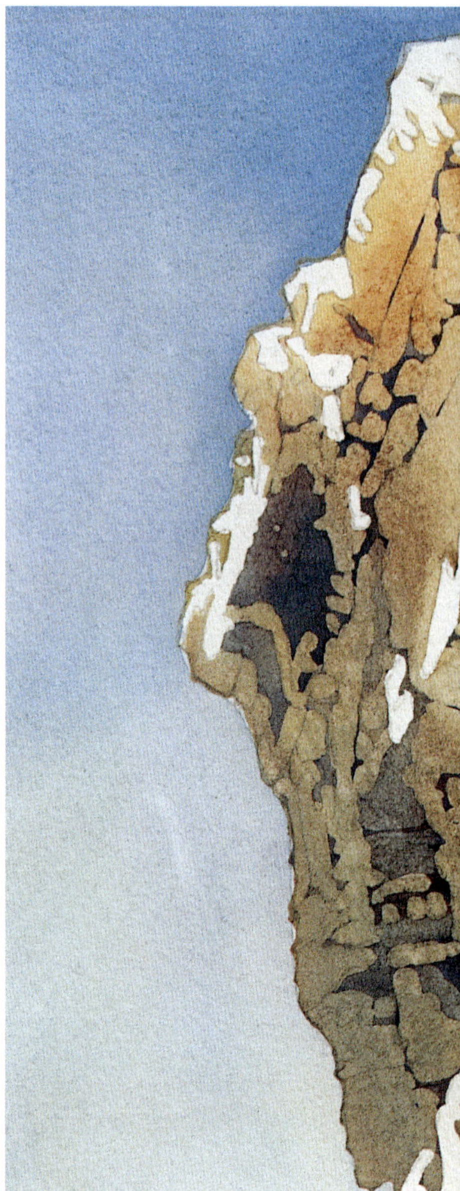

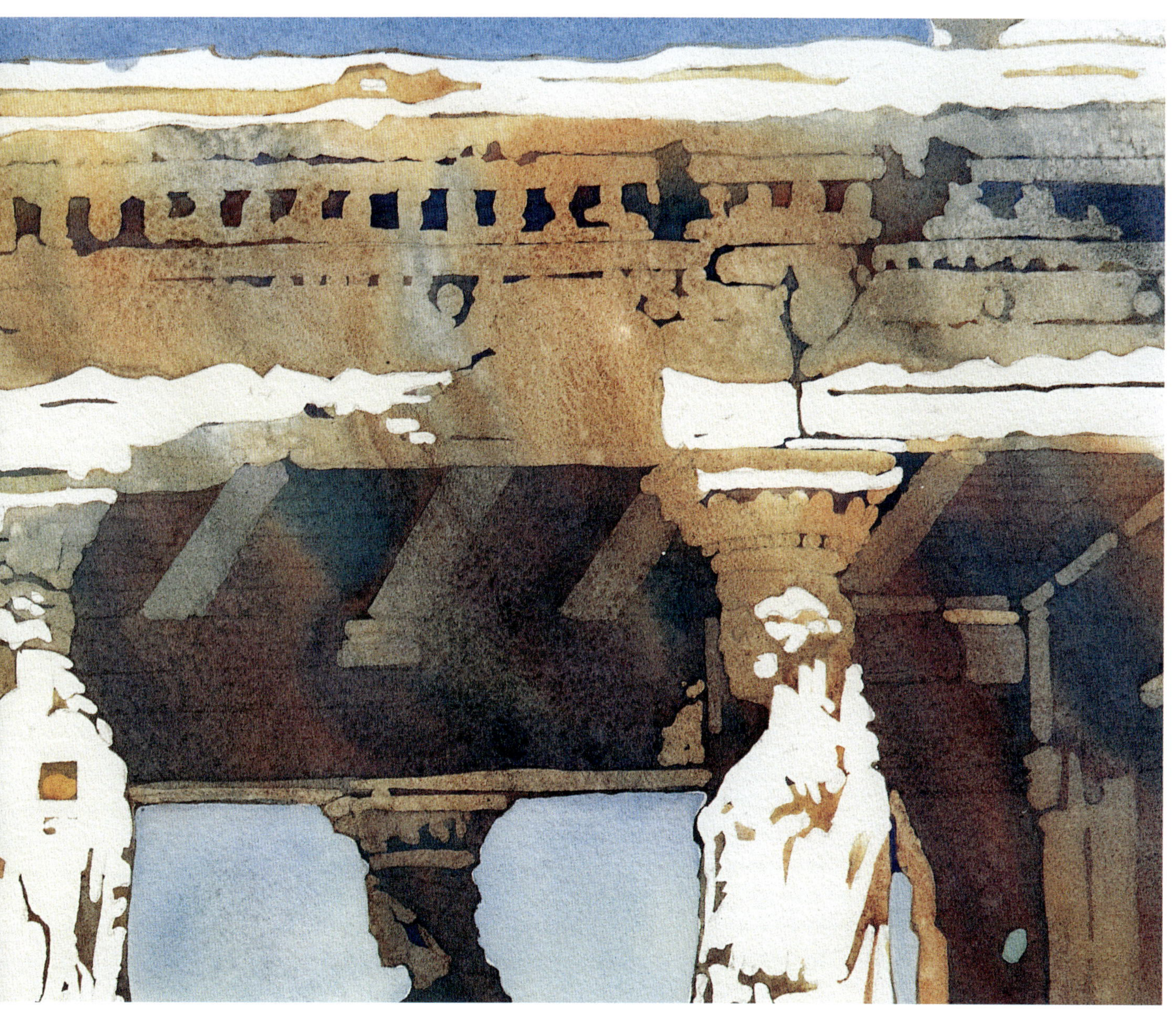

Parthenon by Jean Grastorf, *15" x 20" (38cm x 51cm)*
The key contrasts are exemplified here: desaturated oranges next to a saturated blue, and darks next to lights; the shadowed areas are modulated with a variety of assimilating colors.

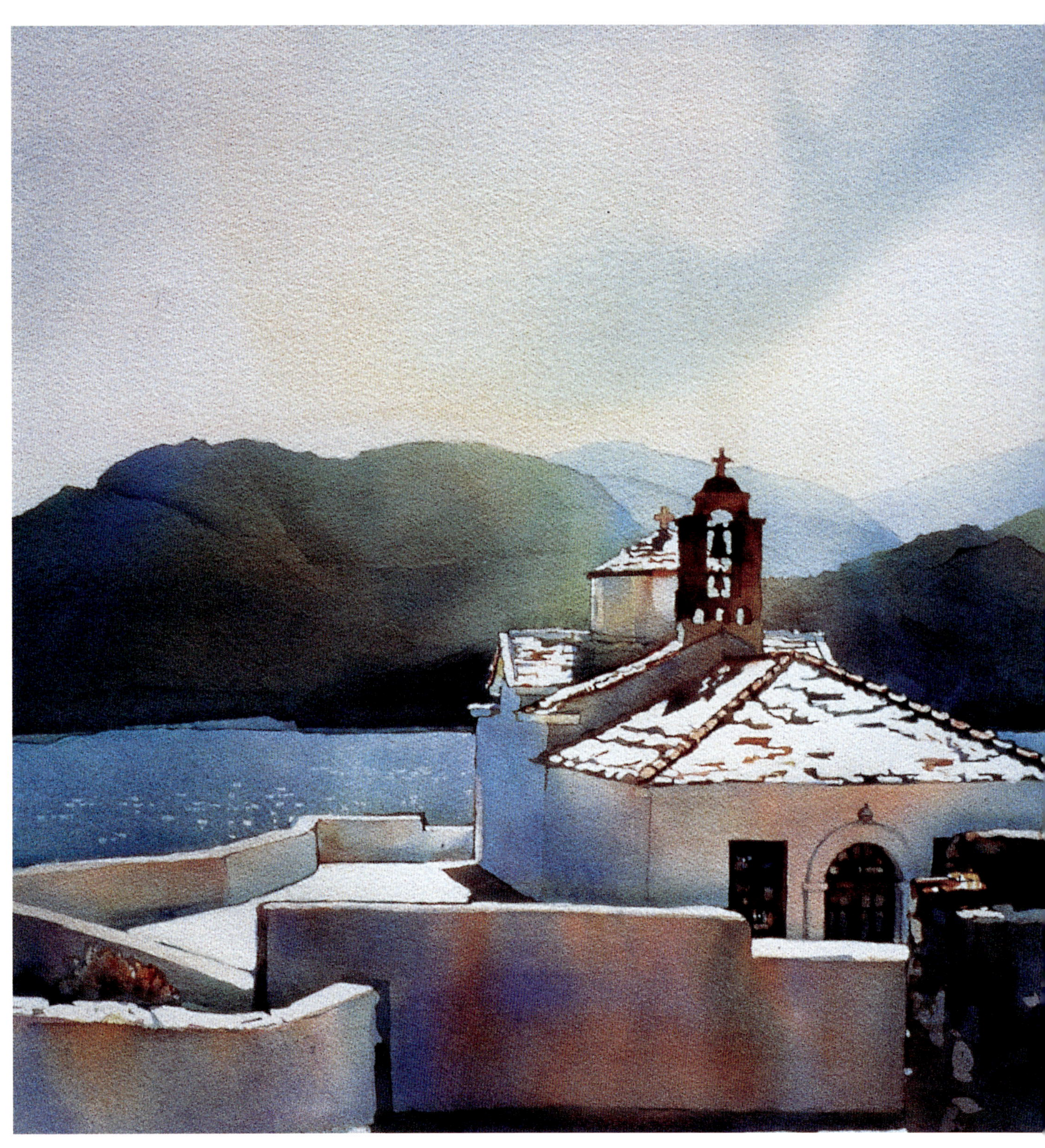

Gradations: Getting Colors to Work Together

A key element of old movies is the way the camera carefully and slowly pans across a scene, letting the eye move with it at a certain pace. The main character's sudden entrance into the scene provides the focal point, but the mood has already been set by the tempo of the camera movement. Had the camera jumped and jolted all the way through the build-up, there would be much less of an impact when the star appeared. The eye moves across the surface of the painting in a similar way. It settles on the key points of interest, which are often areas of high contrast. These most often do not take up the majority of the painting. In fact, if these high-contrast areas appear throughout the painting, it loses interest as every element fights for center stage. Gradations of colors set the scene for these touches of higher contrast colors to be seen clearly. Without gradations the painting fails; with them the painting shines.

Bridges of Color

Gradations of colors are gradual shifts in colors, from one color to another similar to it. They constitute the bridges viewers can use to travel from one point of interest to another. These can occur as subtle washes that mingle colors so they blend into one another across an area. But they can also be separate strokes of color that have been carefully mixed from two colors. The question of what color to paint next to something, or in a specific area, is answered by gradations. By starting with one color and mixing a second, slightly different color, and then a third, and so on, a chain of colors is created that spans problem areas and ties together points of interest (diagrams 7.1-7.2).

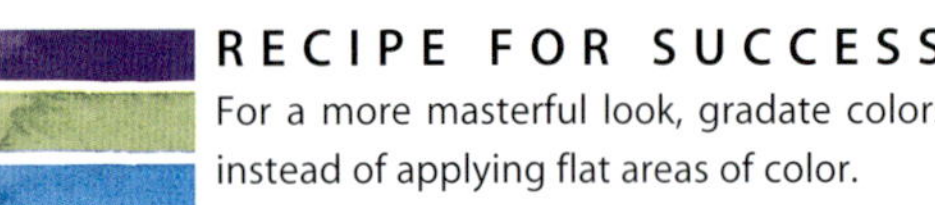

RECIPE FOR SUCCESS

For a more masterful look, gradate colors instead of applying flat areas of color.

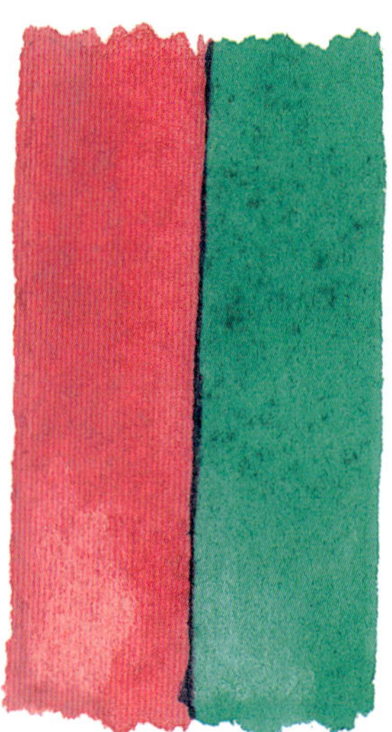

Diagram 7.1 The red-violet and green appear jarring when placed side by side.

Diagram 7.2 The two colors are bridged by gradations that link them more harmoniously.

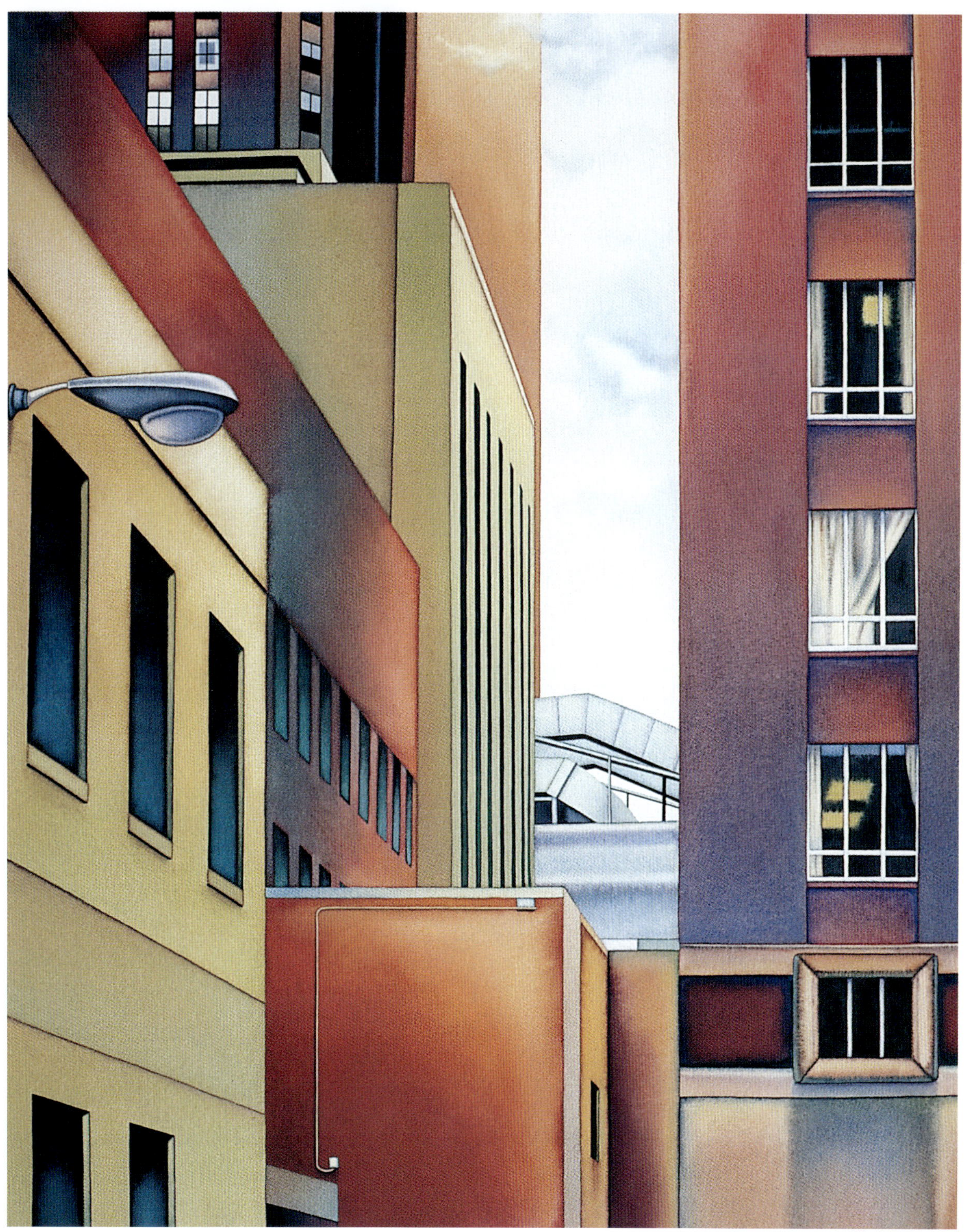

City of Color by Ann DeLaurentis, *21" x 27" (53cm x 69cm)*
The shifts from one color to another are gradations that are made by blending one color into another. Gradations add life to otherwise flat areas of color.

The gradation of colors also creates harmony. The eye-jarring effect of an adjacent bright red-violet and green is greatly alleviated by a bridge of transition colors found by mixing them together. First a little of the red-violet is mixed into the green to create a mixture color, and likewise a little green is mixed into the red-violet. Eventually, a point will be reached where the mixtures appear to sit in the middle between each color, neither too red-violet nor too green.

The difference between beginning painters and more advanced painters is noticeable in their ability to consider these gradations. For example, in one of the studios where I teach, a grey wall is often used as a background. Beginning paintings will inevitably show this entire wall as one grey of about a middle value. Eventually as the students discover the yellow incandescent lights shining down upon the wall and the bluish light streaming in from the large windows next to it, they discover the grey wall is not a grey at all. Instead it is seen as a pair of color gradations, one from a yellow-grey to a violet-grey and the other from a yellow-grey to a blue (diagrams 7.3-7.4). As these gradations are represented, the paintings suddenly take on a glowing life that causes other students to remark upon their beauty and life-likeness.

Diagram 7.3 A gradation from a yellow-grey to a violet-grey.

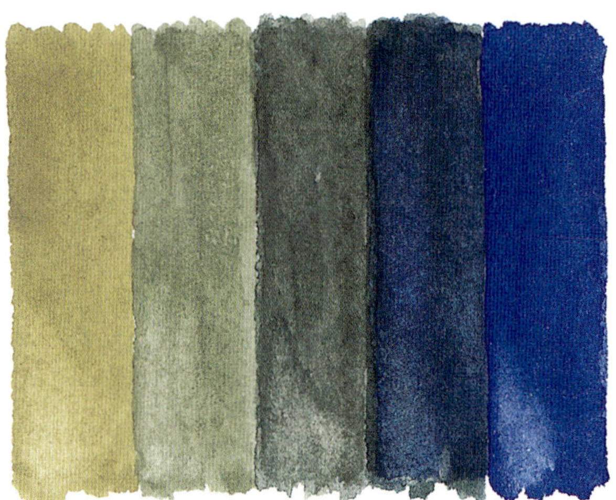

Diagram 7.4 A gradation from a yellow-grey to a blue.

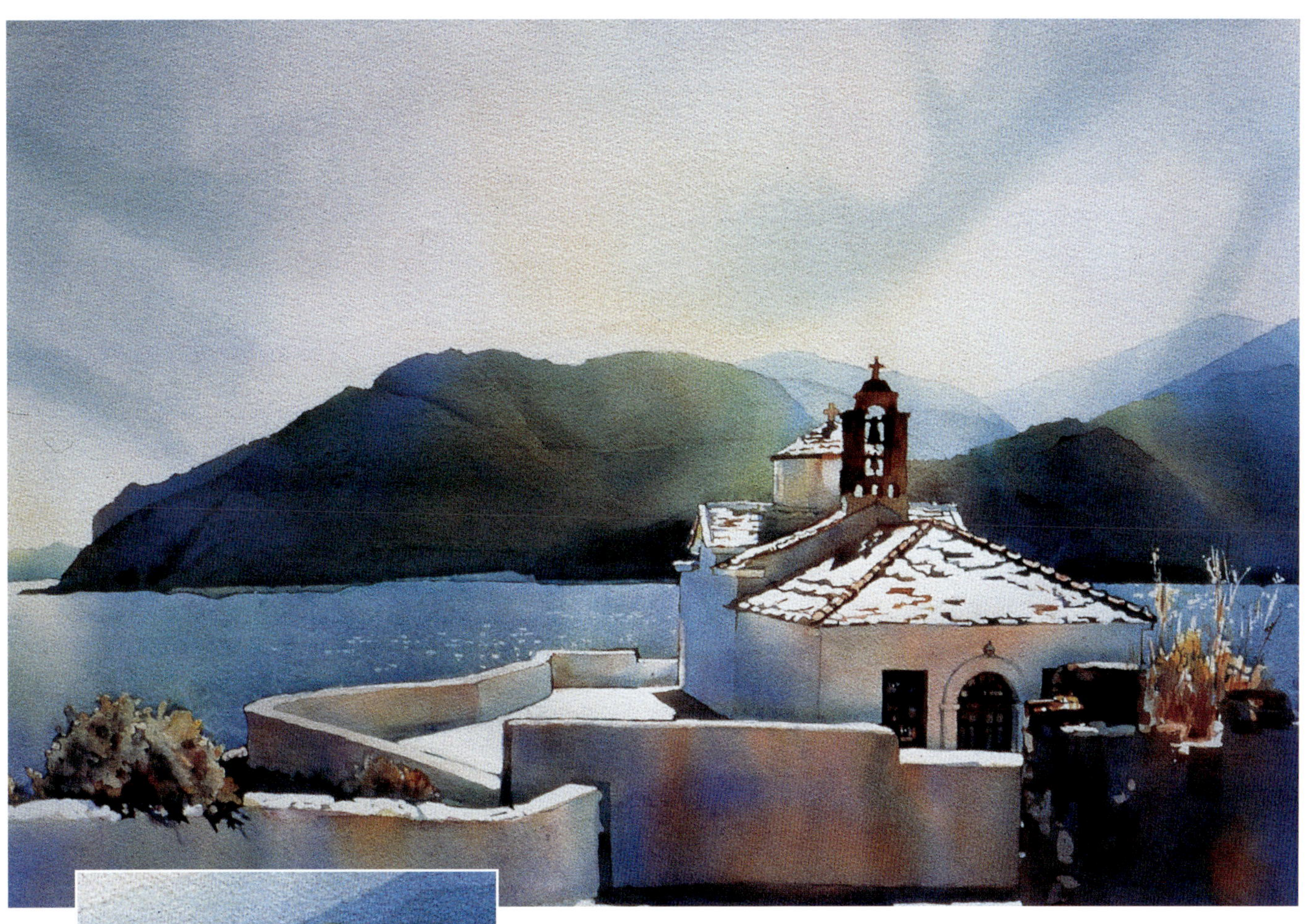

Skopelos Church by Jean Grastorf, *21" x 36" (53cm x 91cm)*
Gradations between darker to lighter colors cause the background to appear hazy while the gradations from blue to red-orange on the stucco walls establish the effect of reflected water.

(Detail) Almost every color of the detail is part of a gradation—shifting in hue or in value. When carefully observed, gradations are apparent in the colors of nature.

Diagram 7.5 Graduations of the value of blue can produce the sensation of light or volume.

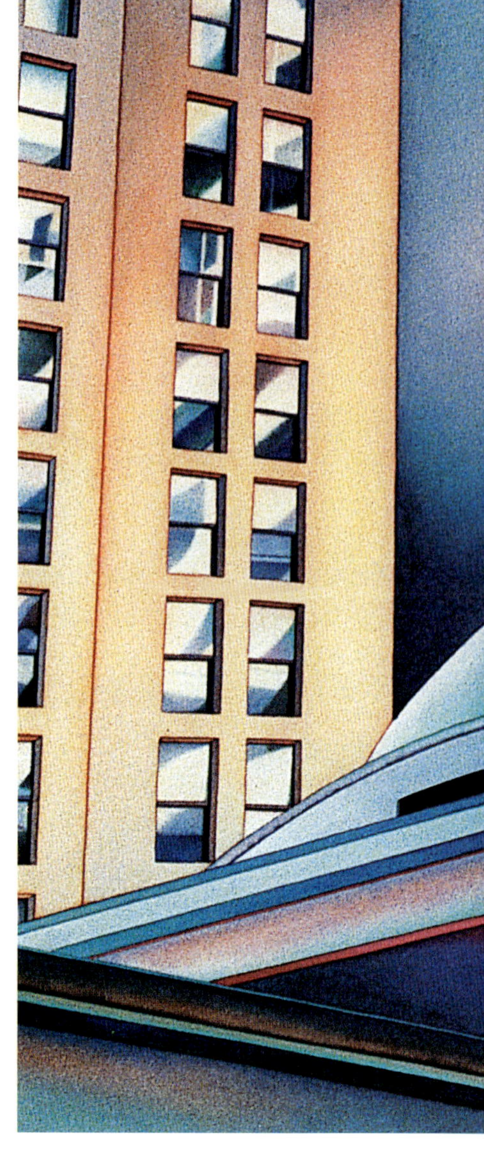

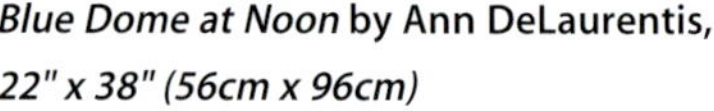

Blue Dome at Noon **by Ann DeLaurentis,**
22" x 38" (56cm x 96cm)
The volumetric quality of the dome is heightened by gradating the color on it from a lighter blue-green at the left to a saturated blue-green in the middle to a lighter, and more pink color at the right.

Gradations should not just occur in a background, but everywhere in a painting: on objects, over a curved edge, across a cheek of a portrait. Gradations are important because they reflect the way things are in the real world.

Gradations are key to two types of painterly effects—the creation of light and the creation of form. Realistic effects of lighting are made by gradating the steps from light to dark rather than by using a light right next to a dark. Even a sky, full of light on a clear day, varies from a lighter, yellow-blue near the horizon to a deeper blue directly above (diagram 7.5).

A volumetric object—an apple or a cup sitting in a still life—will look flat

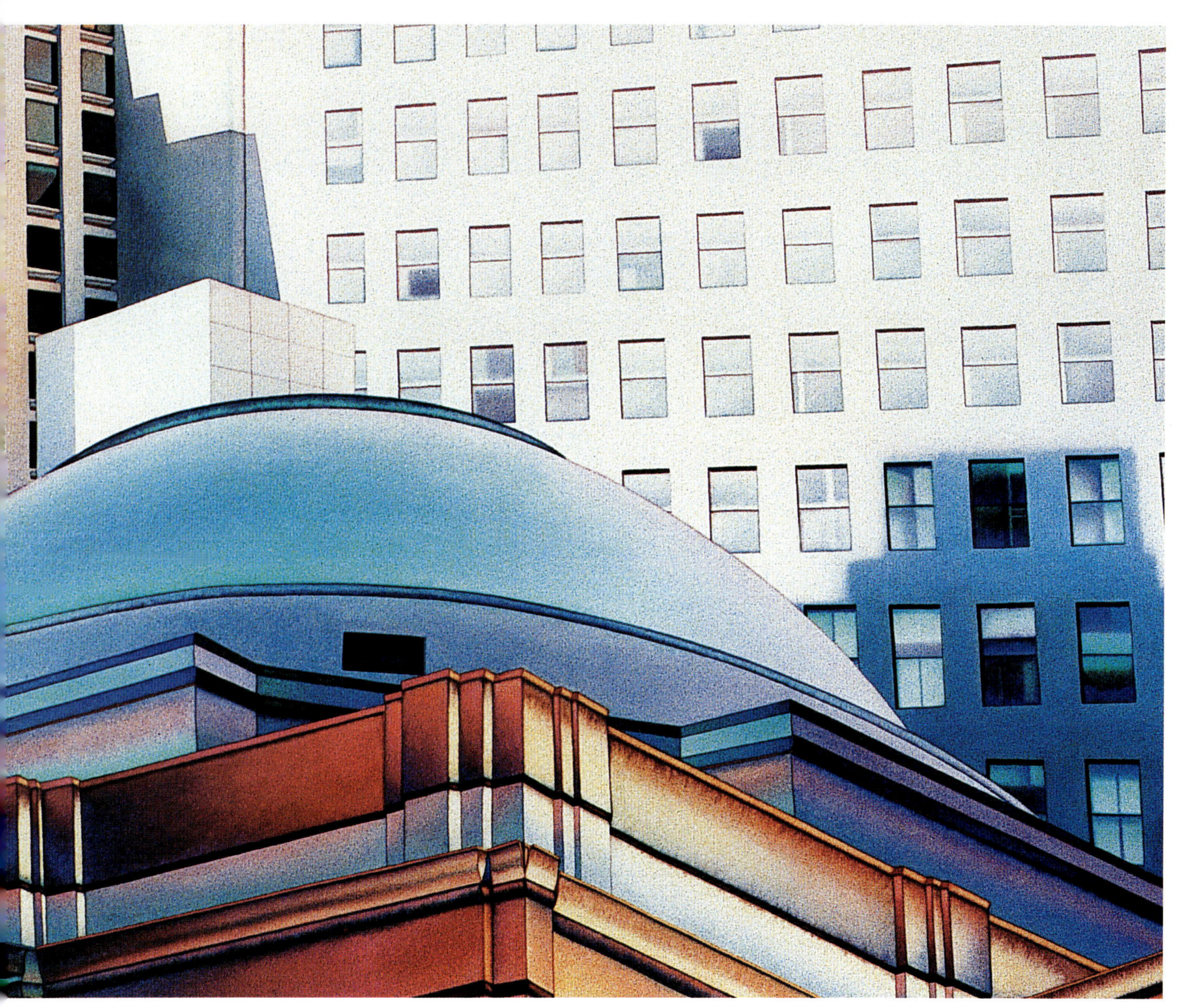

when painted with one color. Careful observation will discover color gradations across the whole form. The red may gradate from a lighter, more yellow red in one area to a bright red and maybe then to a greenish-red in another area.

Many artists look at a still life and see an object placed against a background. If these are painted with very tight, hard edges between them, the objects can sometimes look as though they were cut out from a magazine and pasted onto the background. It is the gradation of colors that will link these two areas together. The occasional abrupt edge is a good contrast, but such hard edges everywhere decrease the overall color sensation of the painting.

Gradation Exercises

Two methods can be used to make gradations a more conscious part of painting. For the first, start with a blank sheet of paper, hide the pencils, and have the watercolors ready. Already this must sound scary to some artists, but remember this can be a sketch rather than a finished work. Next, look at the subject and locate one area that holds special interest. Put down one of the colors in that area, and then put down the color that lies right next to it. From this origin keep enlarging the color area with more observed marks in all directions until the edges of the paper are reached. Don't worry about edges and drawing. Each painted area should represent a seen color. It can sometimes be difficult to see exactly what color is next to the first one, so some diligent looking is required.

The second way to focus on gradations is to put two colors on a palette and mix the gradations between them on a sheet of scrap paper. These can go from the saturated color to another saturated color, from a light to a dark color, from a saturated to a desaturated color. Each exercise increases the awareness of what combining the various colors can accomplish.

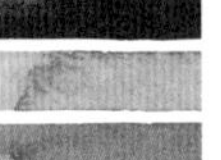

RECIPE FOR SUCCESS

Gradations are particularly important at the edges between two colors or between objects and backgrounds.

Golden Palm **by Jean Grastorf, *30" x 40" (76cm x 102cm)***
Every painted area of this highly complex painting is gradated with color. The color shifts intensify the sunlight streaming through the leaves.

(Detail) The bottom fruits are painted with separate lines of colors; this shows how the paint does not have to be carefully blended to be a successful gradation of color.

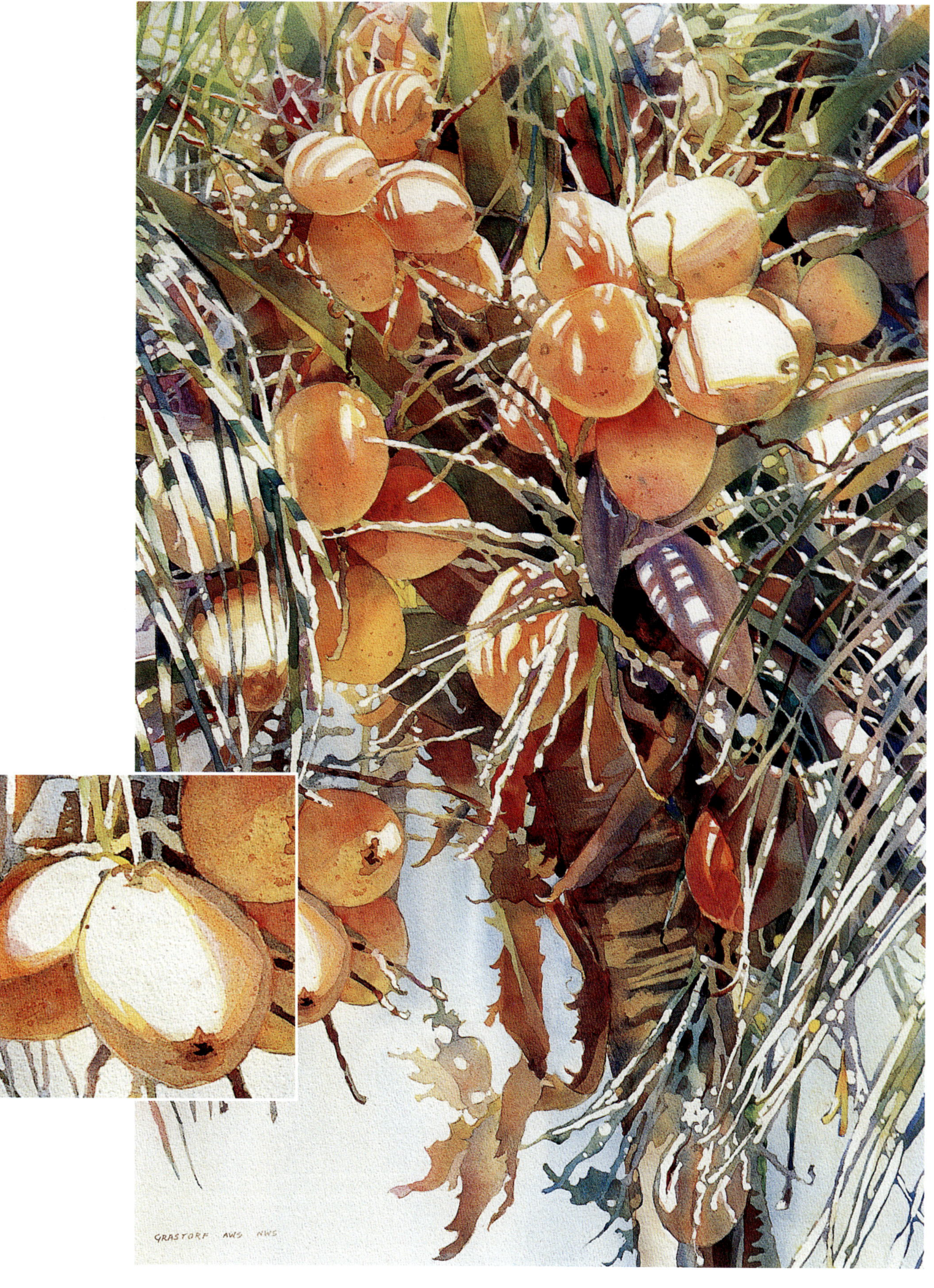
GRASTORF AWS NWS

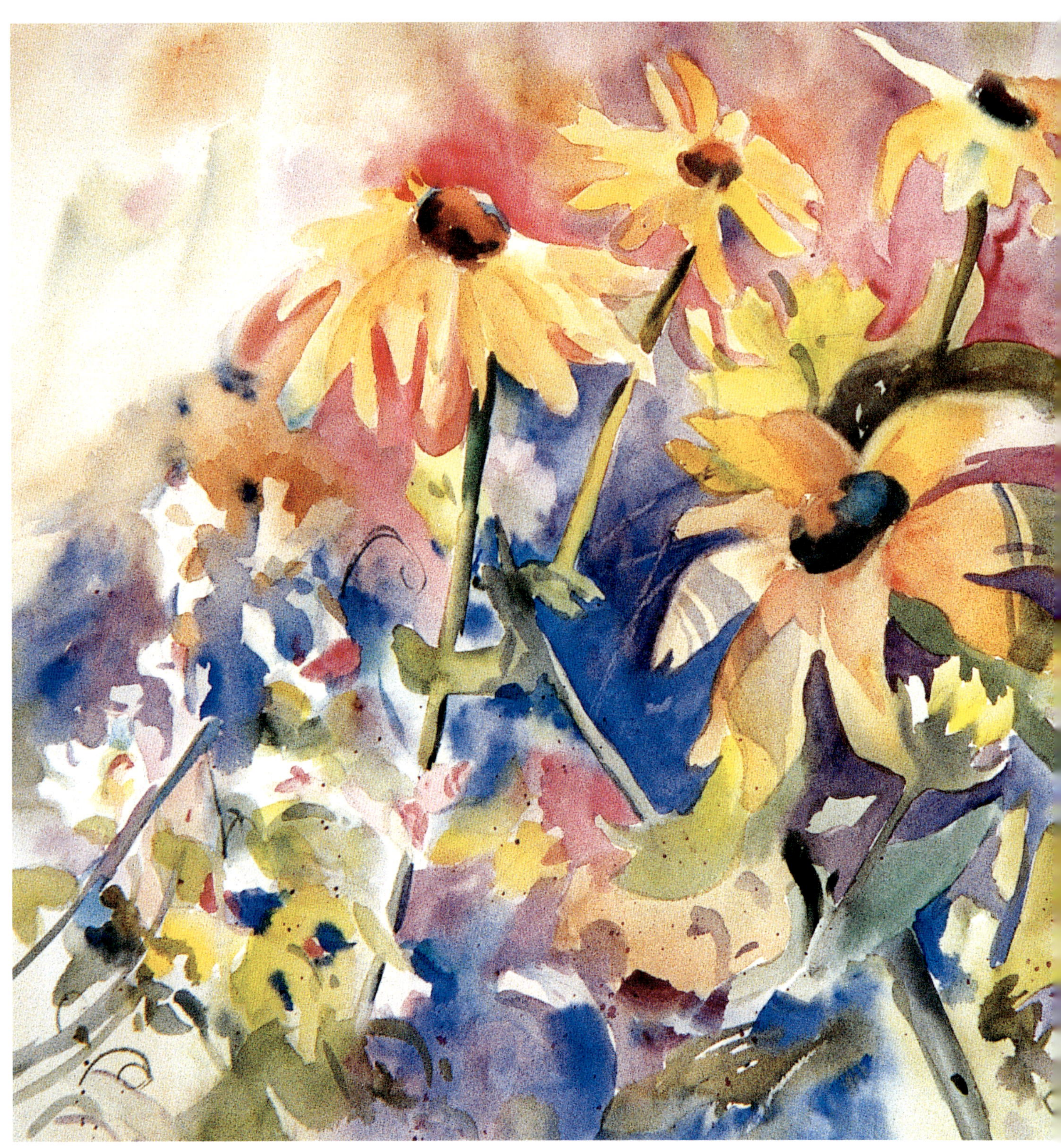

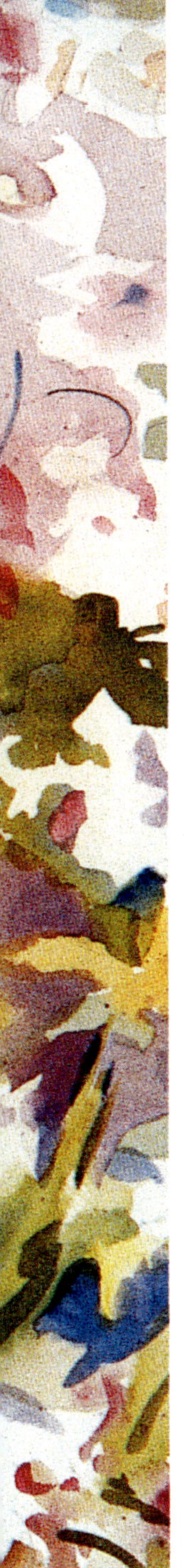

Making Paintings Vibrant:
Modeling with Spectral Colors

As when a rainbow, opposite the sun
A thousand intermingled colors throws.
With saffron wings then dewy Iris flies
Through heaven's expanse, a thousand varied dyes
Extracting from the sun, opposed in place.

—Virgil

Who hasn't seen a rainbow and felt a sense of awe and magic? Rainbows are rare fleeting events. They appear almost out of nowhere and disappear just as quickly. Their colors are ethereal, moving. They only occur in the early morning or late afternoon, and when there is a double rainbow, the colors of the second are in the reverse order of the first. The red appears on the bottom of one and on the top of the other. A rainbow seen from an airplane is seen as a circle.

A rainbow is nature's way of showing us how white sunlight can be broken into colors. Isaac Newton set up an experiment to prove this in 1666. He covered all of his window except for a small hole and he directed the sunlight shining through this hole into a glass prism that he picked up at the Stourbridge Fair. He found that when light exited the other side of the prism, it was a sequence of colors similar to the rainbow. We now call this sequence of colors the visible spectrum (diagram 8.1).

Newton tried to define exactly what colors were in this spectrum in the same way many have often tried to ponder the colors in a rainbow. He started out with eleven but eventually revised it to comprise red, orange, yellow, green, blue, indigo (a blue-violet), and violet.

Amazingly, the spectrum was not always depicted with these colors. Numerous pre-Renaissance paintings depict a rainbow with only red and green or red, yellow, and green.

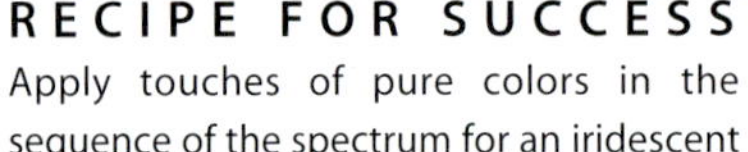

RECIPE FOR SUCCESS

Apply touches of pure colors in the sequence of the spectrum for an iridescent effect.

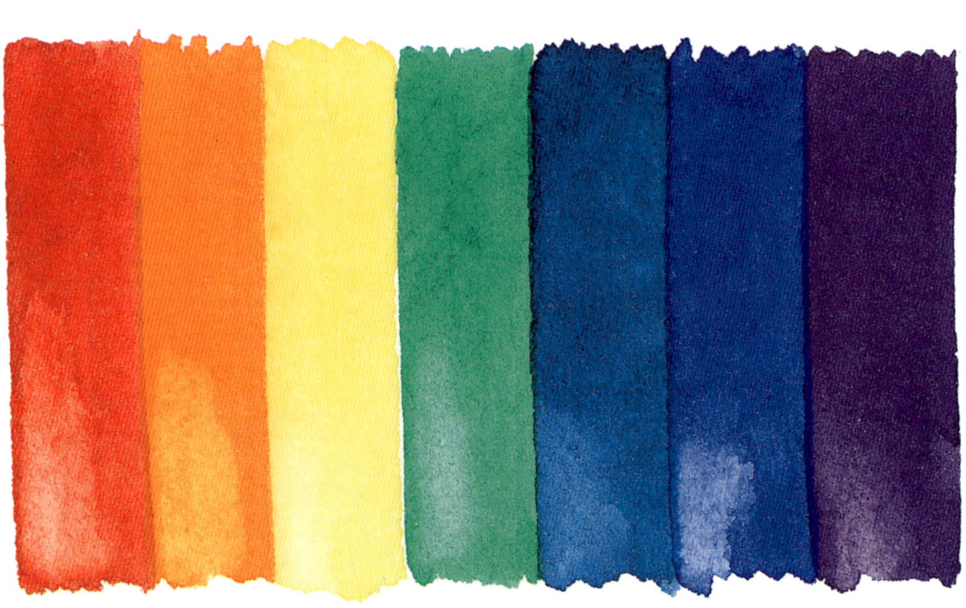

Diagram 8.1 The colors of the rainbow, or visible spectrum: red, orange, yellow, green, blue, indigo, violet.

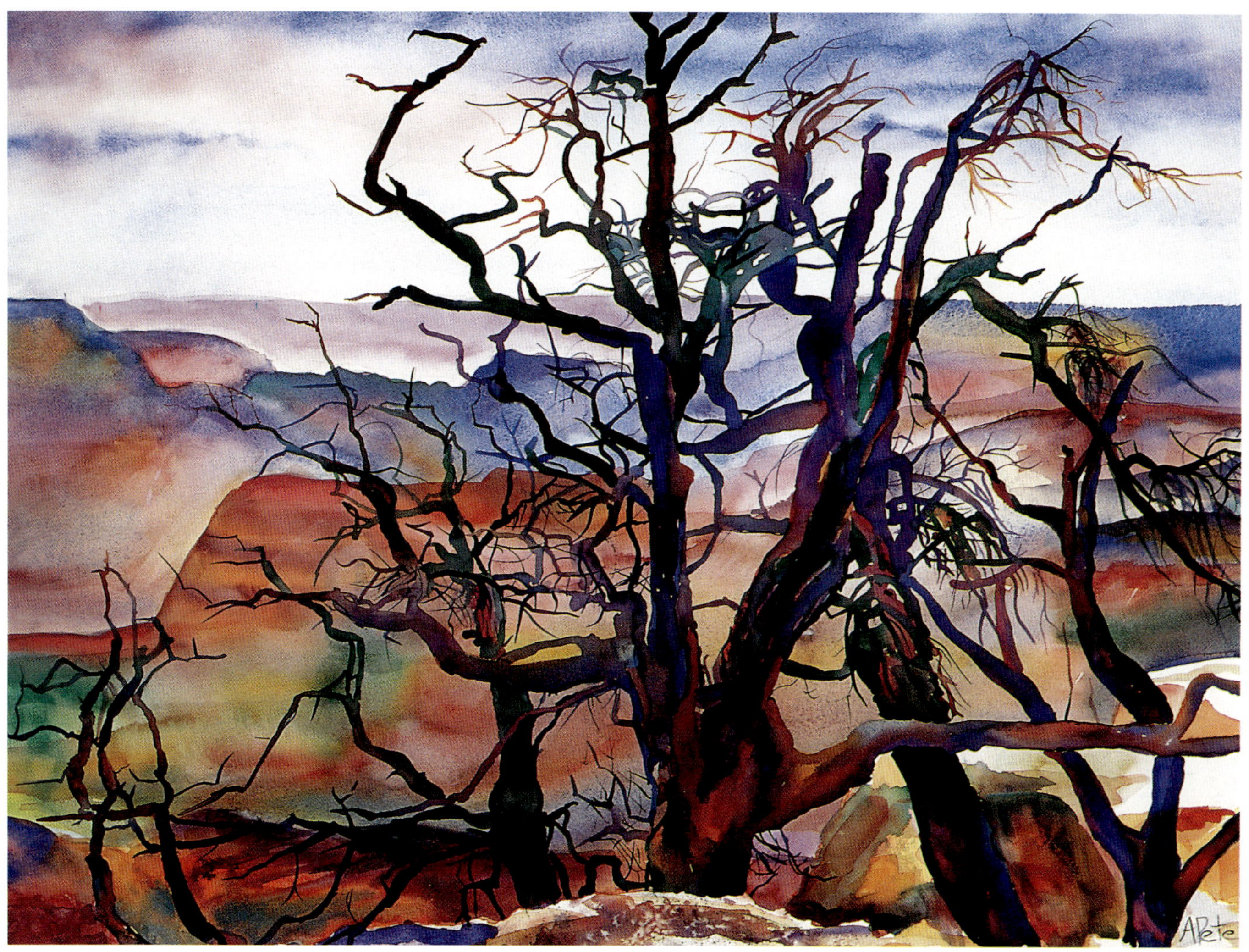

Growth by Ashley Peter, *22" x 30" (56cm x 76cm)*

The eye-catching dazzle of the painting arises from the way the colors are placed next to their neighbors on the color wheel and ordered similar to the sequence of the rainbow.

The Spectral Sequence

Spectrums are found not only in the rainbow but on signs and products everywhere because their color quality is unlike any other color combination. The seven colors are fully saturated and are arranged in the sequence they occur in naturally in the rainbow. The uncommon brilliance of the color wheel occurs because the arrangement of its colors is similar to the visible spectrum (diagram 8.2).

This natural brightness can be used in watercolors very successfully by using a technique of modeling with spectral colors. This is a special form of gradation where the gradation from one color to the next strictly follows the sequence of colors of the spectrum or the color wheel. The first step is to identify the color of the object. If it is red, the color placed next to the red is a red-orange, followed by an orange, followed by a yellow-orange, and so on. Of course, the modeling can also head in the other direction through red-violet to violet. The direction chosen depends on the situation to be represented.

Diagram 8.2 The twelve hues of the color wheel arranged in a rainbow sequence.

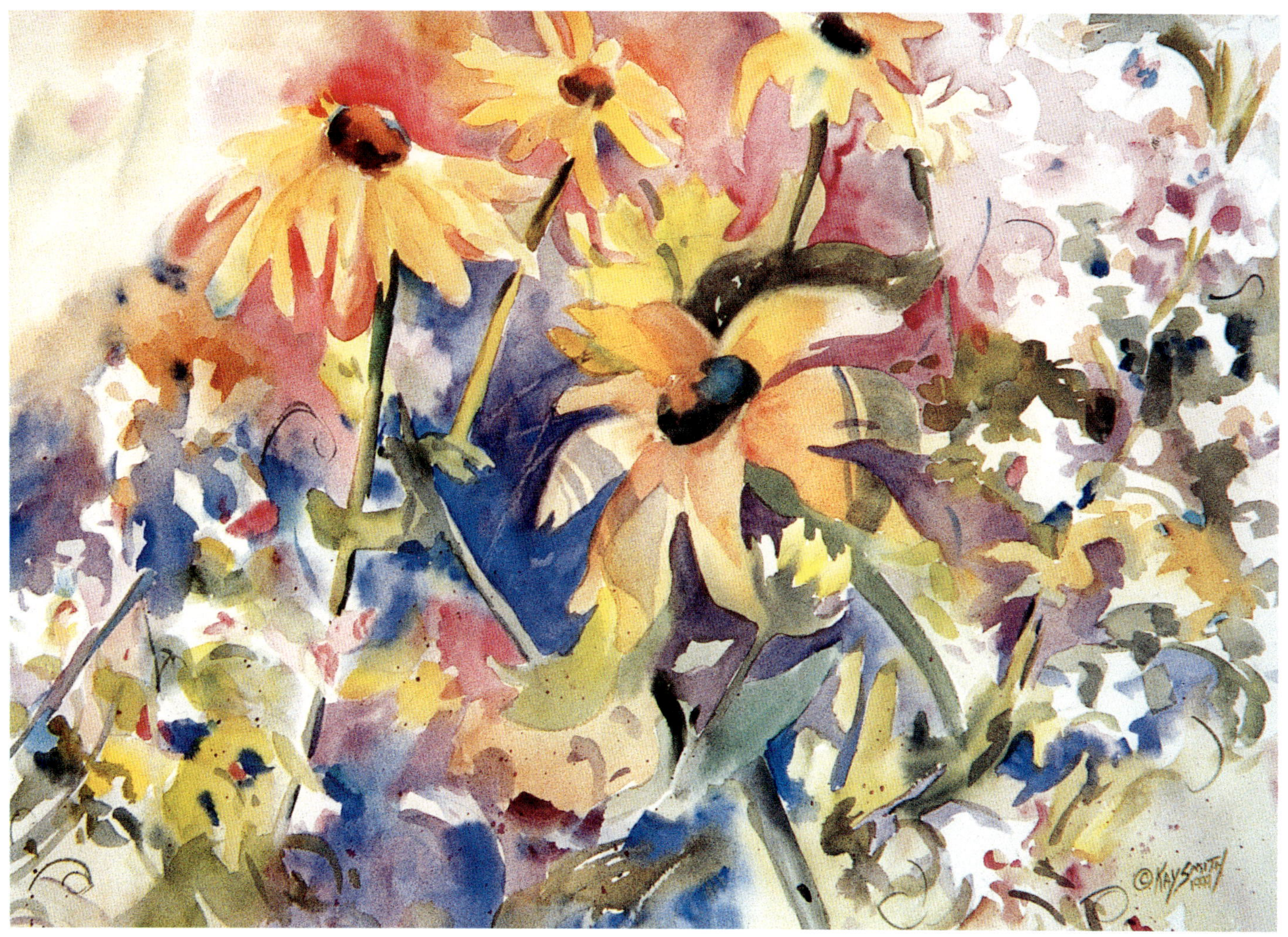

Blackeyed Susans by Kay Smith, *16" x 20" (41cm x 51cm)*
The background is a free spectral ordering of colors from red-violet to violet to blue. The flowers, meanwhile, shift through a spectral sequence roughly opposite on the color wheel, from yellow-green to yellow to yellow-orange.

Colors of the color wheel are different values, so modeling means paying careful attention to these value differences. For example, yellow is a naturally lighter value; violet is a darker value; and red and green are more medium values. In modeling a light area, the dark violet would have to be lightened in order to avoid the high-value contrast from ruining the light's effect.

If a shadow is to be depicted, it will be necessary to use darker colors. If the fully saturated colors are used, the darkest colors are violet or blue-violet and the object will need to move from its color to these shadow colors very quickly (diagrams 8.3-8.4). This means if the color of the object is orange, the touches of red-orange and red and red-violet will be small. As the colors progress to the violet and blue-violet, the area of each color will grow larger. Or, if the situation calls for a more flushed shadow, the same original orange could move through the colors giving more room to the red, red-violet, and violet.

Movement from a bright light to shadow might start with yellow moving through yellow-orange to orange and so on (diagram 8.5). The movement would also occur just as nicely by starting with yellow and moving through yellow-green to green.

A painting can be constructed with numerous places where these passages of spectral colors move across the boundaries between areas to link them together. It is important when modeling in this way to use the technique in a number of places throughout the painting. A painting

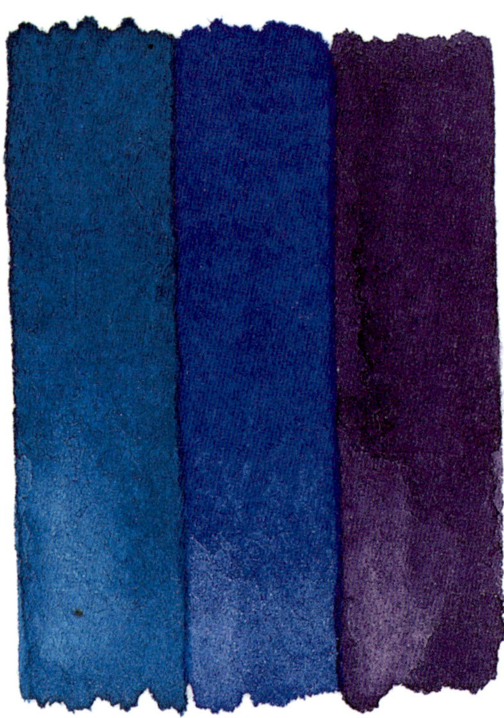

Diagram 8.3 Cool shadows can be created by modeling from blue to violet.

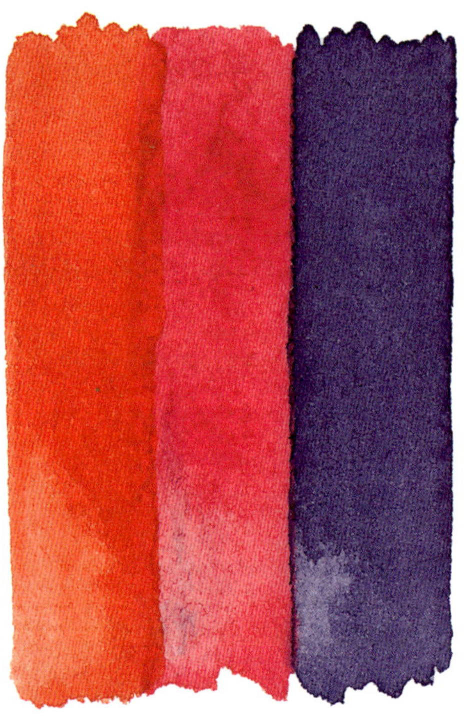

Diagram 8.4 Warm shadows can be created by modeling from red to violet.

showing only one area of spectral modeling is much like a rainbow sign near a country landscape. Its careful arrangement of highly saturated colors outshines the other, more grey colors, and therefore doesn't harmonize with the surrounding countryside. A few passages throughout the painting will solve this problem, as each passage creates a direction and movement the eye enjoys following. Consistency of technique is a hallmark of innovative techniques that work.

For the daring, whole paintings can be constructed in this way. Each object can be modeled out of spectral colors. Of course, not all the colors need to be the same size. A red apple, for example, can have a fair amount more red than it does the spectral colors the red moves to. The contrast of sizes of color pieces helps to create interest (diagram 8.6).

Diagram 8.5 Modeling starting with yellow and moving through the hues in order until violet is reached.

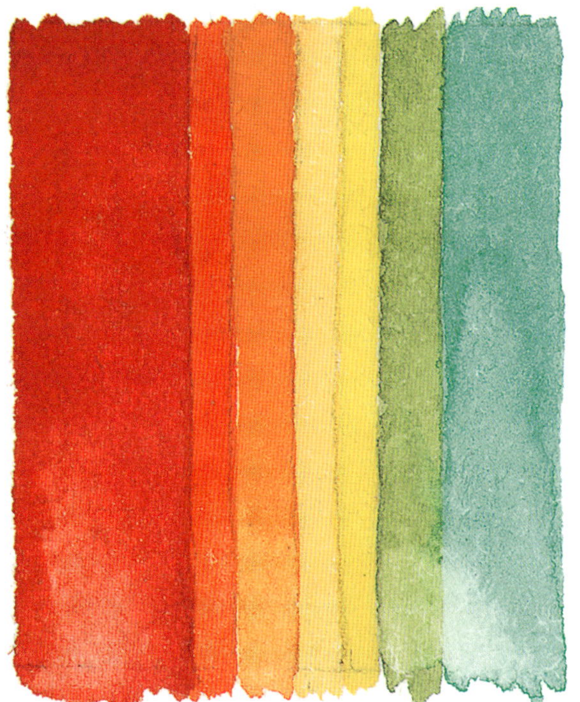

Diagram 8.6 The spectral modeling from red to green with unequal sizes of colors.

RECIPE FOR SUCCESS

Paint spectral sequences of colors in areas that move from light to shadow instead of applying a single flat shadow.

Spectral Modeling

Examining an apple more closely can demonstrate another fascinating effect found with modeling. The great painter Caravaggio (1583–1610) demonstrated how fast transitions from light to dark could give a painting dramatic power, and the impressionists showed painters how the shadows of objects would most often contain colors complementary to the object. Merging these two discoveries means shadows will most often include colors opposite to the lit areas. For example, the spectral modeling of a red apple will include its green shadow. But the rules of spectral modeling mean the red cannot be placed right next to the green. It has to get there by a walk, or in this case a run, through the colors that separate the red from the green, either through the oranges and yellows or through the violets and blues.

This rainbow-like set of colors may also be adjusted for value and saturation. How many artists have tried a rainbow made of very light colors or, even odder, a rainbow made of very dark spectral colors? Such sequences produce unexpected results. The yellows become very greenish when black is added, while the violets and blues retain their color until a fairly dark point. A greyed rainbow would be an oddity in the real world, but the colors found in such a sequence are perfect colors for spectral gradations that possess natural luminosity.

Lastly, the same progressions of pure colors can be broken up so the spectral colors group together rather than strictly follow one another. These can hover around a center much like moons hover around a planet, or they can be grouped into a specific area. A method such as this retains the resplendent characteristic of the spectrum and satisfies artists who do not wish to adhere to the more rigid sequential gradation.

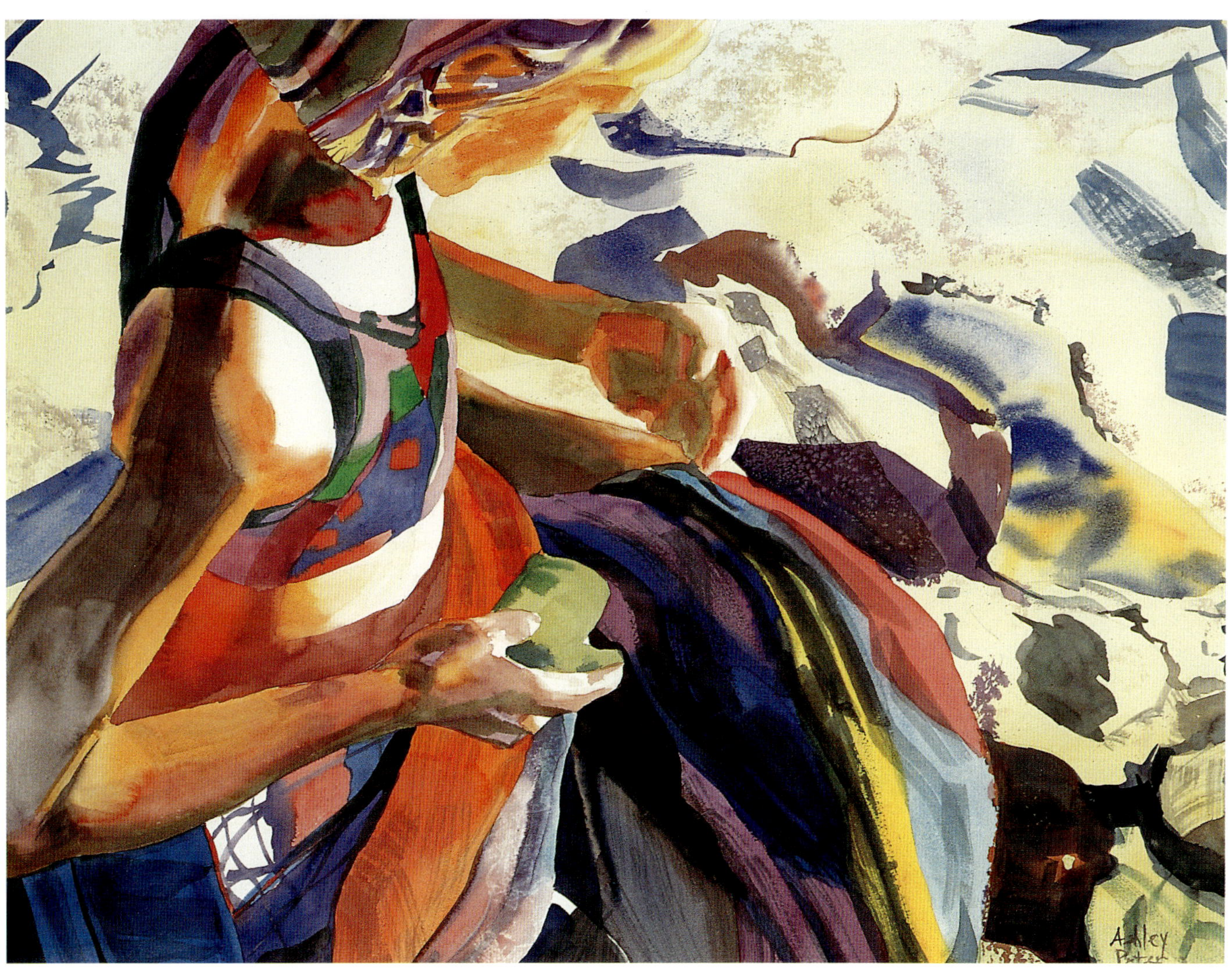

Light of Day by Ashley Peter, *22" x 30" (56cm x 76cm)*
The bright quality of the spectrum is retained by short spectral gradations and more free-form groupings of the spectral colors in small areas.

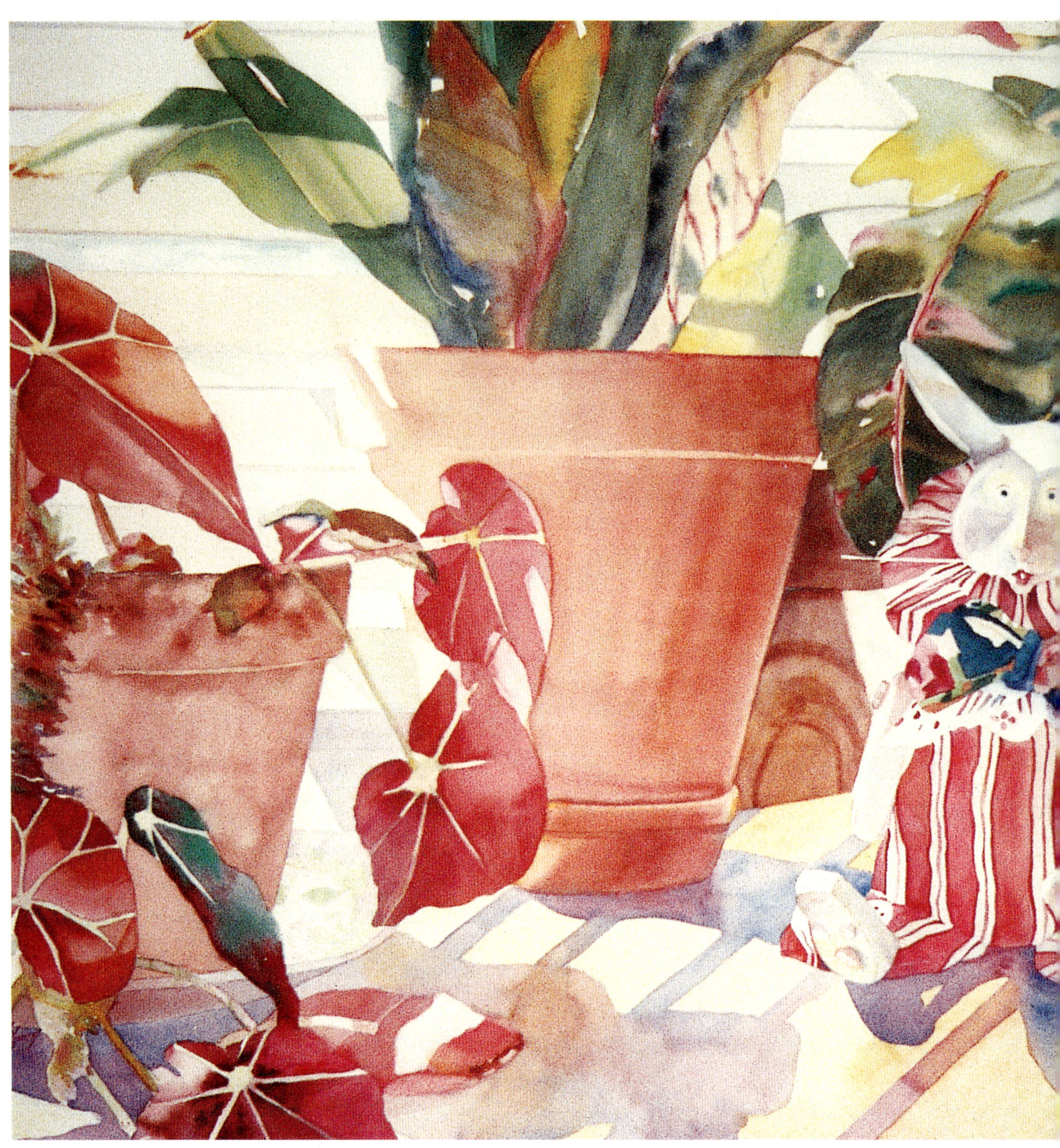

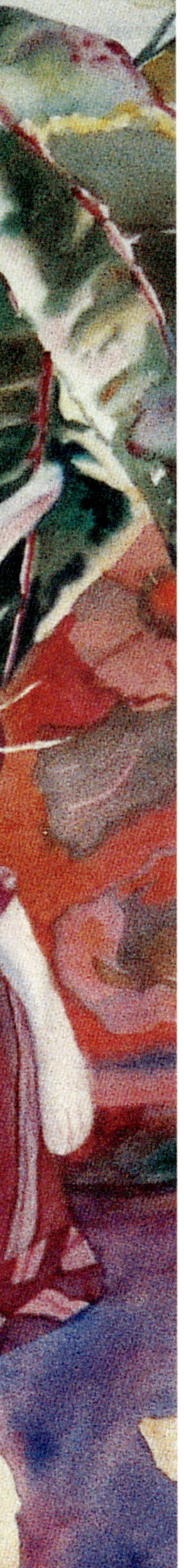

9

Less Is More: Working with a Two-Color Palette

A complex problem is often better grasped if it is broken into smaller, easily digestible chunks. These small parts can be figured out separately until finally the whole is understood. This means that not all of the color fundamentals I have discussed in this book can be used in one painting. After trying out the ideas, one artist may go wild over tetrads while another may find that careful constructions with complementary colors is their favorite. I recommend experimenting with the many ways of using color I have presented, but sometimes it is also good to pull back and focus on one or two ideas for a while.

The Appeal of Two Colors

Color is a complex issue for artists because they not only wish to use it well, they also desire to discover certain colors or ways of applying these colors in a manner that holds personal meaning. It is also not uncommon for artists to have preferences for certain colors. There have been times when I preferred using blue or red, times when I knew I had to paint with black, times when I have loathed yellow and times when I just had to use yellow. It is important to trust these feelings and to go with them. By doing so, the paintings become full of meaning and the process of exploring one color offers the possibility of discovering new solutions.

The best way to get to know the colors one has a preference for is to create two-color paintings. One-color paintings, called monochrome paintings, although interesting, do not offer enough substance for learning about color combinations. Colors are most effective when used in combinations—by putting them

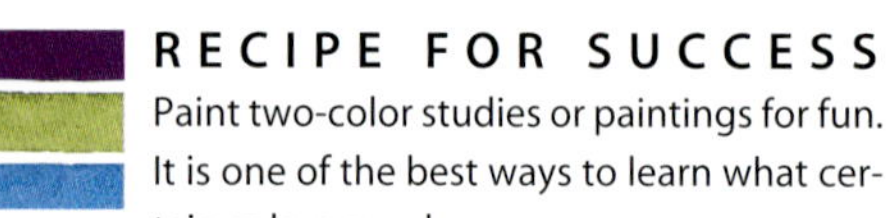

RECIPE FOR SUCCESS

Paint two-color studies or paintings for fun. It is one of the best ways to learn what certain colors can do.

Diagram 9.1 Blue-violet and yellow-orange, similar to the two hues Sargent used in at least one Venice painting, and their mixtures provide support for the pure hues in the painting.

together in two-color paintings, the special qualities of each are easily uncovered.

Furthermore, two-color combinations are appealing. Holidays, the special events in people's lives, are often characterized by two colors—the Christmas season is known by red and green, Halloween by orange and black. The people who have to choose between different red blouses or ties or dresses for the office party probably learn more about red because of that holiday than they might on a typical day.

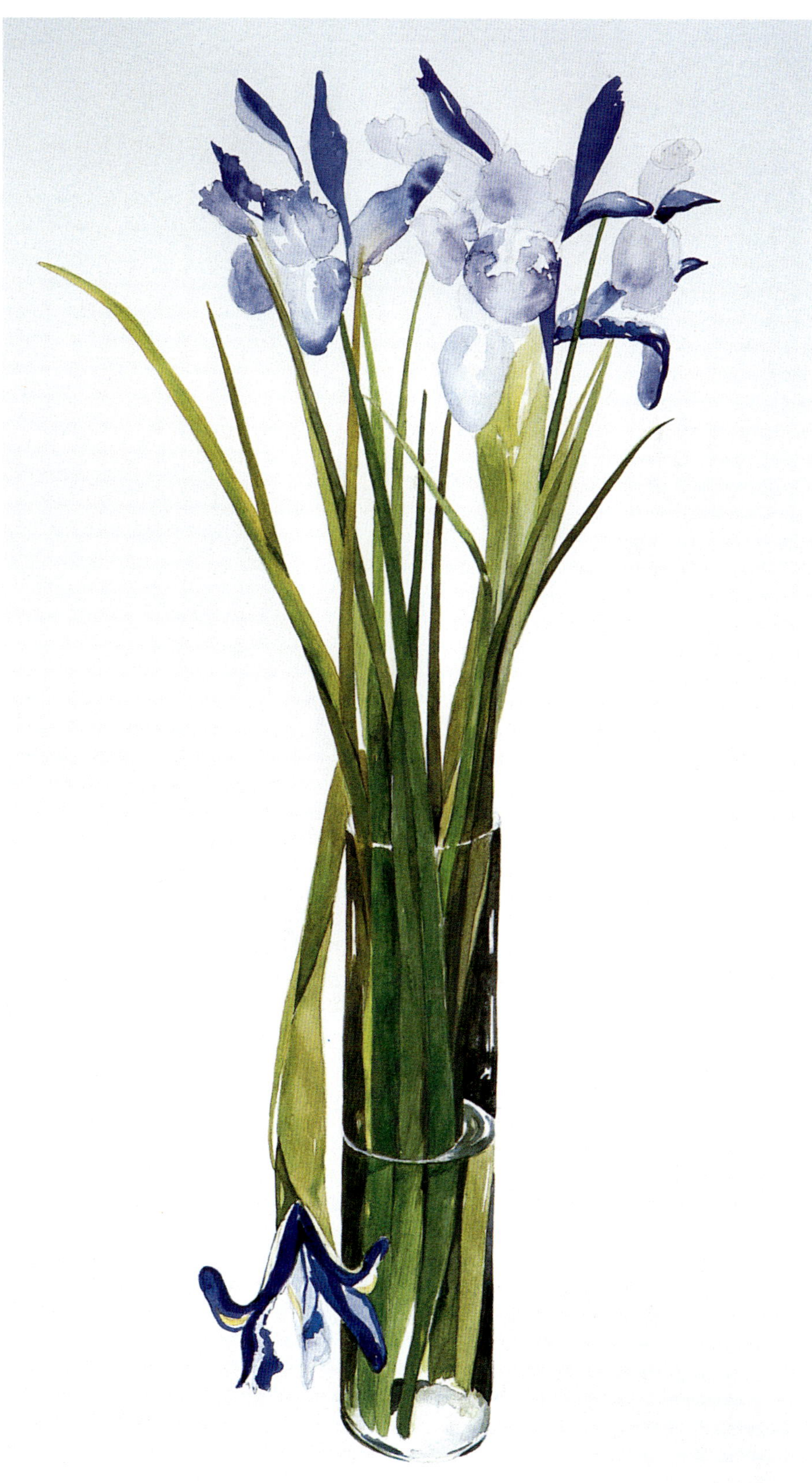

Iris Defeated **by Nancy Carey**
22" x 15" (56cm x 38cm)
A two-color painting can be full of excitement, as this one done in yellow-green and blue-violet demonstrates.

Two-Color Constructions

Watercolors that are made of two colors become very powerful. They catch the eye because of their bold simplicity and special daring. John Singer Sargent, who painted roughly seven hundred watercolors between 1900 and 1914, was an expert at using a two-color foundation. One view of a white building on the Grand Canal in Venice (*on the Grand Canal*, c. 1907) is painted on white paper using primarily the two colors of blue-violet and yellow-orange in their many values (diagram 9.1). It is stunning for its freshness, and the captured light makes complete sense because shadows in yellowish light often appear blue-ish.

Two-color paintings can begin with complementary colors such as red and green. Such a limited palette calls for immediate decision making. Since using colors in absolutely equal amounts throughout a whole painting can make it monotonous, the first step is to choose one color that can dominate. A painting made mostly of red can be successfully contrasted by a few well-placed greens.

The next step is to decide what range of reds to work in. Should the painting be built of dark reds, medium reds, light reds, or a whole value range of reds? How many of the reds should be desaturated or saturated? And once the

Diagram 9.2 Two examples of the mixtures and contrasts of red and green.

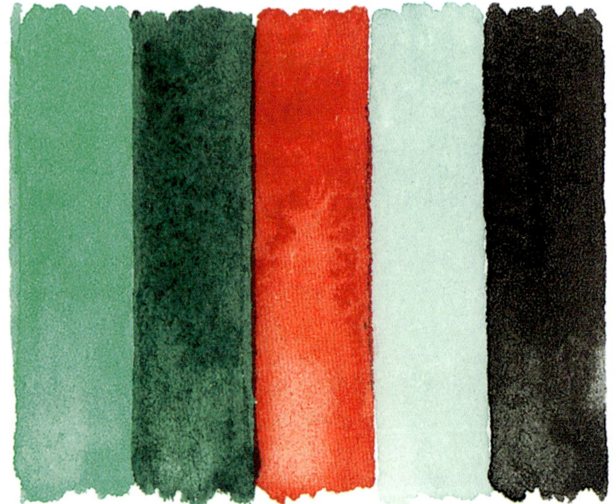

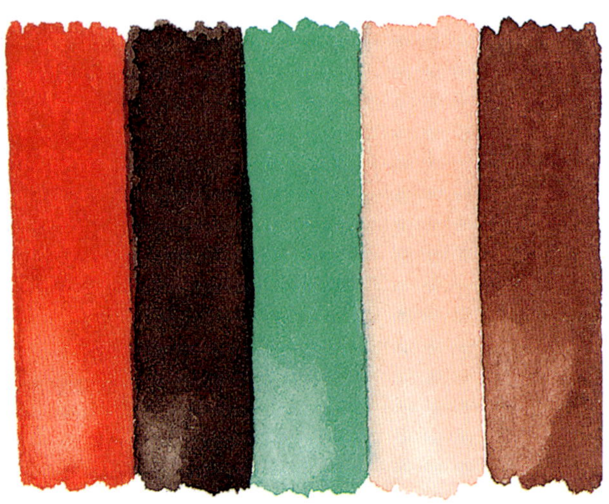

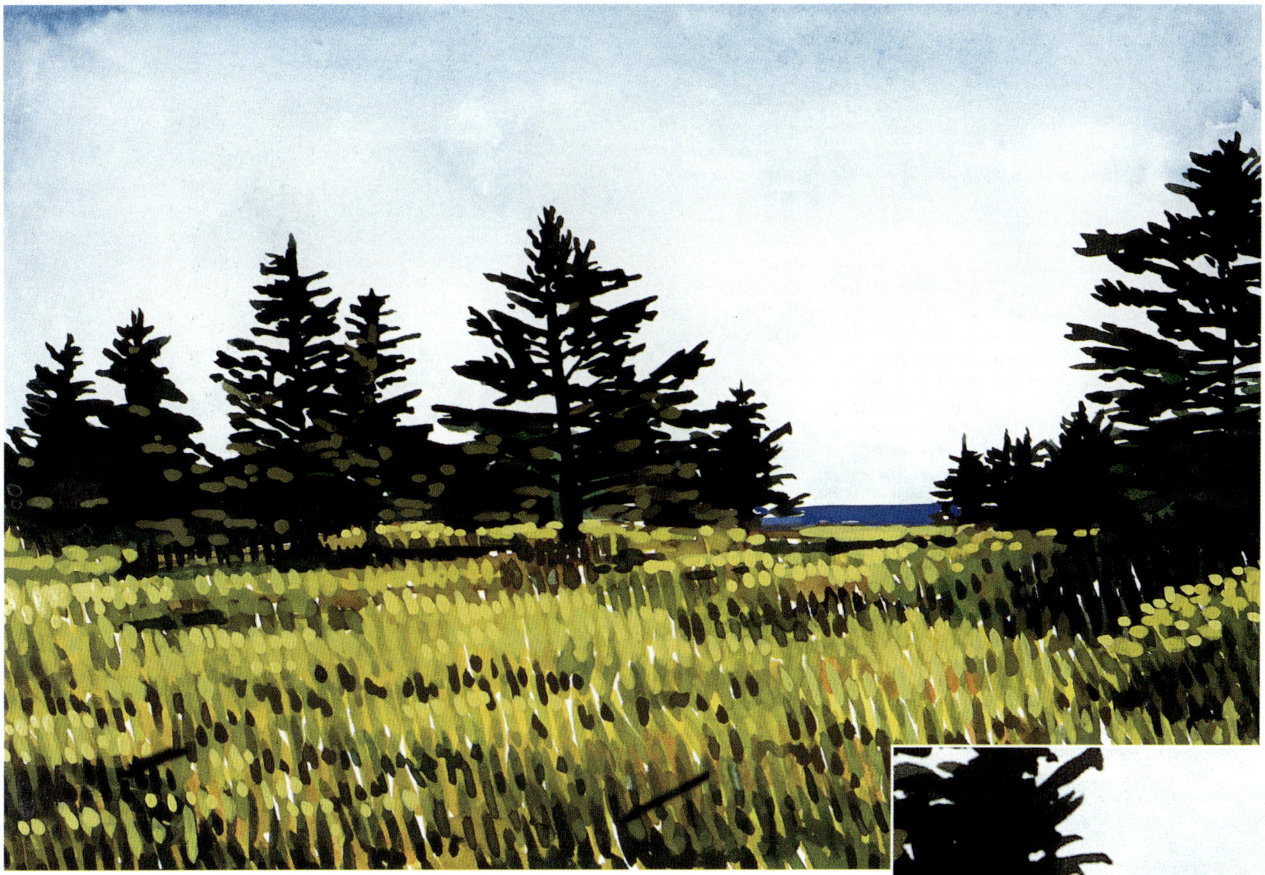

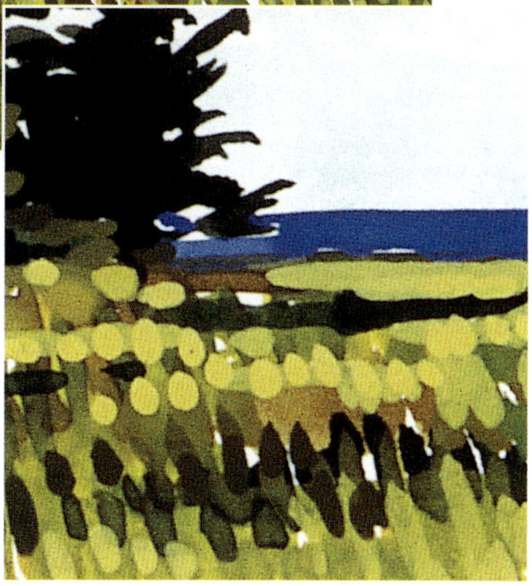

Study for *Just a Glimpse* by James Linehan *6" x 10" (15cm x 25cm)*
Blue and yellow make up the basis of this landscape. The two colors are applied as both pure colors and as a variety of mixtures that are desaturated and altered in value.

(Detail) A strong color contrast of blue and yellow combined with a strong value contrast of the light sky and the dark trees all comes together to create a point of interest.

green is introduced, should the green be altered in value and saturation as well? A painting created from very light versions of red and green will have a completely different character than one created from dark reds and dark greens. A whole different color impact can be made by using the same complements, but mixing the two colors together a great deal so the pure red and green are found only as small touches against a larger colored grey field.

RECIPE FOR SUCCESS

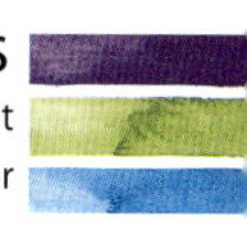

Vary the techniques of applying the paint for even greater contrasts with a two-color palette.

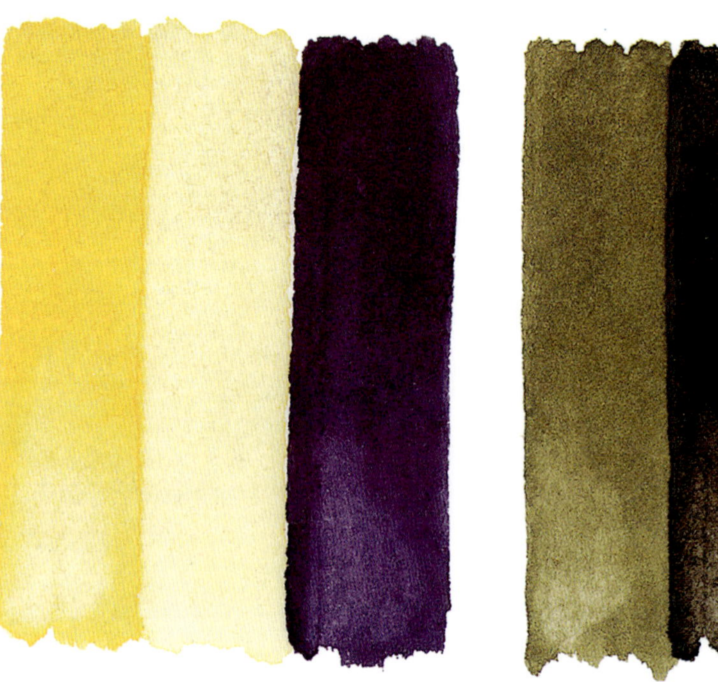

Diagram 9.3 Yellow and violet in their natural values compared to the same colors with reversed values. Black has been added to darken the yellows.

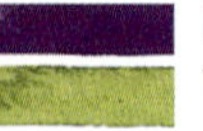

RECIPE FOR SUCCESS

The main color contrasts are:

Contrast of Hue

Contrast of Value

Contrast of Saturation

Contrast of Extension

Yellow and violet are great for two-color paintings because they naturally have a very wide value difference, the violet being dark and the yellow light. These complements in juxtaposition are good for capturing high contrast lighting conditions. If the values are reversed, the yellow slightly darkened and the violet lightened, the result is often very bright and unexpected (diagram 9.3).

Other colors can be used for two-color paintings. The trick is to make them strong by using many different variations of each color or the color mixture. There are a whole host of ways to apply the two colors: combining dots of colors, large washes of rich color, a wash layer over the dried first color, bleeding the colors into each other using a wet-on-wet technique, a dry brush technique, or scumbling one color over another.

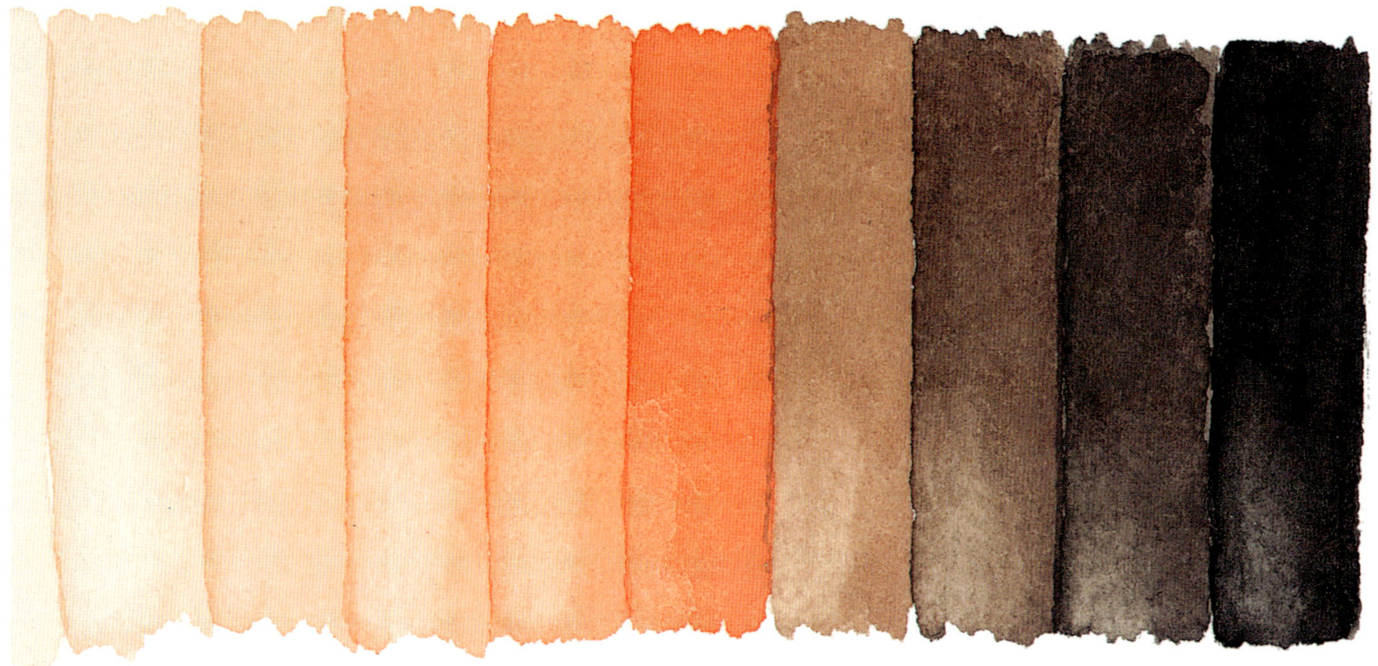

Diagram 9.4 A value scale of orange with ten steps shows a beautiful transition from light to dark.

The two-color paintings can be final products in themselves or function as ways to learn specific things about color usage and application that can later be used on more colorful paint-ings. Combine a few other small pieces of color with the strong foundation of two bold colors, and the painting steals the show.

A more subdued approach is found by meticulously altering the two colors with white and black. The goal in this instance is to make not one or two different values of each color but to try to make ten or even twenty different values of each (diagram 9.4). This exercise in itself is good for learning how to subtly modify a color. The beauty of such extensive mixing is found in two-color paintings that look as though they were painted with more than two colors.

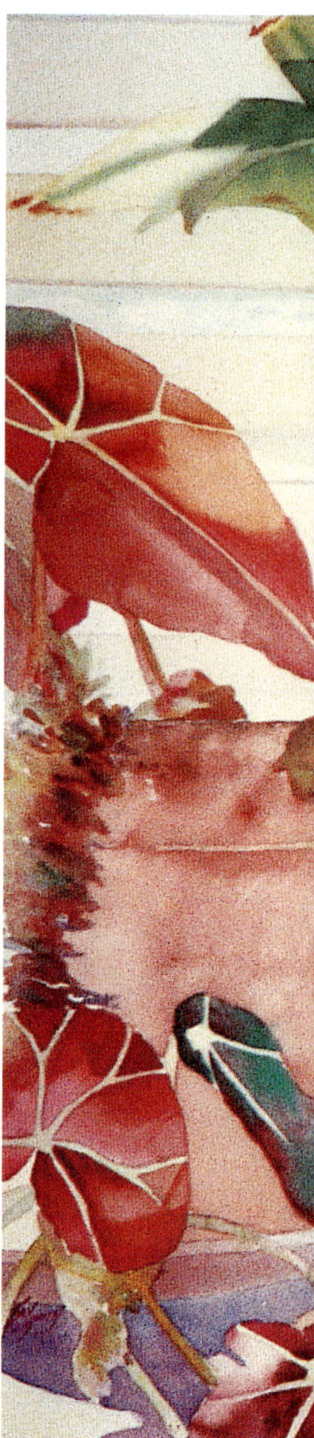

Analogous colors, or those next to each other on the color wheel, also become interesting in a two-color painting. A watercolor created with only yellow and orange does not give too much leeway for contrasts, since they innately wish to assimilate. Adjusting the values—painting some areas as washes and others as rich pieces of paint—or allowing some of the brilliant white of the paper to shine through are both aids to success with analogous colors (diagram 9.5).

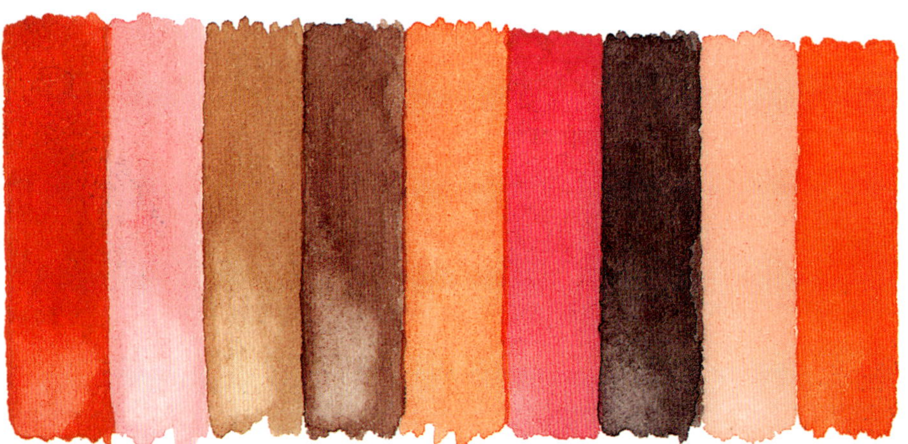

Diagram 9.5 The analogous colors here—red-orange, red, and red-violet—are positioned together with a variety of values.

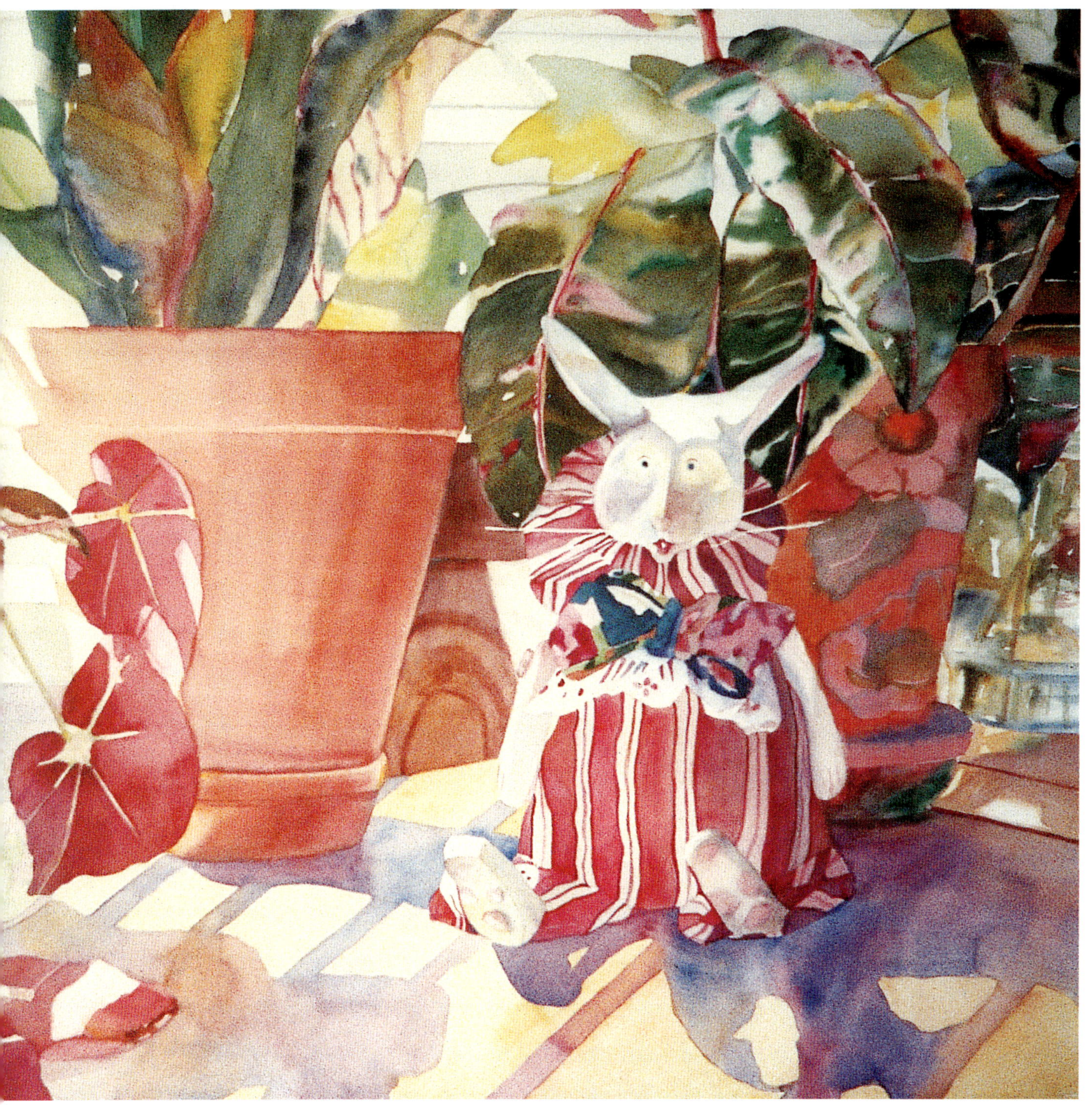

The White Rabbit by Kay Smith, *22" x 30" (56cm x 76cm)*
While not a strict two-color painting, two sets of analogous colors are hard at work here. The pots, shadows and rabbit are in red, red-orange, and red-violet, while the leaves are done with yellows, greens, and blues.

Painting with two colors breaks both expectations and preconceived notions about what colors are used for and what they can do. And it is critical to break such notions in order to become an excellent colorist. Many of these notions are founded in language. For example, the mind says a sky is blue; an apple, red; a tree, green; but with careful observation the eyes will see that there are many more colors in each of these items.

Two-color experiments with unusual, weird, eccentric, and outlandish color combinations are fun and easy to do. Very frequently, the strangest combinations produce the best results. The most interesting of these combinations can then developed into larger, more substantial paintings.

The knowledge learned by creating two-color paintings is also useful in other contexts. For example, if the artist is out painting water and sky, the two color studies done with blues will help the artist to know what blue might work best in the observed landscape as well as what color might be placed alongside the blue for a vibrant interaction.

RECIPE FOR SUCCESS

Make two-color paintings with weird and eccentric color combinations in order to break stereotypes of harmonious color combinations.

Courthouse Column **by Ann DeLaurentis,**
8" x 14" (20cm x 36cm)
The colors are simple—blue-green and red-orange—but their many variations cause the painting to look complex and harmonious.

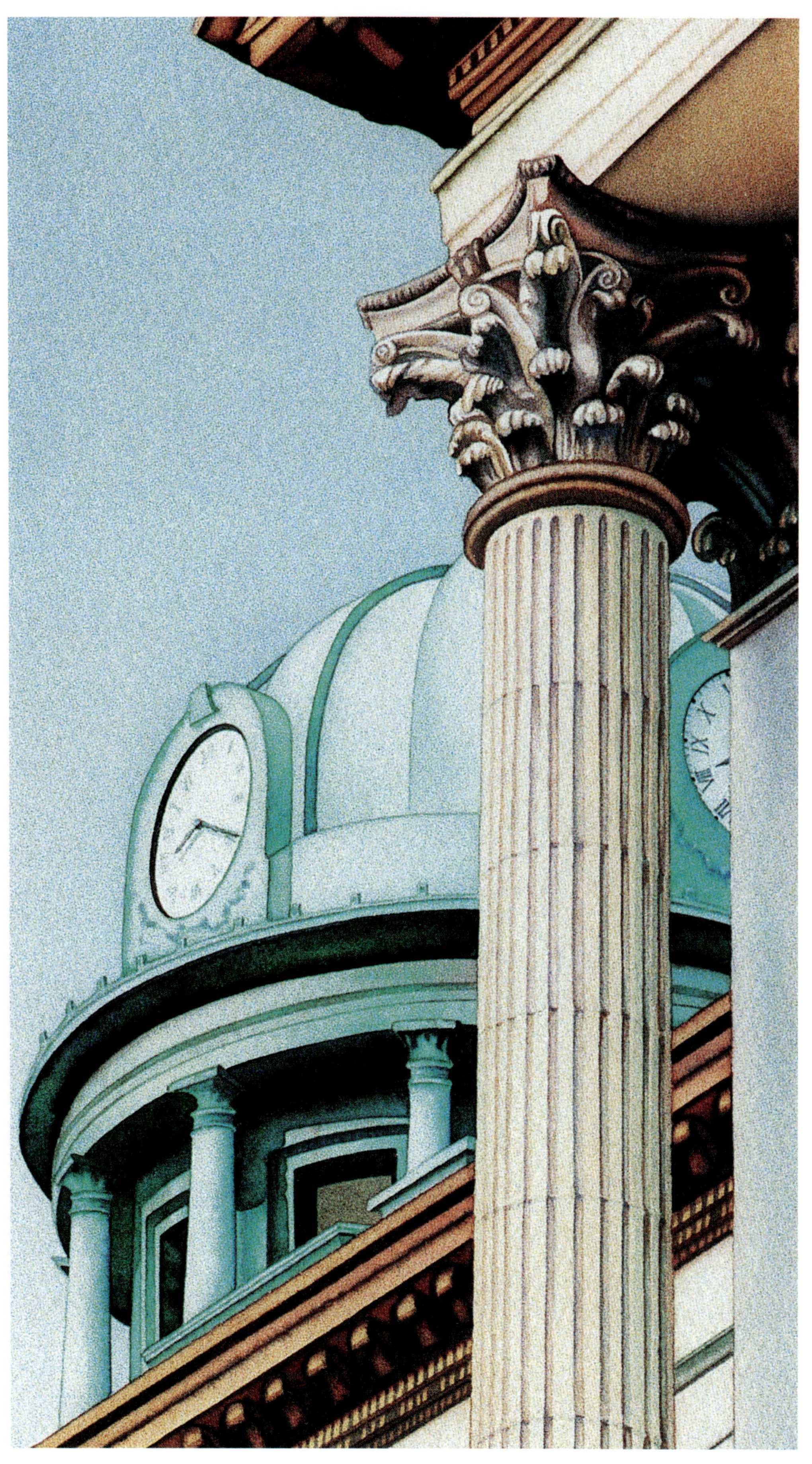

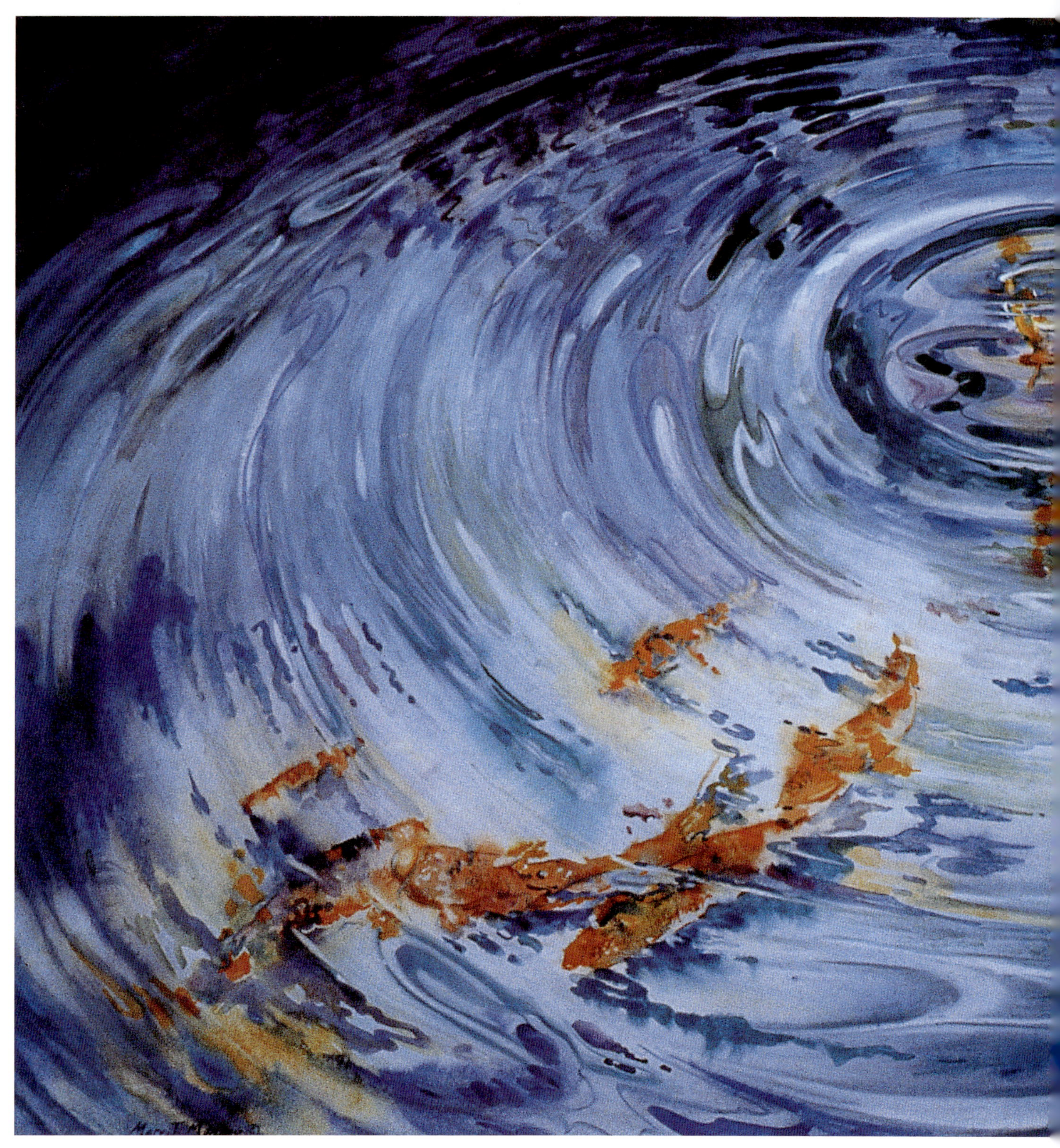

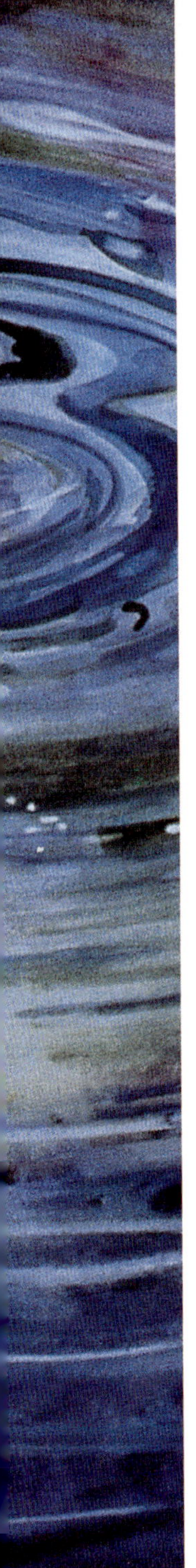

10

The Wow Effect: Using
Unexpected Colors

One of the secrets to making great paintings is always to be surprised by what you see. If artists get too comfortable with colors, if they always use the same tricks in each painting, then their color usage eventually becomes rote and looks preprogrammed.

One strategy that works to keep painters on their toes is to use unexpected colors. These are often found by looking long and hard at things in the real world. In such looking, it is critical not to prejudge the colors but to just let the eyes dictate what colors are where. A sky is thought to be blue, but at sunset the blue turns to pinks and oranges, and before storms it can appear as blue-green as any swimming pool. Clouds are known to be white—unless they sit full of water and appear as grey masses much darker than the blue of the sky. During autumn, clouds can appear strikingly iridescent, as though they were painted with the exact technique of spectral modeling.

Seeing the Unexpected

One of Winslow Homer's watercolors represents a hurricane in the Bahamas (*Hurricane, Bahamas* 1898), with the wonderful invention of a heavy, dark grey-blue across the whole top of the painting. In 1905, a group of painters including Henri Matisse were called wild beasts because instead of copying light they expressed it by using unexpected colors. It is always striking to be drawn into a painting unexpected colors or marks, only to find out they work really well.

The great thing about unexpected colors is that by themselves they may look completely out of place, but in a specific context they make complete sense. A painting that uses unexpected colors demands attention.

The impressionists were at first laughed at when they painted many different spots of color on their canvases. However, it was through very careful observation of nature that they were able to see these spots. They didn't make them up, but tried instead to represent exactly what they saw. And they probably saw nature better than their more classical contemporaries. When painting, they would try to use colors that mimicked nature as intensely as possible. The watercolors of Van Gogh are masterpieces that captured the Provence light with its loud blues, yellows, and greens all mingled together to form lyrical cypress trees. Against this palette he would often throw in touches of red-violet, a color opposite on the wheel to the three tree colors, as an unexpected contrast that is often attributed to his taste for the exotic. Exotic or not, my bet is he saw these colors in nature.

RECIPE FOR SUCCESS

Some of the oddest combinations of colors are found by looking very carefully at nature. Spend a long time looking before painting.

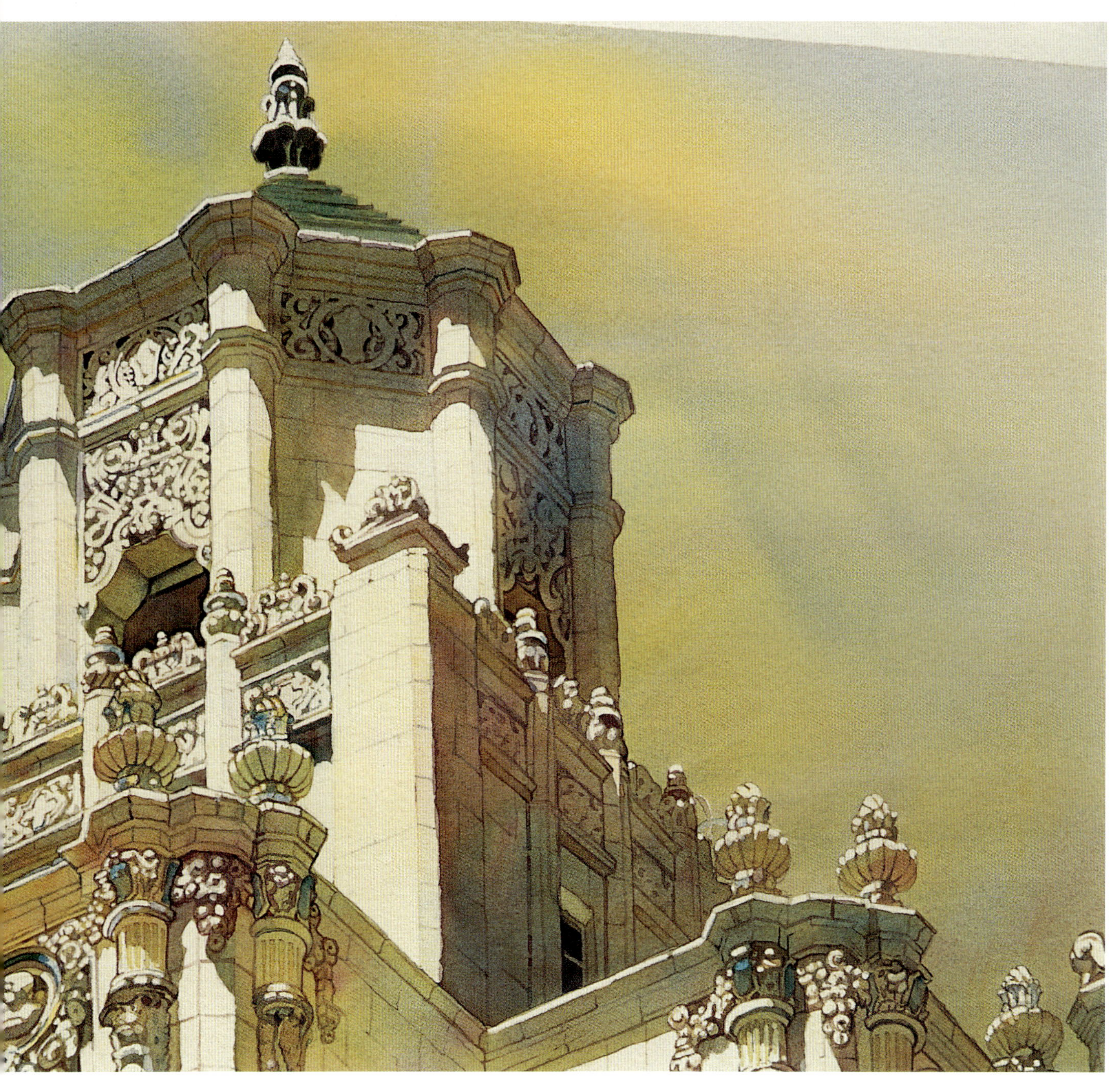

Snell Arcade by Jean Grastorf,
20" x 28" (51cm x 71cm)
A yellow sky! Such an unexpected color choice provides a jolt of excitement, yet it makes complete sense given the combination of yellow toned colors used for the painting.

The general rule for using unexpected colors is to make sure they fit within a whole coordinated key of color. Choosing triads or tetrads as a base for the watercolor is one way to accomplish this. Then use contrasts of extension or saturation to add a great deal of excitement to the combination. The contrast looks unexpected, but the nature of the color chord allows the painting to look harmonious.

Great results using unexpected colors often come from questions beginning with the question, "What if ... ?". What if the sky were painted yellow instead of blue? What if the interior wall were blue-green instead of grey? What if the shadow were painted a dark red combined with spots of green instead of a single blue-violet? What if one side of the face were painted green and the

RECIPE FOR SUCCESS

Use paintings to answer color questions beginning with "What if ... ?".

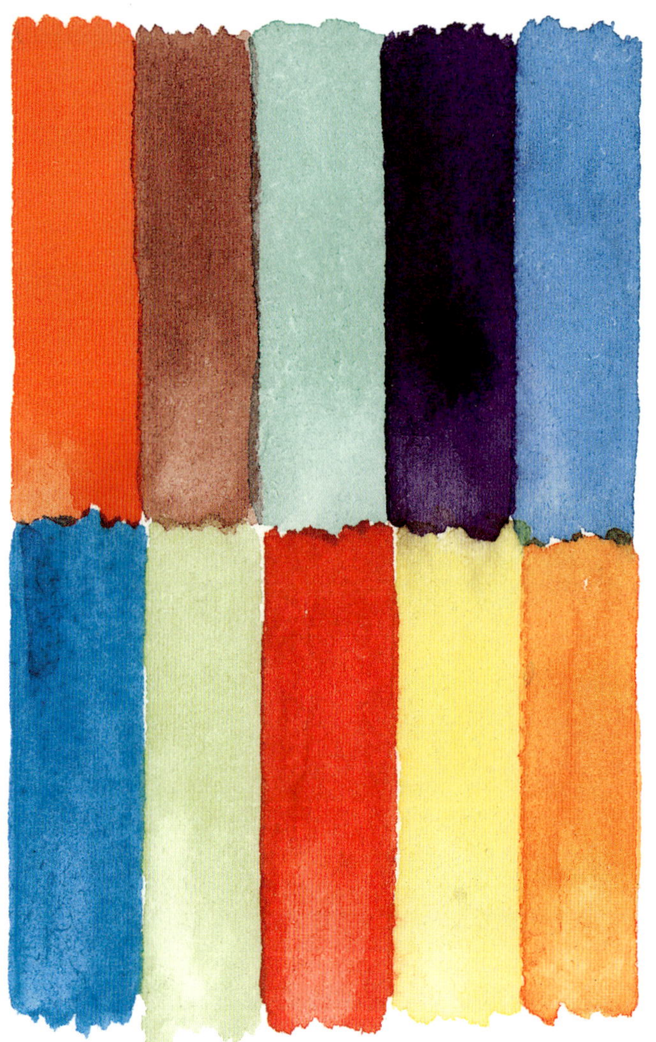

Diagram 10.1 The colors of the top row are what is normally seen, but the opposite colors on the color wheel, as shown on the bottom row, are painted as a way of using unexpected colors.

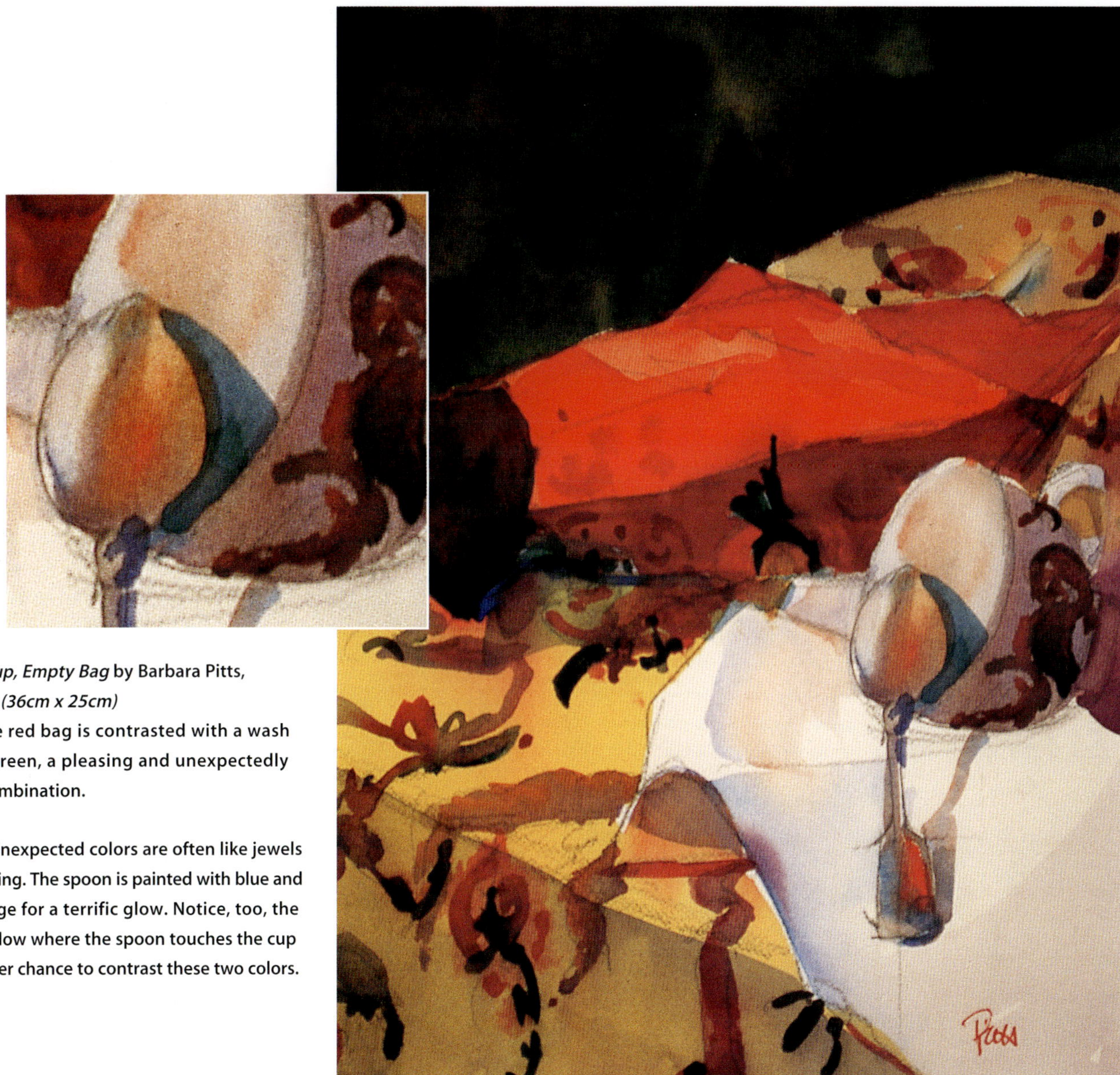

Empty Cup, Empty Bag by Barbara Pitts, *14" x 10" (36cm x 25cm)*
The large red bag is contrasted with a wash of dark green, a pleasing and unexpectedly bright combination.

(Detail) Unexpected colors are often like jewels in a painting. The spoon is painted with blue and red-orange for a terrific glow. Notice, too, the blue shadow where the spoon touches the cup for another chance to contrast these two colors.

other yellow? The answers to such questions have yet to be seen. The mind is terrible at visualizing what the results would look like, and this is why it is important to answer these questions by making watercolors rather than merely thinking about them.

Striking paintings with unexpected colors are also created by using the opposite color of every color seen in a motif (diagram 10.1). For example, where an orange is seen, paint that area blue; instead of the perceived violet, paint that area a yellow.

RECIPE FOR SUCCESS

Track colors to discover preferences and aversions. Good colorists use every color successfully.

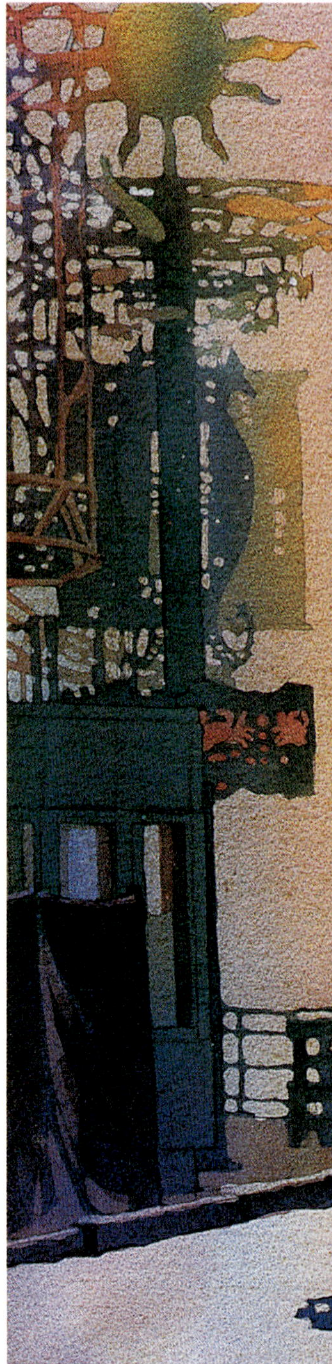

Another method is to bump the colors a certain number of steps around the color wheel. It is like shifting letters in a secret code. Thus, if one area is red, the color might be shifted two colors clockwise on the color wheel, so a violet would be painted in that area. Any other colors in the painting will also be shifted two steps clockwise.

Watercolor is a transparent medium, and part of its richness comes from seeing the paper or the edge of one color through another. Some surprising results can be obtained by applying colors and, when they are dry, overlapping them with new colors. Try using yellows under reds, or red-oranges under violets, or even yellows under violets, for interesting results. These mixtures can be tried first on pieces of scrap paper that are then kept around as guides to the different results.

In addition, I often recommend tracking the colors used in paintings over a few days, weeks, or months. Record on a separate sheet of paper a small swatch of each of the colors used in a painting—reds go on one sheet, violet on another, and so on. This way it is possible to objectively discover color preferences and to find out if a range of colors is being avoided. For example, if the green and blue sheets show many color swatches while the yellow sheets show only one or two, a good goal is to paint two or three watercolors in which yellow becomes the color that takes up most of the painting. Good colorists cannot be afraid of any color.

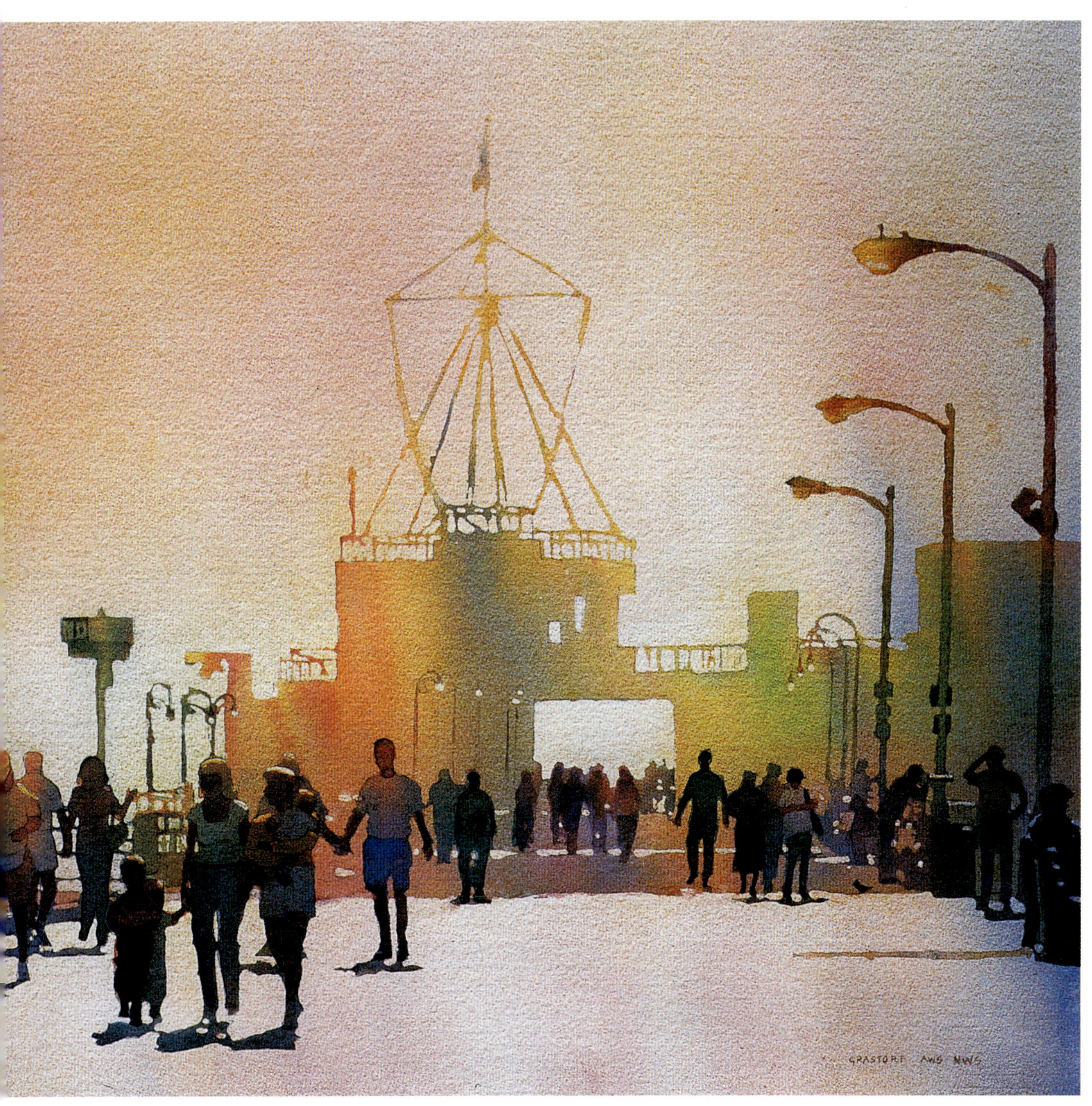

Santa Monica Pier by Jean Grastorf, *20" x 28" (51cm x 71cm)*
Unexpected colors work best when the fundamentals of choosing colors and color contrasts are kept in mind. Here, value contrasts and gradations are combined with unexpected colors for a striking impression.

Trying New Colors

Throughout the book I have presented and referred to twelve colors that form the basis for the ideas here. Yet I know artists may also have preferences for particular colors that are not a part of this color wheel. One artist may prefer a permanent magenta or a cobalt violet instead of the permanent rose I have chosen. The goal behind my choice of colors and ultimately any choice of colors is to make sure their combinations are decided upon with knowledge rather than happenstance.

After readers feel confident with the twelve colors that make up the exercises of this book, it can be fun to switch one color for another. Perhaps switch magenta for the rose used here. Or if one painting requires a large amount of some strange green that is difficult to mix, it is easy to buy a tube of that green and then substitute it temporarily for the closest green on the color wheel. Once the key techniques of combining colors are understood and used in day-to-day practice, the palette can even be expanded to include two of each of the twelve colors, realizing of course that the exact nature of the triads and tetrads will change.

Sienna, umber, and other desaturated colors could be added to the palette, sitting near their parent hues. A brown would be placed near the orange so it is always remembered that this brown is a desaturated orange and should be used as such. This way browns do not slide back to the area of colorless filler that goes on the sides of trees and old barns. This can be handy if a painting requires a tremendous amount of such colors. However, these same browns could be premixed using colors from the wheel for more colorful browns.

I also believe that a lifetime of painting can be accomplished, and accomplished well, with the twelve colors and the fundamentals in this book. Using color well is in itself very unexpected. Ultimately, it is not the number of colors the artist uses that makes a strong painting, but what he or she does with those colors.

I do not think artists can ever learn enough about using color. Trying out new ideas or setting up problems guarantees a continual focus on color. The fundamentals presented in this book allow one to go beyond simple color usage in an easy manner. At that point, experimentation and using unexpected

RECIPE FOR SUCCESS
Learning about color is a lifelong process. Always try out new color ideas and look for new problems to solve.

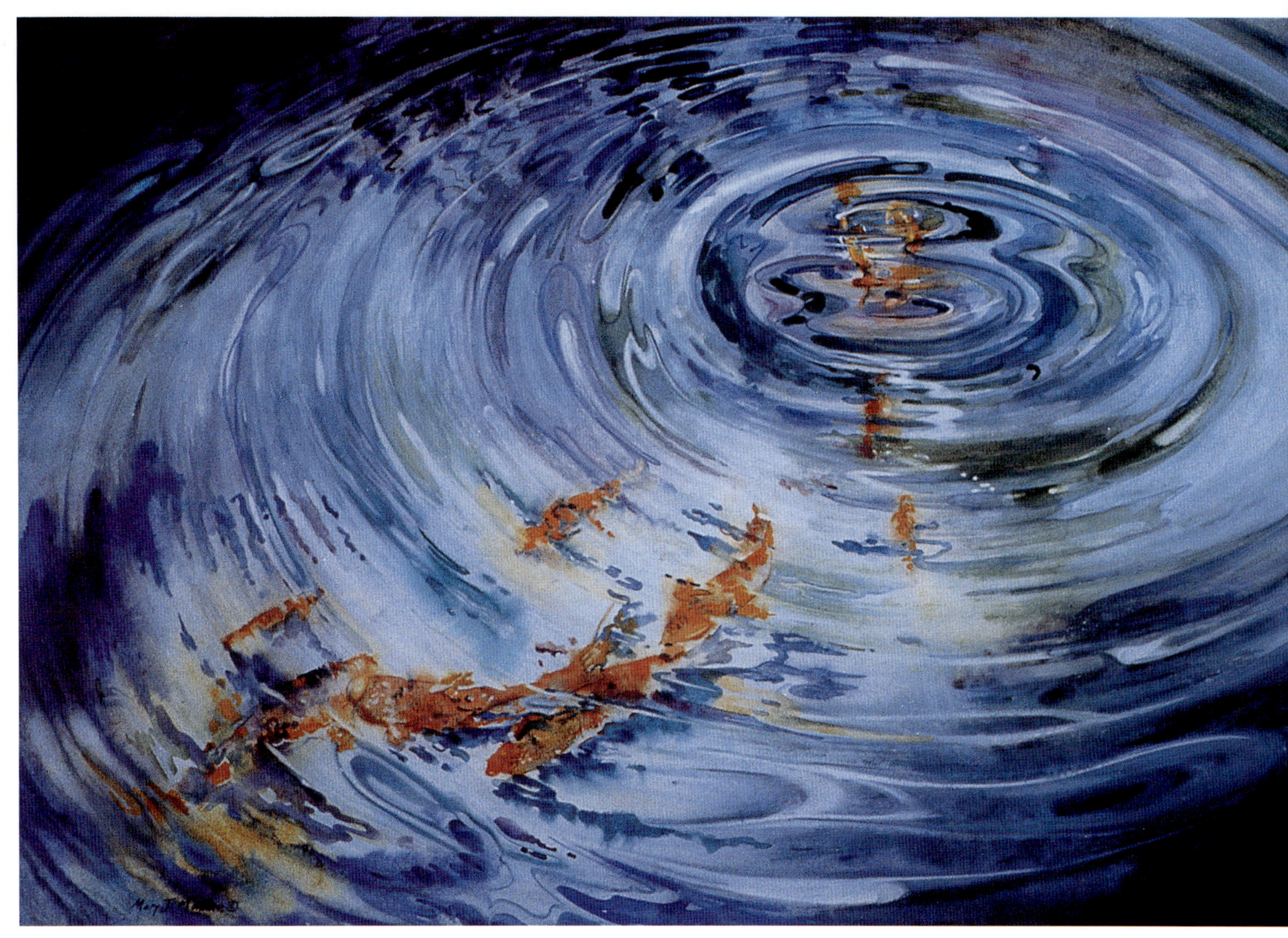

Ten Koi II by Mary Maxam, *22" x 30" (56cm x 76cm)*
Everything about this complex painting of the koi is unexpected, from the active composition to the variety of colors. Painting with a daring attitude often produces outstanding results.

colors becomes a rewarding challenge that is easily surmounted by the accumulated knowledge.

Being extremely daring with colors should produce a successful painting more often than not, especially when the colors are chosen from a position of color understanding.

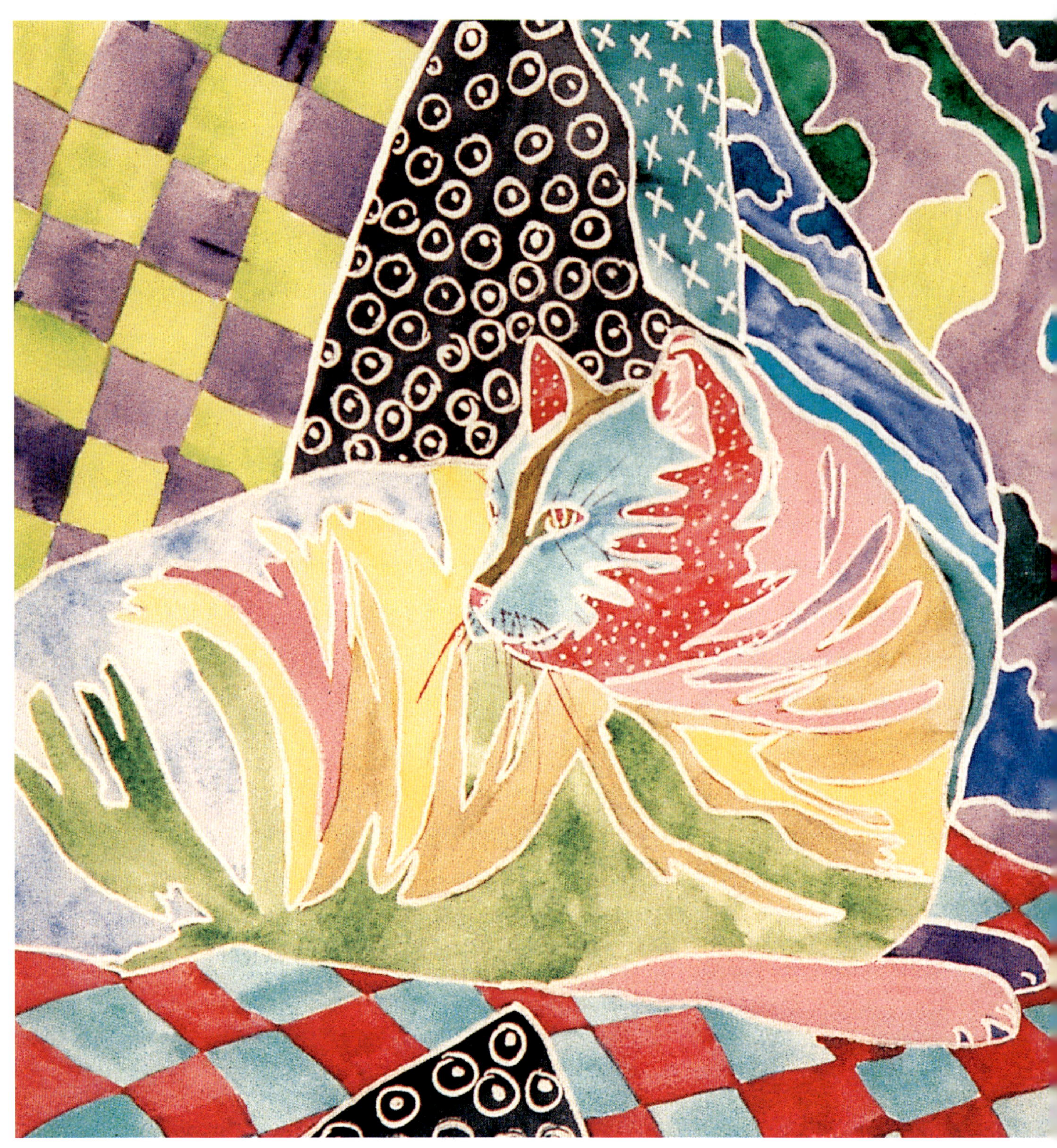

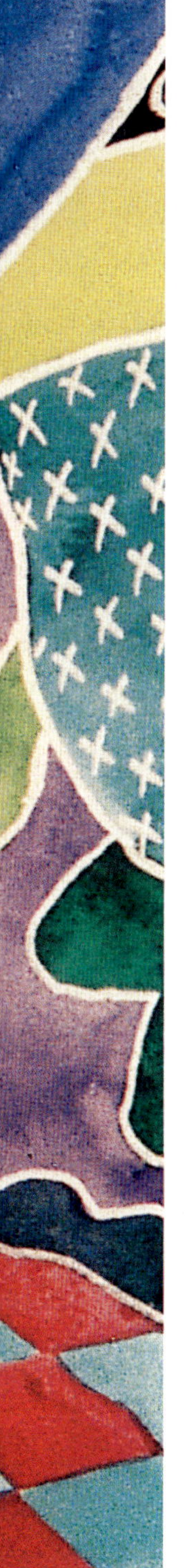

11

The Road to
Color Mastery

"The painter who is truly a colorist ... will never have to fear that an excess of color will make his work appear gaudy. He will leave it to more timorous souls to wish for 'not color, but just a nuance' and will not fear to seek brilliance and power by all possible means."

—Paul Signac

I've often seen students sign up to take my color classes a second and third semester, mainly because they wish to preserve color awareness as a constant companion. They are aware of how easily they could slip into using color as they once did, without thought or reason. Furthermore, they see that the paintings they've done after studying color are generally much more colorful than their earlier works.

Recording Colors

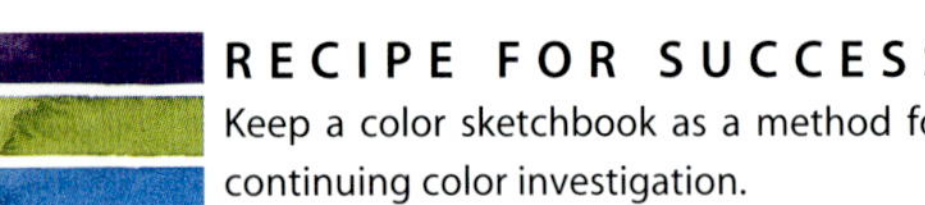

RECIPE FOR SUCCESS

Keep a color sketchbook as a method for continuing color investigation.

The road to masterful color usage is like learning any skill. It's important to keep learning as well as to periodically revisit the fundamentals. What was once a chapter can suddenly become a wondrous field for intense study, because the artist suddenly sees the concepts in a new way.

There are a few tricks one can use to maintain that focus on using color. Many artists keep inspirational sketchbooks full of thumbnail drawings and notes about painting. They find that these often give an insight into their work or provide the foundation for making a painting. Sometimes ideas that were not originally developed can take on a special significance years later, mainly because one cannot pursue every avenue at once. I know many artists who turned these early ideas into paintings years down the road. If a sketchbook is such a useful tool, then I ask, why not keep a color notebook too? In fact, such a notebook might be the perfect place to track color usage as described in chapter 10.

Often an artist sees a beautiful color combination but doesn't have the time to do a finished painting on the spot. A line drawing can capture the composition but not the color. Two weeks later the simple notations—"luminous blue" or "Wow! What a vibrant red!"—do not tell exactly what blue and red those colors were that made the scene so compelling. The sketchbook and the twelve colors of the color wheel provide a shorthand to capture the scene's vibrancy. To analyze a scene, one must ask what colors give the subject such an allure, and to answer that question, one needs to dissect the colors. What is the dominant hue? What is its value and saturation? What are the colors around it, and what are their values and saturations? How much of each color is there? With some practice this can be done very quickly.

The next step is to paint swatches or stripes of the colors, much like the swatches I've illustrated this book with. Mix up the first color and paint a swatch into the notebook. Then apply a swatch of the second color. That second color might be contrasting, such as a blue sky against orange rocks, or it might be similar to the first in hue or in value, such as the sky often appears as it blends from a pink to a green. The number of swatches needed to capture an electrifying color effect will vary depending on the subject. However, the goal is to do this with the

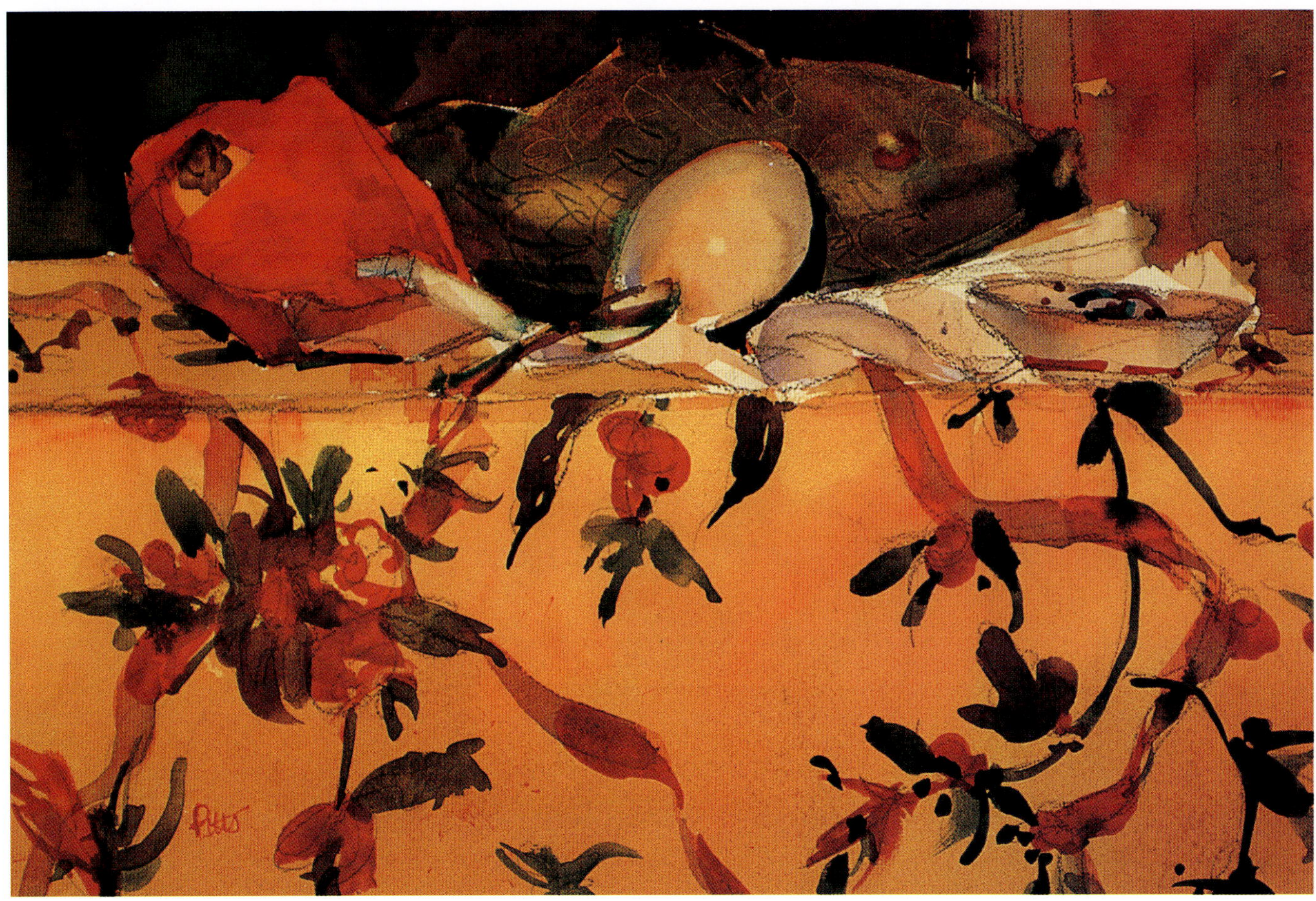

High by Barbara Pitts,
12" x 17" (30cm x 43cm)
The visual punch of the still life is created by the counterpoint of the delicate variations of green found in the brass fish to the bold bright pattern of the cloth.

minimum of colors necessary. Later, with a line drawing and a few notes about how the colors change, this color study can provide a basis for a more finished watercolor. This procedure works for landscapes, still lifes, and even just for an attractive area of color, whether it be the whole subject or only a small part.

One should also look for appealing color combinations in any form. I often skim store catalogs and magazines for fascinating colors. I keep a box of clipped rectangles of colors that I then arrange together into interesting combinations. When I find one I like, the colors are pasted into my color notebook. The next step is to try to duplicate the colors with paint in order to understand the colors and what mixing is necessary to duplicate the sensation they create together. Often subtle gradations from one color to another are needed in order to nail down the effect of the shifting light of a photographic background.

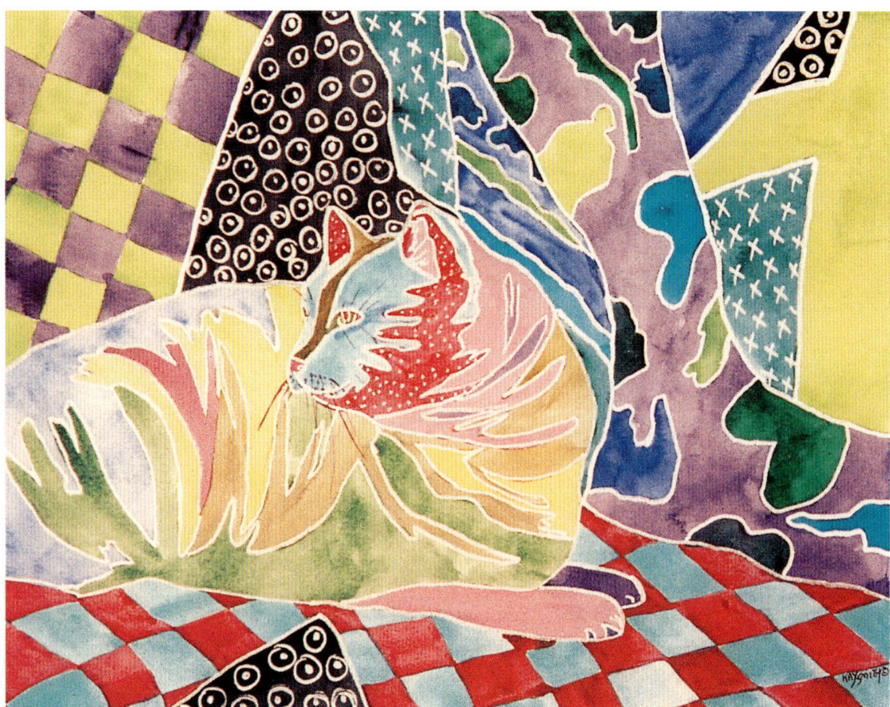

Kaleidoscope Kat by Kay Smith, *5" x 22" (38cm x 56cm)*
Daring color usage can often result in electrifying painting. Note how complementary colors of equal value are found in many areas, one way to tie together these uncommon colors.

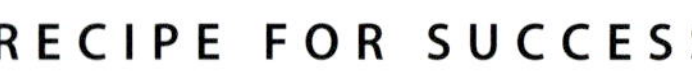

RECIPE FOR SUCCESS

Arrange swatches of appealing colors into interesting combinations and paste the best ones into the color notebook for later reference.

Snapshots are helpful reminders for painters, too, but it is important to understand that they are no substitute for these color studies. Photographs are generally small, they lack the depth of the original subject, and they are better at capturing value differences rather than subtle changes in color. Furthermore, the many colors of nature are reduced to mixtures of three film dyes, which are then translated into photographic printing dyes. Because of this translation, the color of the subject is greatly diminished.

Invitation and Theory

Whether one is painting from real life or considering a more abstract approach, artists often position their intuitive preferences for colors as completely opposite from the process of consciously choosing colors. Becoming a great colorist means finding ways to combine the two approaches. When that happens, the fundamentals presented in this book begin to affect the intuitive selection process.

An intuitive approach can be roped in by pausing to consider the three or four dominant colors of the subject. By dominant I mean the larger or most striking areas of color. These are then written down and compared to the twelve-hue color wheel. The artist can then see if the group of colors conforms to a known grouping such as triads, tetrads, complements, or analogous colors. When a set is found to match, the painting can be structured with that set of colors as a guide. None of the magic of choosing colors intuitively has been lost; rather, a bit of knowledge is applied to the colors to make the set more meaningful. These colors can also be altered slightly to conform to a set by carefully adjusting the hue of one or two.

Another trick to keep thinking about color is to use one of the fundamentals in the book as the basis for a still life. Colored objects and cloths can be selected that match the colors of a triad or tetrad, or an orange can be placed on a blue cloth to emphasize the complementary aspect of the relationship. Then, with the still life carefully arranged according to a play, the artist can let intuition take over for the remainder of the process.

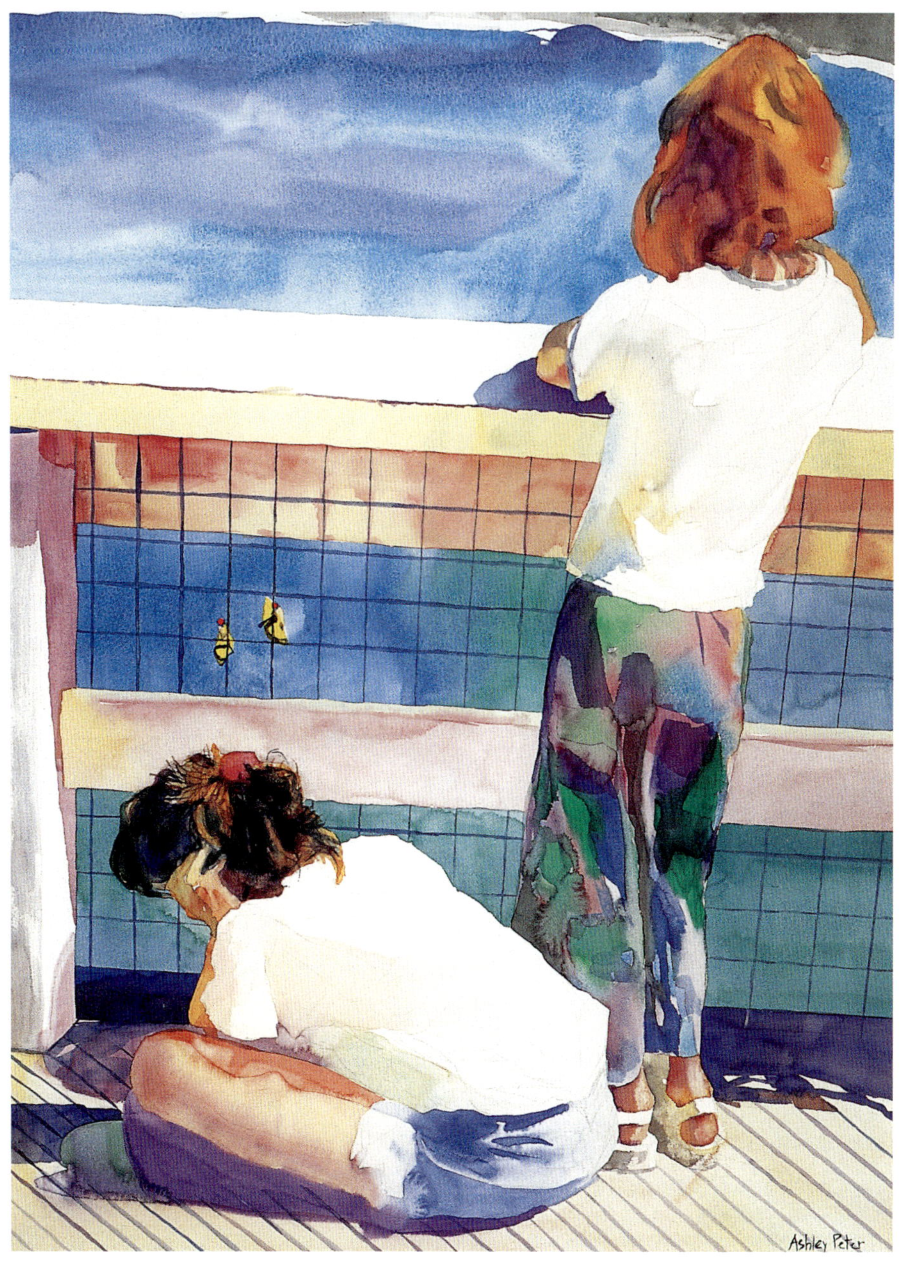

Two Boats **by Ashley Peter,**
30" x 22" **(*76cm x 56cm*)**
The small yellow boats down on the water are a contrast of extension combined with a complementary contrast when compared to the large violet shadows.

The Painting Process

The path to great color usage is paved by careful observation, precise color mixing, and conscientious analysis of how the paint works on the painting. These should be examined separately at first, but with practice they will become a linked group of innate skills. The first is to develop the skill of seeing. Thinking about some of the fundamentals actually helps this process. For example, shadows are very often complementary to the subject. Taking the color wheel, finding the color of an object, and then looking for its complement in the shadows is a method that often allows artists to finally see the color of those shadows. In addition, after staring at a.particular color for too long, it may begin to flicker as the eye begins to fatigue, so a green can appear to be laced with touches of reds. Adding these small touches of the complement can really liven up a painting.

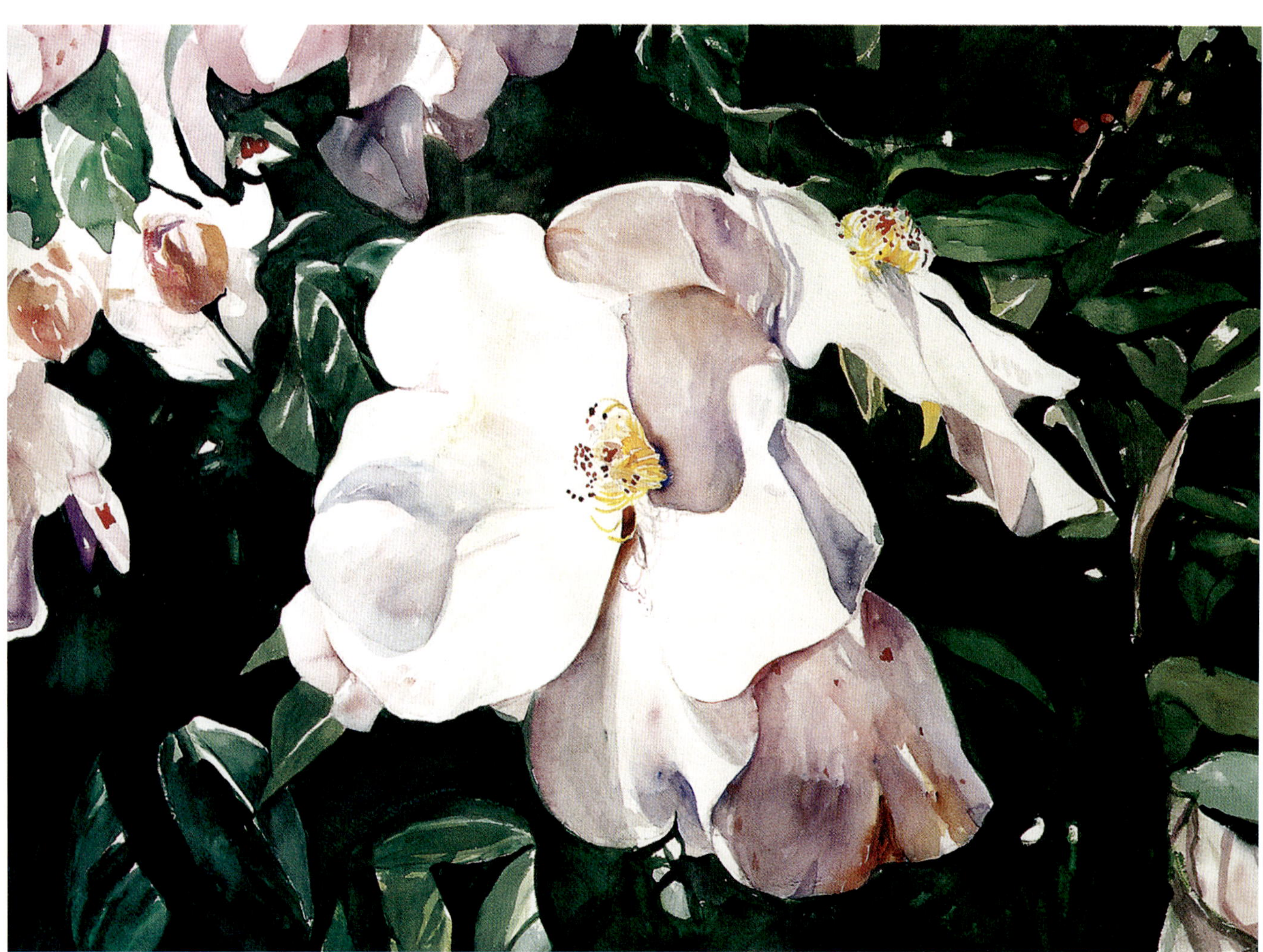

Pink Roses by Nancy Carey, *30" x 22" (76cm x 56cm)*
A few colors only make up the watercolor: green, violet, red, and yellow. The painting appears to contain more colors because each are adjusted with many variations of value.

Once the colors are seen, the next step is to mix them. Getting the exact color means trying to mix it and then trying again. At the beginning, this can take three or four tries. If one color just isn't working, it's good to try other primaries. A better pink might be made from the cadmium red deep or the quinacridone red, and one cannot always guess the final color mixture by looking at the primary hue.

The last step after mixing the color on the palette is to place the color on the paper and then compare the sense of light and color of the subject to the watercolor. If the watercolor is not as luminous as the original, the colors need to be adjusted. Surprisingly, it's often not the color of the object so much as it is the colors around it. For example, I've had students painting a very bright orange who just couldn't nail that citric brightness until they started adding the complement blue into the shadows of the cloth and the wall around the orange. In fact, careful observation showed that the blue complement showed up everywhere around the orange, including the highlight on the orange, which was discovered to be a light blue instead of white or light orange.

Analyzing Painting

Using the fundamentals to analyze paintings is also a great method for continually improving color knowledge. In color classes I will often show slides of master paintings and ask students to figure out the main colors of the work. I then plot the colors they find on the simple twelve-hue color wheel so they can understand how they relate. I put the saturated hues on the rim of the wheel and the desaturated colors on the inside, toward a theoretical grey center of the wheel. Value differences are not plotted on this two-dimensional structure. This plotting of the colors makes evident their relationship, and often a painting that appears to be painted with twenty different hues will be found to utilize only about three hues that are shown in many variations of saturation and value.

Artists can analyze their own work in the same manner—a process that is best done a few days or weeks after the piece is completed. Artists often see their own work more clearly with a bit more distance, and this is why some artists start a painting and turn it to the wall for a few months. Only when they have the objective distance will they turn it back around to continue painting. Getting together with another artist and offering critiques of a painting or two is also useful if the focus is an analysis of color rather than a general like or dislike of the painting.

RECIPE FOR SUCCESS

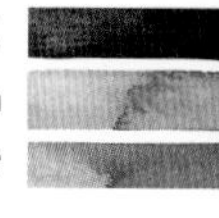

To make objects appear brighter, darken and desaturate the colors around the object.

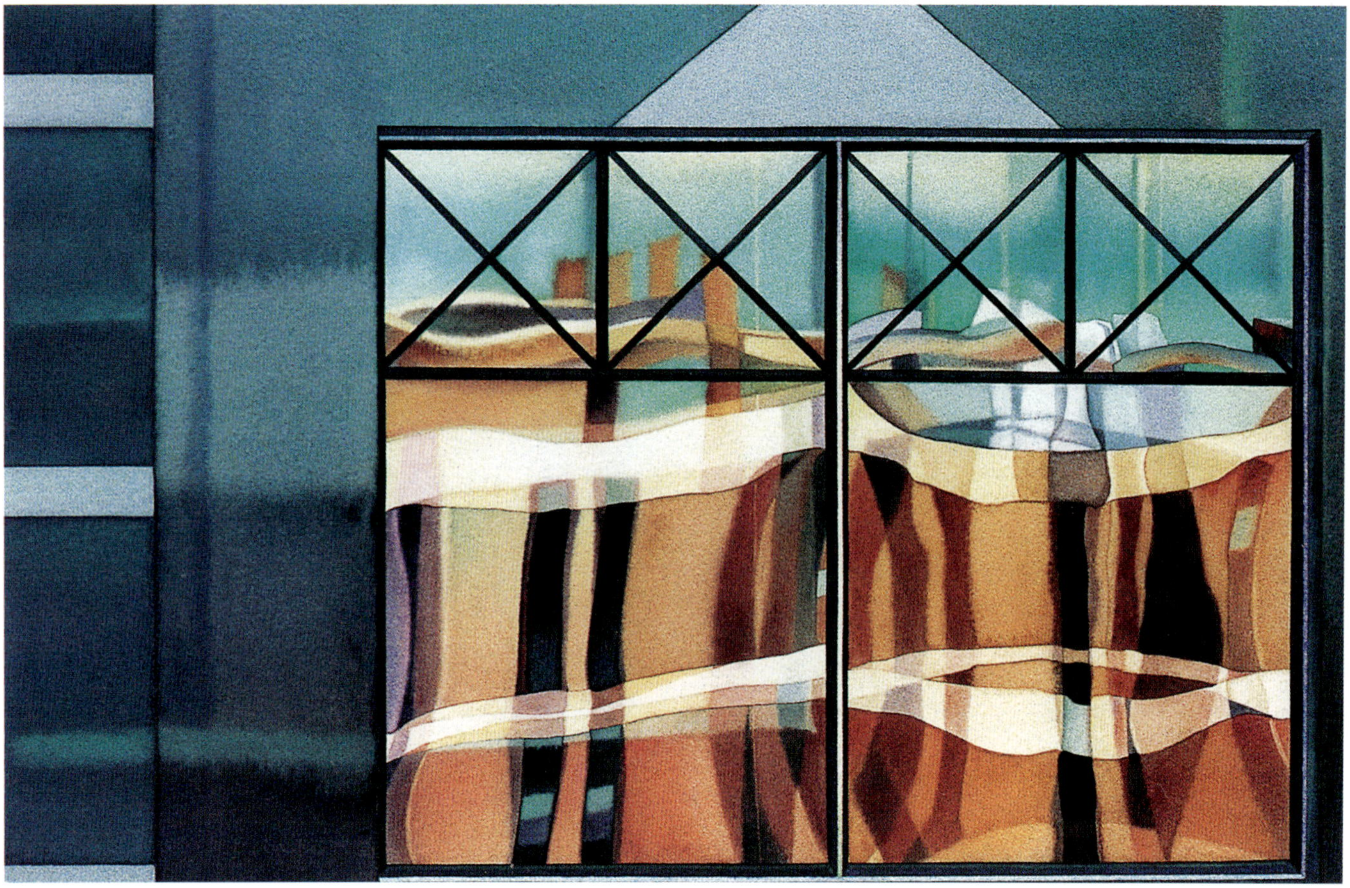

Warp Series II by Ann DeLaurentis, *10" x 14" (25cm x 35cm)*
The reflections of buildings in the windows of a modern skyscraper provide a playful structure for combining colors. Exciting color combinations can often be found in unexpected places.

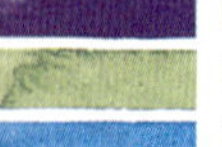

RECIPE FOR SUCCESS

Learn to analyze the colors in master paintings to learn what makes them work so well.

Finally, I would like to share an anecdote that I believe is helpful to those wishing to evaluate their work that occurred in one of my color classes. Two students had revised paintings and brought them in to the class for feedback. One had pared down the composition considerably by removing many extraneous items, while the other had greatly increased the number of elements in the composition. Each had taken a different tack, but they both felt that their work was not quite up to par. Something was lacking, but they couldn't put their fingers on it. I asked the class what they thought, and many agreed that the works were good but not really exciting—and they didn't quite know why, either. I asked the class to analyze the works based on what they knew about contrasts of hue, value, saturation, and extension. The students discovered that each work, while compositionally opposite, failed to use any contrast well. Each had a number of hues taking up roughly equal areas of the painting. The colors were of approximately the same values through the paintings. The saturations were virtually identical everywhere. In a nutshell, there were no strong contrasts of any type. I suspect that, from now on, these students will find that looking for and developing contrasts in their paintings will always be at the top of their lists.

Artists who use color well all have one thing in common—they are rarely satisfied with their first efforts. They become masters with color by consciously using color and daring to make color an especially strong part of the paintings. The nice thing about color, however, is that when we strive to use it well, it's generally forgiving. But I warn you—it's also addictive. An old painter I knew once talked about vibrant colors as though they were flavors of ice cream; indeed, a mastery of color is a real treat for the eye.

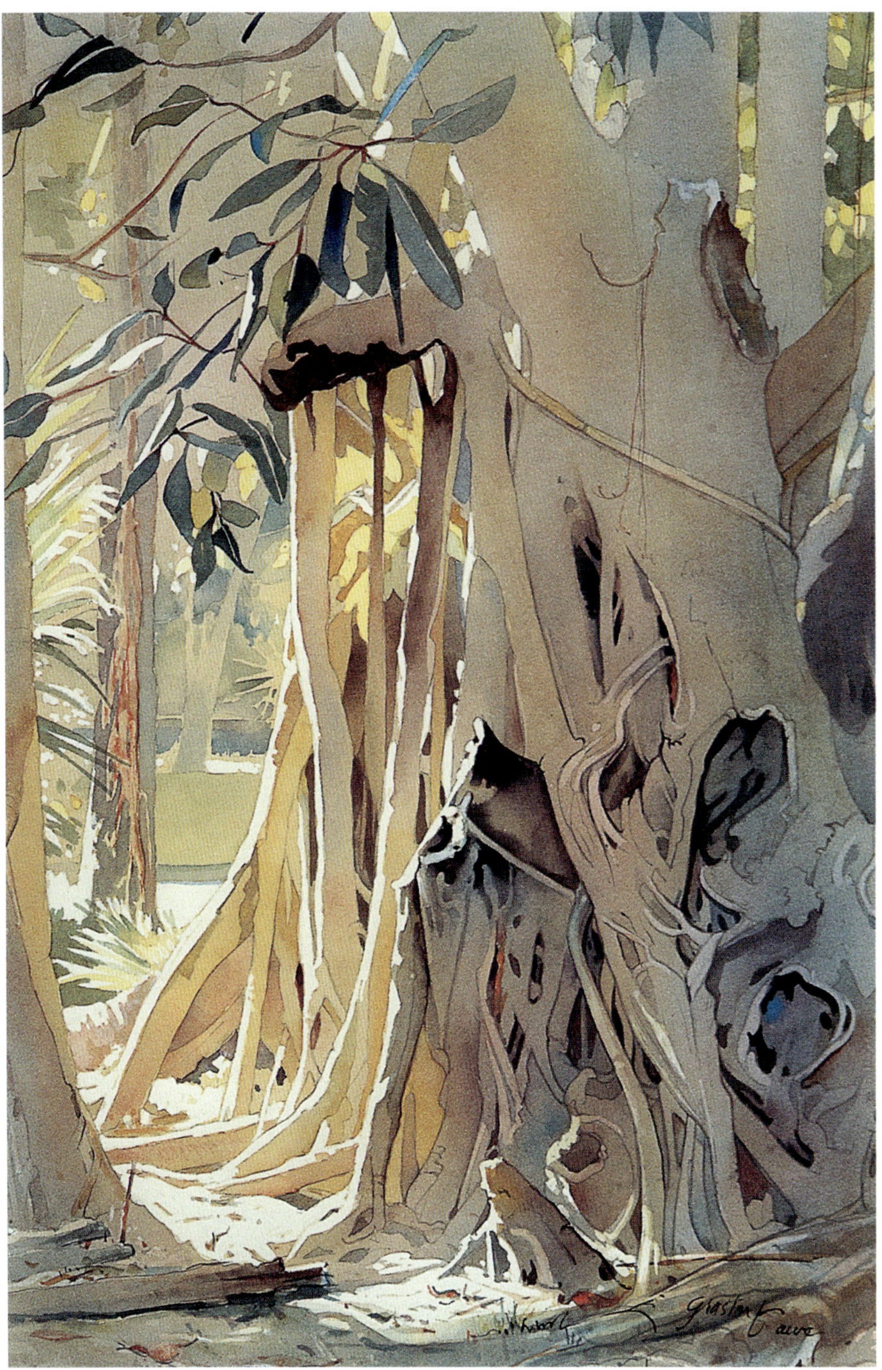

Banyan **by Jean Grastorf, *28" x 20" (71cm x 51cm)***
The mysterious beauty of the greyer chameleon colors allow the more saturated yellows to appear as sunlight while the white highlights are a masterful touch of value contrast that makes the painting sparkle

Contributor Biographies

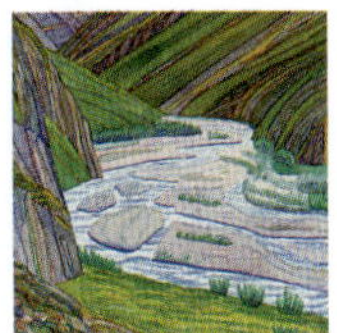

James Behlke
7659 Burnham Way
Dublin, CA 94568

JAMES BEHLKE has shown his watercolors, paintings, prints, and drawings since 1978, and recently won the Mayor's Award at the 1999 Water + Color juried show at the Bedford Gallery in Walnut Creek, California. Raised in Alaska and now living in California, he has had numerous solo shows, including ones at the Anchorage Museum of History and Art, the Alaska State Museum, and the Visual Arts Center of Alaska. His work is on display in numerous collections, including the Anchorage Museum of History and Art, the Alaska State Museum, the University of Alaska Museum, Parks Canada, and Progressive Insurance Corporation. Behlke received a bachelor of fine arts degree in printmaking from the University of Alaska, Fairbanks, and a master of fine arts degree in painting from the University of Southern California in Los Angeles. His art may be seen at http://www.behlke.com.

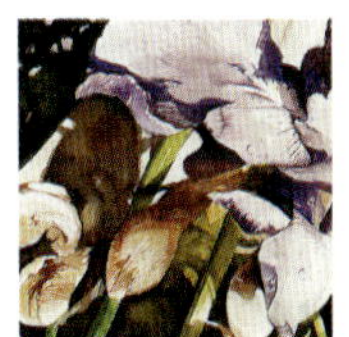

Nancy Carey
563 5th Street
Brooklyn, NY 11215

NANCY CAREY is a member of the Brooklyn Watercolor Society. She has worked as a graphic designer for many years and recently returned to her first love, painting, by way of watercolor classes at the Brooklyn Botanical Garden. Carey concentrates on flowers in her paintings, and she works in pastel, charcoal, and oil sticks as well. She earned a bachelor of fine arts degree in painting from the Rhode Island School of Design.

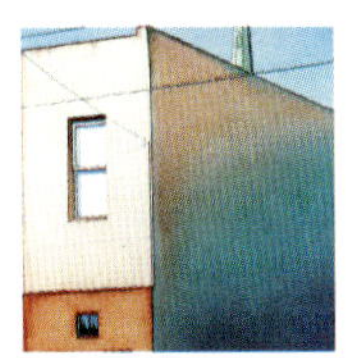

Ann DeLaurentis
432 North Christian Street
Lancaster, PA 17602

ANN DeLAURENTIS has exhibited her watercolors and etchings in twelve solo exhibits and numerous group and juried exhibits. She is a signature member of the Pennsylvania Watercolor Society and the Philadelphia Water Color Club. Her work is represented by the Rosenfeld Gallery in Philadelphia, Pennsylvania; the Central Market Art Company and DeLaurentis Studio in Lancaster, Pennsylvania; and the William Ris Galleries in both Camp Hill, Pennsylvania, and Stone Harbor, New Jersey. DeLaurentis teaches watercolor workshops in her studio and has taught courses in painting and photography at the college and high school level. Her work has been featured in *American Artist Magazine*. DeLaurentis' watercolors can be viewed at her website at http://www.delaurentis.simplenet.com.

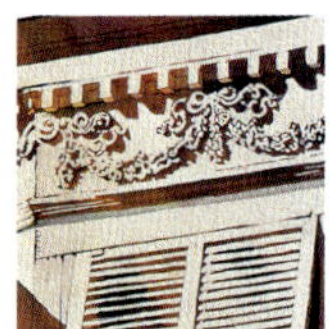

Jean Grastorf
6049 4th Avenue North
St. Petersburg, FL
33710

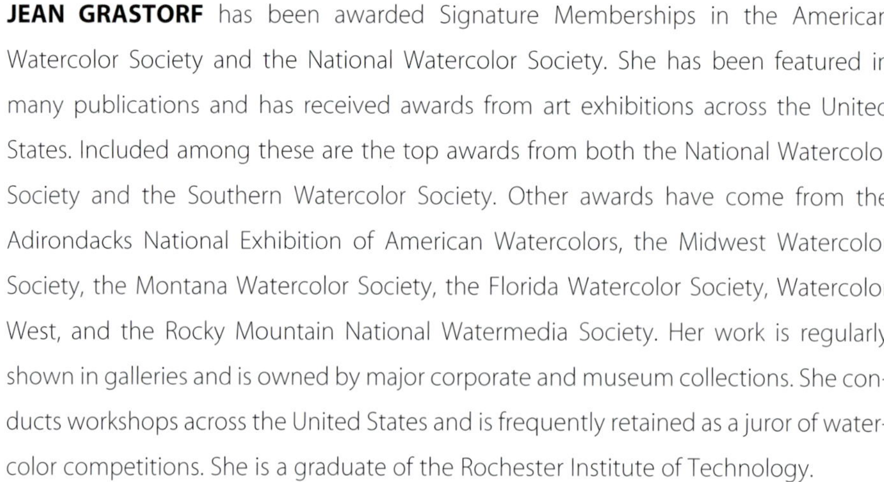

JEAN GRASTORF has been awarded Signature Memberships in the American Watercolor Society and the National Watercolor Society. She has been featured in many publications and has received awards from art exhibitions across the United States. Included among these are the top awards from both the National Watercolor Society and the Southern Watercolor Society. Other awards have come from the Adirondacks National Exhibition of American Watercolors, the Midwest Watercolor Society, the Montana Watercolor Society, the Florida Watercolor Society, Watercolor West, and the Rocky Mountain National Watermedia Society. Her work is regularly shown in galleries and is owned by major corporate and museum collections. She conducts workshops across the United States and is frequently retained as a juror of watercolor competitions. She is a graduate of the Rochester Institute of Technology.

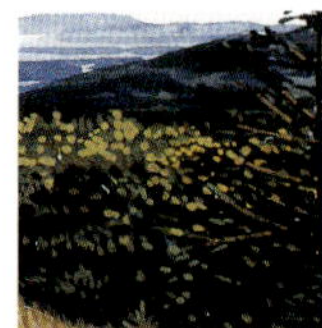

James Linehan
336 Center Street
Bangor, ME 04401

JAMES LINEHAN is represented by Sherry French Gallery, New York, NY. His work has been included in over one hundred group shows and twenty solo shows in the past fifteen years. He has completed twenty public commissions, including fifteen for the Maine Arts Commission's Percent for Art Project, and is represented in twenty-two public and corporate collections. Born in Melbourne, Florida, on January 22, 1953, he was raised in North Easton, Massachusetts; Lewiston, New York; and Tempe, Arizona. After receiving his bachelor of fine arts degree in painting at Arizona State University in 1974, Linehan continued his studies at the University of Wisconsin-Madison where he earned a master's degree in painting in 1976 and a master of fine arts degree in 1978. Prior to moving to Maine in 1983, he taught for five years at St. Andrews College in North Carolina. He is now a professor of art at the University of Maine. Linehan and his wife, Karen, have four children: Flynn, Anna, Clare, and Connor.

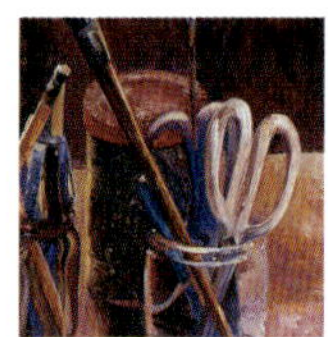

Mary J. Maxam
1535 Meadowbrook
Acres Road
Coeur d'Alene, ID
83814

MARY J. MAXAM is a signature member of both the Northwest Watercolor Society and Montana Watercolor Societies. Her paintings have been in exhibitions sponsored by the National Watercolor Society and the Midwest Watercolor Society, winning the Grumbacher award in Montana's "Waterworks 98" show. Maxam received a bachelor of fine arts degree from Boise State University in Boise, Idaho. She has continued her study through painting workshops with several nationally known instructors, such as Irving Shapiro and Linda Doll. Her works can be seen on the Makart Internet site at http://www.makart.com/mjmgallery.

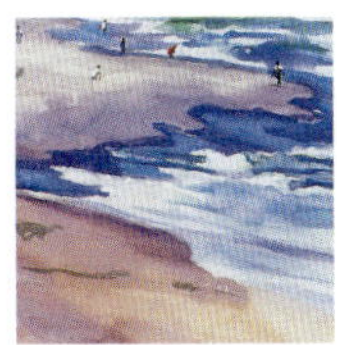

Ashley Peter
P.O. Box 1341
Simi Valley, CA 93062

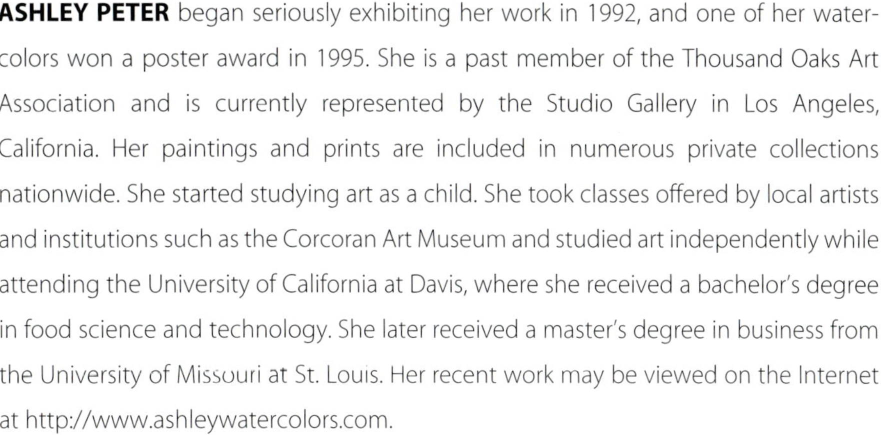

ASHLEY PETER began seriously exhibiting her work in 1992, and one of her watercolors won a poster award in 1995. She is a past member of the Thousand Oaks Art Association and is currently represented by the Studio Gallery in Los Angeles, California. Her paintings and prints are included in numerous private collections nationwide. She started studying art as a child. She took classes offered by local artists and institutions such as the Corcoran Art Museum and studied art independently while attending the University of California at Davis, where she received a bachelor's degree in food science and technology. She later received a master's degree in business from the University of Missouri at St. Louis. Her recent work may be viewed on the Internet at http://www.ashleywatercolors.com.

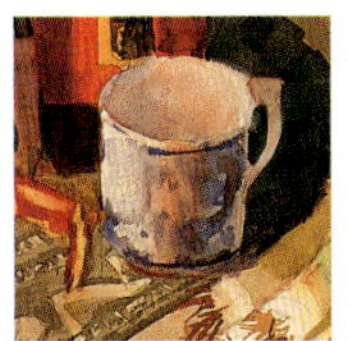

Barbara Pitts
2515 East Marion Street
Seattle, WA 98122

BARBARA PITTS has exhibited and taught internationally. Her watercolors have received awards in many national juried competitions in the United States, including those of the Northwest Watercolor Society, the Texas Watercolor Society, and the Red River Watercolor Society. She has organized international cultural exchanges and exhibitions. As a printmaker working in non-toxic techniques, she has been Visiting Artist at the Seacourt Print Workshop in Bangor, County Down, Northern Ireland.

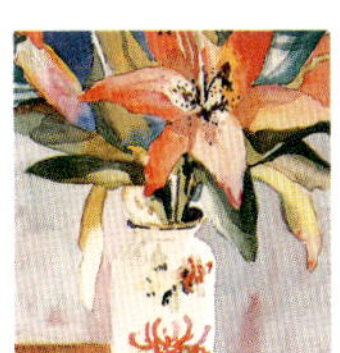

Kay Smith
800 Caprock Drive
Big Spring, TX 79720

KAY SMITH is a member of West Texas Watercolor Society (attaining signature status) and Odessa, Midland, and Big Spring Art Associations. Her work is recognized in national, regional, and local competitions with multiple best of show and people's choice awards. She owns Brushworks Studio Gallery in Big Spring, Texas, and is represented by Caravan International. Brilliant use of color is a hallmark of the loose, painterly style she uses in creating original transparent works that hang in collections around the world. Since 1978, she has been employed as a registered nurse. Smith began her career as a watercolorist in 1993 after attending one of Ken Hosmer's annual workshops. An oil and pastel painter since grade school, she has studied with Tony Couch, Frank Webb, Judi Betts, Betty Lynch, and Jo Beth Gilliam. Her watercolors are shown on the internet at http://watercolor-online.com/KaySmith/.

Resources

Easy Solutions: Color Mixing Watercolor How to Mix the Right Colors for the Subject Every Time, by M. Stephen Doherty, Rockport

The Best of Watercolor: Painting Light & Shadow, selected by Betty Lou Schlemm, edited by Sara Doherty, Rockport

The Best of Watercolor: Painting Color, selected by Betty Lou Schlemm, edited by Sara Doherty, Rockport

Color Harmony Workbook: A Workbook and Guide to Creative Color Combinations, by Lesa Sawahata, Rockport

The Enjoyment and Use of Color, by Walter Sargent, Dover Publications, Inc.

Paul Signac and Color in Neo-Impressionism, by Floyd Ratliff, Rockefeller University Press

Color and Culture: Practice and Meaning from Antiquity to Abstraction, by John Gage, Bulfinch Press

Colour: Why the World Isn't Grey, by Hazel Rossotti, Princeton University Press

The Color Compendium, Augustine Hope and Margaret Walch, by Van Nostrand Reinhold

Hawthorne on Painting, by Charles W. Hawthorne, Dover

The Art Spirit, by Robert Henri, Harper & Row

About the Author

Christopher Willard was born in Bangor, Maine, in 1960. He has always had a passion for visual arts, and one of his first remembrances is of melting crayons on a hot radiator to see the color mixtures.

He received his master's of fine arts degree in painting from Hunter College (City University of New York) in 1992, and his bachelor of fine arts degree in painting and drawing from the Portland School of Art (now renamed the Maine College of Art) in Portland, Maine. Mr. Willard has exhibited in numerous national and international shows, most recently in the group show "Clinton AKA Hell's Kitchen" at Gallery @ 49, New York, New York, and at the Casements, Ormond Beach, Florida.

His paintings are included in numerous public collections, including the Metropolitan Museum of Art, *Reader's Digest,* Key Bank, and the Alberta College of Art and Design. Awards include the E.D. Foundation Grant, the Manhattan Graphics Center Grant, the Hunter Alumni Association Scholarship, the Hunter Faculty Travel Grant, and the Veritas Award for Outstanding Creativity, among others. Mr. Willard has led numerous seminars, including "A Short Course on Color," "Discovering the Creative Self," and "Painting and Color." Public commissions include the New York Philharmonic, Goliard Concerts, the off-off-Broadway show "Minor Problems," and the Errol Simpson Dance Company.

Keenly interested in playing an active part of a larger art community, Mr. Willard is a member of the College Art Association and the Inter-Society Color Council, serving on their interest groups in art, design and psychology, and fundamental and applied color research. He was invited to speak most recently at international conferences for the Association Internationale de la Couleur, (AIC), Göteborg, Sweden; the International Conference on Colour Education, Helsinki, Finland; and at the Society for Photographic Education, Northeast Regional Conference, Hartford, Connecticut. As a member of the AIC, he serves on the committee for visual illusions. He recently presented a paper at the CAA conference in Toronto, Ontario, Canada, titled "A Dystopia of Color Education in a Utopia of Color Experience."

Among his visiting artist positions are the Alberta College of Art and Design and the Glen Oaks Community College, where he was awarded the Flora Kirsch Beck Visiting Artist Grant. Mr. Willard is currently adjunct professor at Hunter College (CUNY) and at the Westchester Art Workshop (Westchester Community College), Westchester, Connecticut. He has authored more than 40 articles and book chapters, and writes a monthly column for *American Artist* magazine.